John Lavan Kirby

John Lavan Kirby, who was educated at Oxford and London, is the Librarian of the History Faculty Library in Oxford. He is a Fellow of the Royal Historical Society and a contributor to *History Today* and the *English Historical Review*. His study of Henry IV is the first full-length biography for over seventy years.

Henry IV of England

Henry IV, from an illuminated manuscript

Henry IV of England

J. L. KIRBY

CONSTABLE
LONDON

First published in 1970
by Constable & Company Ltd
10 Orange Street London WC2

Copyright © 1970 by John Lavan Kirby

ISBN 0 09 457210 0

Printed in Great Britain by The Anchor Press Ltd,
and bound by Wm. Brendon & Son Ltd, both of
Tiptree, Essex

Uxori Dilectissimae

Acknowledgments

The footnotes to this book form a very inadequate guide to the debt which I owe to the writings and private help of many scholars. Here I should like to thank especially Professor V. H. Galbraith for his highly original views on Henry IV, and Dr Pierre Chaplais for the benefit of his exact scholarship on occasions too numerous to remember. It is also a great pleasure for me to be able to thank all those members of the staff of the Public Record Office, who over a period of thirty years have helped me in many ways with this and other work. Finally I should like to mention the name of the late K. B. McFarlane, whose lectures first aroused my interest in the fifteenth century nearly forty years ago.

Contents

Contents

Illustrations

Chapter 1

Introduction – The sources

THE dividing line between medieval and modern history is not very easy to draw, but for the historian the most important difference lies in the nature of the sources, and in this respect the fifteenth century is very much of the Middle Ages. In the modern period the historian, and still more the biographer, is able to work from letters and memoirs. For the Middle Ages there are hardly any memoirs, and in England letters were written, usually by a clerk or secretary, in either Latin or Anglo-Norman, with a formality of style through which it is rarely possible to discern the real character of the person from whom they purport to come. It is true that private letters began to be written in English in the fourteenth century, but very few have survived even from the fifteenth, and the first king to have English letters written in his name was Henry V. Owing to the lack of such sources, and indeed of any personal records, most medieval men and women – including even some kings and queens – remain shadowy figures to us. Their biographies can never be written with the fullness with which more recent, even sixteenth- or seventeenth-century, characters can be described. For kings we are usually limited either to a comparatively bare recital of the facts of 'life and reign' with no intimate detail; or to imaginative reconstruction, lending them the thoughts and words which we think that we ourselves might have had in a similar situation.

It may well be said that offered these two alternatives the only policy is to give up, and refuse to attempt biography at all; and this in the main has been the policy of recent historians. To write about individuals, especially kings, instead of about movements and people in the mass, has now indeed a somewhat old-fashioned air, but history is still about people, and to some of us individuals remain more interesting than masses. More can, of course, be discovered about kings than about other people, but it is rarely possible to separate a king's life from his reign, or to distinguish between his own actions and those of his counsellors or ministers. The King had no private income and there are no records of his private life apart from his kingship. His biography is bound therefore to be mainly the story of his reign.

Late medieval England was before all else a monarchy, and the King's first duty was to provide good governance. 'He mynestrith to his reaume defence and justice' said Sir John Fortescue,[1] the constitutional lawyer of the century. It was such good governance that Richard II and Henry VI conspicuously failed to provide, and failure cost both of them their thrones and their lives. Henry V and Edward IV on the other hand may be regarded as notably successful kings. Henry IV is perhaps not so easily judged.

Henry IV has not been well treated by historians. The most memorable history of the reign is provided by the plays of Shakespeare, from which it is certainly not the King who emerges as the sharpest character. From Shakespeare, of course, we can never escape whether we wish to or not, and this is one of the greatest problems for the historian of this period. The chronology, the sequence of events, with which Shakespeare took liberties even when his sources were correct, can be restored, brought back from drama to reality; but who can ever write of Henry Percy and Henry, Prince of Wales without being haunted by Hotspur and Prince Hal?

Neither the sixteenth-century writers who provided Shakespeare's narrative nor their successors over the next three hundred years can be regarded as authorities now. The fullest account of the reign is that of James Hamilton Wylie, the *History of England under Henry IV*, published between 1884 and 1898 in four volumes containing over 2,000 pages. This is a fascinating book full of learning, a massive work, which can never be superseded for students of the period. Some may be attracted and some repelled by the enormous conglomeration of archaisms in which Wylie delighted, but none can deny that it remains a great work of scholarship. It is however overloaded with facts, and not very easy to read or to use. All, or more than all, the facts are there but they have to be sought out, and Wylie's attitudes as well as his treatment of his facts are now somewhat dated. The only other modern work devoted exclusively to Henry, *King Henry IV*

[1] Fortescue, *Governance*, p. 127

by J. D. Griffith Davis, published in 1935, is very much more
of a lightweight. Two good recent accounts of the reign are by
K. B. McFarlane in *The Cambridge Medieval History*,[1] and by
E. F. Jacob in *The Fifteenth Century*.[2]

The sources for the life of Henry of Bolingbroke before his
exile in 1398 are mainly scattered references in the chronicles of
the time, and in the national records. The only important single
source is provided by the sadly incomplete records of his father's
duchy of Lancaster, which now survive in the Public Record
Office. The outstanding examples of these were edited for the
Camden Society in 1894 by Lucy Toulmin Smith as *Expeditions
to Prussia and the Holy Land made by Henry, Earl of Derby (afterwards Henry IV); accounts kept by his treasurer during the years
1390–91 and 1392–93*. From these accounts comes all the knowledge that we have of these two expeditions, and the fact that the
two years which they occupied are the only ones out of the first
thirty-two years of Henry's life which are so fully documented
means that we are bound to over-emphasise the importance of
these two years. To Henry looking back in 1399 they were
probably not the outstanding years of his life. To us, with but
little knowledge of the other thirty years, they are bound to
be so.

From 1398 until his death Henry was at the centre of affairs,
so that all chronicles and national records are potential sources
both for his life and for his reign. The chronicles,[3] although
at first sight numerous, are in reality few, and all so closely related
to each other that is it very difficult to distinguish between them
or to assess their independent value. Almost all are partially
copied or compiled from each other, or from common originals
now lost, and most of them exist in a number of different versions;
for before the invention of printing no copy of a book was ever
quite the same as any other, and no version was final. Some
chronicles, and some versions, add very little to the common story
which emerges, yet almost every one has some small contribution
to make, and none can be safely ignored. Especially for the period
1398–9 some chronicles are clearly related to the *Rolls of Parlia-*

[1] 'England: The Lancastrian Kings, 1399–1461', *C. Med. Hist.,* vol. viii, chap.
11, pp. 363–79 (1936)
[2] Chaps. 1–3, pp. 1–120 (1961)
[3] For the chronicles see Kingsford, *Eng. Hist. Lit.*

ment,[1] which, although supposedly a formal record of proceedings, were clearly at times compiled to express the official view of the Government of the day. Copies circulated for propaganda purposes – to explain how Henry came to displace Richard and to justify the change – doubtless found their way into the chroniclers' hands.

It is convenient to divide the chronicles for this period into three groups, firstly those of the St. Albans school, secondly those related to *The Brut*, and thirdly the French chronicles, although any such division is bound to be arbitrary, and there are some which refuse to fall into any group.

The chronicles for the years from 1376 to 1420 at St. Albans were the work of Thomas Walsingham, a worthy successor to the long line of chronicle writers at that abbey. His two main works survive in a number of copies,[2] but neither has been printed in full in a single edition. The larger has been printed in four parts, of which the third and fourth cover this period, from 1393 to 1406 as the *Annales Ricardi II et Henrici IV* in *Johannes de Trokelowe*,[3] and from 1406 onwards by V. H. Galbraith as *The St. Albans Chronicle 1406–1420*. Walsingham also covered the period with a shorter history, and that part of it for the years 1392–1422 is printed in the *Historia Anglicana*.[4] The *Ypodigma Neustriae*[5] which Walsingham compiled between 1419 and 1422 was copied, for this period at least, from his other works. Walsingham stands out as the great chronicler of his day. The King often visited the abbey, and on occasion met his council there, so that the monks were in a position to learn at first hand of the events of the day, and their chronicles may be expected to reflect the official government view of such events. It is the fullest account that we have, and the only authority for some of the events of the reign, with all the faults and virtues of monastic annals. But the days of monastic annals were drawing to a close, and although nothing was to provide an adequate substitute, the chronicles of towns, especially of London, came nearest to doing so, at least in the fifteenth century.

[1] Printed as *Rotuli Parliamentorum*, 6 vols. and index, 1783–1832
[2] Galbraith, *St. Albans Chron.*, Introduction, *passim*
[3] *Annales R. II et H. IV*, pp. 155–420
[4] Walsingham, *Hist. Angl.*, vol. ii, pp. 211–346
[5] *Ypodigma Neustriae*, pp. 380–437

The Brut[1] was originally a chronicle of Britain from the earliest times written in French and translated into English. The continuation from 1377 to 1419 was however written in English well before the middle of the fifteenth century. Useful for supplying many details not to be found in Walsingham, this chronicle is closely related to the chronicles of London, which exist in several versions, and were probably derived from the same originals. The London chronicles, which were just beginning to be of value in Henry IV's reign, have been fully described by C. L. Kingsford.[2] Another version of the *Brut*, edited by J. S. Davis in 1856, is usually known simply as *Davis's Chronicle*.[3] A number of other chronicles of less outstanding importance should be mentioned. That of Thomas Otterbourne is very similar to the longer history of Walsingham; the Monk of Evesham which goes down to 1402, and *Giles's Chronicle*, which has a good deal in common with the London chronicles from 1403 to 1413, have some independent value. Another short account of the reign is to be found in the continuation of the *Eulogium Historiarum*, also a member of *The Brut* family with some additional matter especially about papal history. A short *Southern Chronicle 1399–1422* of the same family, and a similarly short but apparently quite independent *Northern Chronicle 1399–1430*, were published by Kingsford,[4] but more important for the deposition of Richard II and the coming of Henry to the throne are sections of the *Chronicle of Dieulacres Abbey, 1381–1403*, edited by M. V. Clarke and V. H. Galbraith,[5] and of *The Kirkstall Chronicle, 1355–1400* edited by M. V. Clarke and N. Denholm-Young,[6] the latter being the authority for the timetable of Henry's march after his landing at Ravenspur.

Somewhat different from the other chronicles, and much more modern in style, although written in Latin, is the short chronicle of Adam of Usk.[7] Usk was a Welshman, gifted with a Celtic imagination, who studied at Oxford, became a canon lawyer, and

[1] *The Brut, or the Chronicles of England*, ed. F. W. D. Brie (1906–8), 2 vols.
[2] Kingsford, *London Chrons.*; see also his *Eng. Hist. Lit.* mentioned above
[3] For the full titles of these works see the list of abbreviations under: *Davis's Chron.*; Otterbourne, *Chron.*; Monk of Evesham; *Giles's Chron.*; *Eulogium*
[4] Kingsford, *Eng. Hist. Lit.*, pp. 275–91
[5] 'The Deposition of Richard II' in *Bull. J.R.L.* (1930), vol. xiv, pp. 42–59
[6] 'The Kirkstall Chronicle 1355–1400', ibid (1931), vol. xv, pp. 24–40
[7] Ed. Sir E. M. Thompson, 2nd. ed. O.U.P. (1904)

received a number of benefices partly through the patronage of Archbishop Arundel. From 1397 until 1402 he was at the centre of affairs, present in the Parliament of the former year, and accompanying Henry in 1399 at least from Bristol to Chester, and then in London a member of the commission appointed to discuss Henry's claim to the throne. For these years his chronicle is of considerable independent value, and has something of the nature of memoirs, but it is in a sense disappointing because he could have been less discreet and told us so much more. In 1402, however, he had been found guilty with two of his servants, one perhaps a relative, of stealing a black horse, its harness and some cash, in London in 1400. He deemed it wise to go abroad and sought employment at the court of Rome. Returning towards England some years later he became involved with Owen Glendower in Wales, and also with the rebel Earl of Northumberland in Bruges, so that it was not until 1411 that Henry pardoned him and he was able to land freely in England once more. In consequence his chronicle, although it goes on until 1421, is neither so full nor so reliable – being based on hearsay – for the years from 1402 to 1411, the greater part of Henry IV's reign.

Occasionally useful for casting doubts on the other chronicles is John Hardyng,[1] a squire who began his long career in the service of Hotspur, and was with him right up to the Battle of Shrewsbury. It exists in two versions, both written far too long after the events of Henry IV's reign to be reliable, even if they were not heavily biased in favour of the Percies.[2]

The history of England was so closely bound up with that of France that French chronicles should have considerable value for English history, but they are not on the whole very much help except for Anglo-French relations. Froissart in his later years was usually misinformed about England, and his work is often misleading. His chronicle ended in 1400, when the story was taken up by Enguerran de Monstrelet,[3] who if more pedestrian was little more accurate, and perhaps not very interested in England before 1415. Of the other important French chronicles,

---

[1] Hardyng, *Chron.*
[2] C. L. Kingsford, 'The first version of Hardyng's Chronicle', *E.H.R.* vol. xxvii, (1912), pp. 462–82, 740–53; Bean, 'H. IV and the Percies'
[3] *La Chronique*, 1400–1440, ed. L. Douet d'Arcq (1857–62). Also in English, trans. T. Johnes 2 vols. (Bohn 1849)

the *Journal d'un Bourgeois de Paris*[1] does not begin until 1405 and has no mention of England before the death of Henry IV, and the *Histoire* of Jean Juvenal des Ursins,[2] Archbishop of Rheims, is for this period based entirely on another chronicler, the *Religieux de St. Denys*.[3] The monks of St. Denys were nearer to the court of France than those of St. Albans to that of England, and this brother whose name is now unknown produced a much fuller chronicle than did Thomas Walsingham. His account of events in England is at times, such as the deposition of Richard II, remarkably full and not without value. Two other accounts of the deposition, the one in verse the other in prose, were written in French, but perhaps not in France or by Frenchmen. The metrical *Histoire du Roy d'Angleterre Richard*, edited in England in 1824,[4] and in France in 1826,[5] was long attributed to a Frenchman, Jean Creton, who was said to have been with Richard in Ireland in 1399, and afterwards in the service of the King of France, Charles VI. Recently, however, it has been suggested that the real author was John Trevor, Bishop of St. Asaph,[6] who was certainly with Richard in Ireland, but deserted to Henry in August 1399, and left him in 1405 to take sides with the rebel Glendower. The prose chronicle, which was probably partly based on the metrical one, was edited in England by Benjamin Williams in 1846,[7] and in France from another manuscript by J. A. C. Buchon in 1826.[8] The two chronicles with that of the *Religieux de St. Denys*, which may have drawn on the metrical one, are of interest for their alternative, pro-Richard, account of events, contrasting strongly with the unanimously pro-Henry account of the English chronicles, but they are not, unfortunately, well informed of events after the capture of Richard.

---

[1] *Journal 1405–1449*, ed. A. Tuetey (1881); and in Michaud et Poujoulat *Mémoires*, vol. ii, pp. 631–75

[2] *Histoire de Charles VI*, in Michaud et Poujoulat, *Mémoires*, vol. ii, pp. 339–569

[3] *Chronique*, ed. M. Bellaguet (1839–52)

[4] Ed. J. Webb, in *Archaeologia*, vol. xx, pp. 1–423 (1824)

[5] Ed. J. A. C. Buchon, *Collection*, vol. xxiv (Paris 1826), pp. 321–466

[6] E. J. Jones, 'An examination of the authorship of *The Deposition and death of Richard II* attributed to Creton', *Speculum*, vol. xv, pp. 460–77 (1940)

[7] *Traïson et mort*

[8] *Chronique de Richard II*, ed. Buchon, *Collection*, vol. xxv, suppl. ii, 79 pp. (Paris 1826)

Chronicles are almost always annalistic, often inaccurate, and rarely offer any serious comment on the character or behaviour of individuals, even of the King. They are usually biased in favour of the established order, and do not seek to explain the causes or motives behind events. Aware of these defects historians have increasingly turned to records for their sources, believing that records compiled for the purely utilitarian purpose of carrying on the business of government will be, within their own rather narrow limits, accurate and unbiased.

Records of almost any period may conveniently be divided into three groups, firstly formal proceedings or minutes, secondly letters, in the widest sense of any written communication between two persons or bodies, and thirdly financial records or accounts. The first group is not very well represented in this period. The Parliament Rolls, already mentioned, set down for the record, apparently rather arbitrarily, some of the proceedings of Parliament. Like the formal minutes of almost any meeting they are often more interesting for what they leave out than for what they put in, because the compiler is aware that he is creating a record for the future. On the deposition of Richard II the Parliament Roll sets out the official account of what the King wished to have believed. However, the rolls do give a great deal of information about the dates of sessions, the names of Speakers, and at least some of the proceedings. Of the agenda and proceedings of the King's council only scraps have survived, and these were mostly published by Sir Nicholas Harris Nicolas in 1834–7, in seven volumes entitled *Proceedings and Ordinances of the Privy Council of England*, of which the first two volumes are concerned with the period 1386–1422. The proceedings proper form only a very small part of the whole work, which is really a selection from surviving documents of various kinds, and most of them might more properly be described as letters and papers brought before the council. Apart from these and the proceedings of the courts of law, which are still in manuscript, very difficult to use, and concerned more with private than with public affairs, there are no surviving records which can be classified as proceedings or minutes.

The letter in its widest sense ranges from the formal grant made by the King to the private letter between individuals. Almost all the records of the chancery belong to the more formal part of this group, grants of charters and privileges, and orders from the King to almost every kind of person and institution in the country, as well as some letters to foreign rulers. They provide a mass of detail of an impersonal kind on almost every subject. The privy seal was a slightly less formal office for communicating the orders of the Government, and was much used by the council. Whilst the chancery was fixed at Westminster, the privy seal office did on occasion follow the royal court or council into the provinces. Least formal of the three secretarial offices was that of the signet. The signet was used for sending the King's own letters to the council and to other officers, such as commanders in the field. Whilst the chancery letters were normally in Latin, and those of the privy seal either in Latin or French, Henry IV's signet letters were almost always in French. Some signet letters were written on the King's own immediate orders but even then the clerks formalised them. The office followed the King around the country, and was not usually far from the court, though not necessarily always in the same town on the same day. It is very largely from the signet letters that we can say whereabouts the King was at any given moment. Once or twice he even added a postscript to them in English in his own hand. Unfortunately very few of the records of the privy seal and signet office have survived, and those usually amongst the records of other offices. The surviving signet letters are not therefore very numerous, and non-routine ones are rare. Some have been printed by Nicolas in his *Proceedings*, and a few in other scattered places.[1] Unpublished ones may be found in a number of classes of records in the Public Record Office and occasionally elsewhere.

One valuable collection of copies of letters which survive mainly from Henry IV's reign has been printed as *Anglo-Norman Letters*.[2] This collection was evidently made and copied by some clerk as a formulary, so that he would have examples of how various kinds of letters should be written. Unfortunately he omitted all the dates, and reduced most of the personal names to initials, as these were of no particular interest for his purpose. However, the collection does contain a number of letters to and from Henry as king, from his son, the Prince of Wales, and from

[1] e.g. R. *Letters, H. IV,* ed. F. C. Hingeston; H. Ellis, *Orig. Letters,* 2nd ser.
[2] Ed. M. D. Legge

a number of other magnates, and some of them can be closely dated from other evidence.

The records of the third group, which are mainly records of the exchequer, are voluminous in the extreme. The pipe rolls running from the time of Henry I still recorded year by year the ancient revenues for which the sheriffs accounted. Memoranda rolls contain a mass of information about proceedings in the exchequer, and there are records of customs and other taxes, but of more immediate interest are the many accounts of expenditure by all kinds of royal officers, and the few accounts of the royal household, which give a brief glimpse of the King's daily life. The issue and receipt rolls record all the sums, whether in cash or by assignment, which passed through the lower exchequer, the exchequer of receipt. All these and many other financial records remain in manuscript and are easy neither to understand nor to use. They do however afford a great mass of detail about the administration of the kingdom, and occasionally about the King.

Many other records, the registers of bishops, some of which are printed, some local records, and a number of literary sources, all make minor contributions to the picture, but even so it is rare to find more than two or three consecutive words of praise or blame, of personal description, or explanatory exposition, relating to the King, or indeed to any other person.

Chapter 2

Henry of Bolingbroke, 1366–89

THE future King Henry IV, the only son of John of Gaunt, Duke of Lancaster, and his first wife Blanche to survive infancy, was born at the castle of Bolingbroke on the southern tip of the Lincolnshire wolds. The year was probably 1366, and the month perhaps April. In the fourteenth century no great care was taken to record or remember the birthdays even of members of the royal house, and few men could be sure of their own age. It was, however, the custom for members of noble families to make gifts on Maundy Thursday to as many poor people as there were years in their own ages, and for their officers to keep records of such gifts as of all other financial transactions. In Henry's case even these Maundy gift records are not very full – no doubt some of the early accounts perished when his father's palace of the Savoy was burnt by the rebels in 1381 – nor are they always consistent with each other, but they do suggest that he was born about April 1366. On Maundy Thursday, 3 April 1382, for example, he was fifteen and by April 1392 he was twenty-six, according to the accounts of his receiver for those years.[1] From the royal records on the other hand come two statements which seem to indicate 1367 as the year of Henry's birth. In the summer and autumn of that year two messengers were separately rewarded by the King and the Prince of Wales for bringing news of the birth of a son to the Duchess of Lancaster.[2] These rewards might have been very belated, or more probably might not relate to Henry at all. After Henry, the Duchess Blanche seems to have had at least one other son, who did not survive, so the rewards might have referred to his birth. The doubts remain, and it is only on 31 October 1368 that Henry's existence is firmly proved by the Duke of Lancaster's reference

[1] P.R.O., D.L. 28/1/1, 2 etc. The date is fully discussed in G.E.C. under Lancaster, vol. vii, p. 417n
[2] Devon, *Issues*, p. 191, 1 June 1367; *Cal. Pat.* (1377–81), pp. 194–5 For John of Gaunt's children see: Armitage–Smith, *Gaunt*, pp. 94, 464–5

to 'his very dear son Henry'.[1] In the absence of conclusive evidence it is convenient to take 1366, the most likely year, as the basis for reckoning Henry's age.

Henry's parents were cousins. His father, John of Gaunt, Earl of Richmond and Duke of Lancaster, although by birth the fourth son, was in 1366 the third of the five surviving sons of King Edward III. Blanche, Henry's mother, was the youngest daughter of Henry, Duke of Lancaster. They were married in 1359, just two years after the King's eldest son, Edward the Black Prince, had returned from his victory at Poitiers to celebrate an almost Roman triumph, leading the French King a captive through the streets of London. At that moment Edward III's dream of uniting the crowns of England and France seemed about to be realised, and he might look hopefully towards a future of brilliant marriages and broadening estates for his sons. John of Gaunt, the third son, who had already served in warlike expeditions against the French and the Scots, under the command both of his bride's father and of his own, was just nineteen when the wedding was celebrated on 19 May 1359 at Reading. From there the royal party rode to London to spend three days in jousting, the rough sport of that age which enabled all those of knightly rank to show off their skill in arms, their horsemanship, and the bright colours of their heraldic devices. The King himself took part on this occasion, with four of his sons, Edward, Lionel, John and Edmund, impersonating with nineteen other nobles, the twenty-four aldermen of the City of London,[2] a compliment much appreciated by the loyal citizens, who like everyone else were ever ready to applaud a victorious king. In such times of victory knightly prowess was rated high, and John also might well celebrate his victory, for in Blanche his father had found him an heiress, an heiress moreover to both broad estates and great titles.

Her father, Henry, Duke of Lancaster, a great-grandson of Henry III, died in 1361 two years after the marriage, leaving two daughters and co-heiresses, Maud, who was married to William of Hainault, Duke of Zealand, and Blanche. By thinning the ranks of the nobility, as well as those of the peasantry, the

[1] P.R.O., D.L. 29/4069/262
[2] Walsingham, *Hist. Angl.*, vol. i, p. 286; *Chron. J. de Reading*, pp. 131–2, 264–5

plague was proving itself a builder of great estates; and most fortunately for John of Gaunt and for his son, Henry, Maud too died without issue in 1362 leaving her sister, Blanche, as the sole heiress to the house of Lancaster. John had already been given the earldom of Richmond. After the death of his father-in-law in 1361 he was summoned to Parliament as Earl of Lancaster and Richmond, the former title being held in right of his wife, and in November 1362 he was created Duke of Lancaster. The earldoms of Derby, Lincoln and Leicester also came to him as part of the Lancaster inheritance. Blanche, seven years younger than her husband, was a mere child at the time of the marriage, and was also fated to die young. In September 1369, when she was about twenty-two, the plague killed her as it had already killed her sister. But she had been married for ten years, and besides her lands and titles, she left her husband two daughters, and one son, Henry Bolingbroke.

Both Blanche and her husband were well known to Geoffrey Chaucer, and in her memory Chaucer wrote his *Book of the Duchesse*, a portrait in words:

> And gode faire whyte she hete
> That was my lady name right
> She was bothe fair and bright
> She hadde not hir name wrong . . .
>
> I saw her daunce so comlily
> Carole and singe so swetely
> Laughe and playe so womanly
> And loke so debonairly
> So goodly speke and so frendly
> That certes I trow, that evermore
> Nas seyn so blisful a tresore
> For every heer upon hir hede
> Soth to seyn, hit was not rede
> Ne nouther yelwe, ne broun hit nas
> Me thoughte, most lyk golde hit was
> And whiche eyen my lady hadde![1]

And, although he was to marry twice more, John of Gaunt did not forget his first wife, for in his will thirty years later it was beside Blanche in St. Paul's Cathedral that he asked to be buried.

[1] G. Chaucer, vol. i, 'Book of the Duchesse', p. 306, p. 309

But for Henry, his mother can hardly have been even a memory.

Gaunt's second marriage in 1371 was to Constance of Castile, and the third in 1396 to Katherine Swynford. By Constance he had one daughter, Katherine; and by his last wife, Katherine Swynford, who had been his mistress for many years, he had a family of three sons, John, Henry and Thomas, and one daughter, Joan, all born before the marriage of their parents. The members of this family took the surname of Beaufort from one of the French lordships which had been held by their father, but although declared legitimate both by the Pope, and in 1397 by act of Parliament, they always remained somewhat apart from the house of Lancaster and the royal family. Thus the elder Henry stood alone. He was the only son of Gaunt's first marriage, and the only son on whose legitimacy no doubts might be cast. Moreover he alone was descended on both sides from the royal house of England, and he alone was heir, and heir from the moment of his birth, to the great wealth of the Lancaster estates.

If Henry was born in 1366 he was three years old at the time of his mother's death in 1369. In this same year his great-aunt, Blanche, Lady Wake, eldest daughter of an earlier Henry of Lancaster, and one of the executors of her brother the Duke, Henry's grandfather, was paid a hundred marks ($£66$ 13s. 4d.)[1] by John of Gaunt for looking after the young Henry and his servants.[2] Lady Wake's principal estate was at Bourne, some thirty miles to the south of Bolingbroke; and Bourne Castle, the ancient stronghold of the Wakes on the edge of the fens, was thus probably the first home which Henry would remember. Bolingbroke Castle, however, which had been in the possession of the house of Lancaster since the beginning of the century, long remained an administrative centre of the family estates, and Henry returned there as late as 1391 after his expedition to Prussia, but never, so far as is known, visited it as king.

In 1370 John of Gaunt succeeded his brother, Edward the

---

[1] The English mark was worth 13s. 4d. and, although never a coin, was much used for accounting purposes, especially for large sums. Thus 1,000 marks was $£666$ 13s. 4d. and 600 marks was $£400$. It has often been found simpler to retain this medieval usage rather than translate into £ s. d.

[2] Beltz, *Garter*, pp. 237-8; see account of John Stafford for Bolingbroke, 1368-9, P.R.O., D.L. 29/262/4069 (and perhaps 248/2890). She died 3 July 1380, *Cal. I.P.M.*, vol. xv, p. 181

Black Prince, as lieutenant of Aquitaine, and it was at Bordeaux in that duchy, that he married his second wife, Constance, daughter of Peter the Cruel, King of Castile, who had been killed and supplanted by his illegitimate half-brother, Henry of Trasta-mara. From the time of his second marriage Gaunt claimed the throne of Castile in the right of his wife, styling himself 'King of Castile and Leon', as well as Duke of Lancaster, for the next sixteen years; and although he contrived for a great deal of the time to play a leading part in English politics as well, his main interest was in Spain. That interest was one which his son, as he grew up, could not share, for whilst Henry was heir to the duchy of Lancaster, Katherine, the daughter of Gaunt's second marriage, inherited the claim to Castile. Thus Henry was cut off from his earliest years from playing any part in his father's most ambitious schemes; the Spanish claim stood as a barrier between the common interests of father and son.

Being the son of a royal duke, whose estates were worth more than £12,000 a year and whose household cost £5,000 a year to maintain,[1] figures which must have been far in excess of those of any other subject, Henry was naturally treated as a prince even in childhood. On 29 September 1372 he and his two sisters, Philippa and Elizabeth, had a yearly grant of £200 out of the revenues of the honour of Tutbury, part of the Lancaster estates, for the support of their household; and on the following day John Cheyne, clerk, was appointed receiver of their chamber. In 1374 Thomas de Burton esquire became Henry's 'governor'. Cheyne was one of the leading clerks in the service of John of Gaunt, acting for a time as treasurer of his own household, and Burton was one of the squires of the ducal household. When Henry was ten, in 1376, William Montendre was his tutor, Hugh Herle his chaplain, and Hugh Waterton esquire his chamberlain or keeper of the wardrobe.[2] Herle, who was to remain Henry's chaplain for nearly twenty years, was paid ten marks (£6 13s. 4d.) for buying him a missal and £12 for two horses. Hugh, the second son of William Waterton, belonged to a family serving long and loyally the house of Lancaster. He was one of the earliest members of a trusted group of knights and squires who entered the service

[1] Somerville, *Dy of Lancaster*, vol. i, pp. 90–3
[2] P.R.O., D.L. 28/3/1; *Gaunt's reg. 1372–6*, vol. i., pp. 127, 209, 211, 251; *Gaunt's reg. 1379–83*, vol. i, p. 201; vol. ii, p. 308

of the boy Earl and remained to serve him both as duke and
king, companions both in council and in the field. One at least of
these men, Sir Thomas Erpyngham, was in the service of Duke
John of Lancaster in 1380,[1] served his son, Henry IV, throughout
his life, and lived to serve in the campaign of Agincourt in 1415
under his grandson, Henry V, who greeted him, according to
Shakespeare:

> Good morrow, old Sir Thomas Erpyngham;
> A good soft pillow for that good white head
> were better than a churlish turf of France.[2]

Erpyngham was by that time in his late fifties and still had another
thirteen years to live. Henry, for his part, having no mother or
brothers, and an often absent father, came to rely a great deal
on the comradeship of such knights and squires, and it was in
them rather than in his earls and barons that he was to put his
trust as king.

Whilst Henry was thus spending his childhood in and between
his father's castles surrounded by trusty Lancastrian retainers,
the reign of his royal grandfather was approaching its end. The
heir to the throne, the Black Prince, died on 8 June 1376 at the
age of forty-six. Several years of declining health had followed
his victorious campaigns in France and Spain and prevented
him from taking an active part in either politics or war, with the
result that the Government of the ageing Edward III was deprived of its natural leader. On the Prince's death his son,
Richard of Bordeaux, then aged nine, was recognised as heir to
his grandfather, and in November created Prince of Wales,
Duke of Cornwall and Earl of Chester. On St. George's Day in
the following year (23 April 1377) the old King made his two
grandsons knights, admitting them to the Order of the Garter,
along with their uncle Thomas of Woodstock and others.[3]
Henry was probably just eleven and Richard eight months younger. For the two cousins, who were to reign over England for
the next thirty-six years, this ceremony marked the beginning
of their public careers; for King Edward III, who had reigned
for the last fifty years, it proved to be almost the end.

[1] *Gaunt's reg. 1379–83*, vol. i, pp. 8, 29
[2] Shakespeare, *Henry V*, Act 4, sc. i, ll. 13–16
[3] *Anonimalle Chron.*, p. 106

Edward died less than two months later, on 21 June, Richard became king, and was crowned on 16 July. At the coronation it fell to John of Gaunt, as head of the house of Lancaster and High Steward of England, to bear the sword *curtana*, the sword of mercy, but after High Mass he delegated this duty to his son, Henry. Thus it was that Henry of Bolingbroke came to play a formal part in the inception of Richard's reign, a reign which he himself was to bring to an abrupt end twenty-two years later on 29 September 1399.

After the coronation of Richard II neither he nor his cousin, Henry, was allowed to enjoy the obscurity of childhood. From 1377 Henry was known by one of his father's titles as Earl of Derby, although John of Gaunt did not altogether give up the use of this title himself. In 1378 the Duke exercised the feudal privilege of raising an aid for the knighting of his eldest son, and in the same year Henry was made warden of the regality of the palatinate of Lancaster, whilst his father was overseas.[1] Like all great men the Duke of Lancaster had a council comprising the principal officials of his household and estates, together with some of his household knights and esquires, some lawyers and a number of royal officials who were retained for advice and help in any business which the Duke might have pending in the King's courts, especially the exchequer or the chancery. Over this council it was henceforth Henry's duty to preside in the absence of his father, and indeed he very soon had a similar council of his own, though on a smaller scale. But just as the youth of his cousin, Richard, left the real government of the kingdom in the hands of his uncles and councillors, so Henry's youth left the real authority over the Lancaster estates in the hands of his father's knights and officials.

Shortly before the death of Edward III his youngest son, Thomas of Woodstock, was married to Eleanor, the elder daughter and co-heiress of Humphrey de Bohun, Earl of Hereford and Essex, who had died in January 1373. On 27 July 1380 the marriage of the other daughter, Mary, was bought from the King by John of Gaunt, for 5000 marks which was owed to him for his services in war, in order that she might be married to Henry.[2] Gaunt who had done so well by his own marriage was

[1] *D.K.R.*, vol. xxxii (1871), pp. 350–1 (aid 20 May, *custos* 12 June to 12 August)
[2] *Cal. Pat.* (1377–81), p. 537

naturally eager to see his son also married to an heiress. Thomas
on the other hand, hoping to secure the whole of the Bohun
inheritance for himself, strongly opposed the match, planning
to commit Mary to a nunnery. But he was unsuccessful; within a
few months, either in 1380 or early in 1381, Henry was married
to Mary Bohun. Henry was about fourteen, and Mary probably
ten or eleven.[1] For some time, perhaps until she was fourteen,
she continued to live with her mother, who was paid out of
Lancaster funds for her upkeep.[2] In December 1384 after Mary's
age had been proved, Henry was able to take possession of her
lands, and had for the first time estates of his own independent
of his father's. He secured the castles of Brecon and Hay, with
lands in Wiltshire, Gloucestershire and Hertfordshire, ten
advowsons, mostly in Wales and the west country, and a number
of knight's fees, including those for the earldoms of Hereford
and Northampton. Henceforth he was able to use the titles of
those earldoms along with that of Derby. It did not however
prove easy to secure the records of his new possessions. As late as
1393 his council and legal advisers were still fighting for his
share of the lands, and a final settlement was not reached until
the reign of his son, Henry V.[3]

Henry and Mary had four sons and two daughters. The eldest
son, Henry, the future Henry V, was born at Monmouth in
1387, and the next three years saw the births of Thomas, John
and Humphrey, who were eventually to become respectively
Dukes of Clarence, Bedford and Gloucester. The elder daughter,
Blanche, was born in 1392, and the second, Philippa, on 4 July
1394, her mother dying at her birth. The wives of Lancaster
seemed fated to die young, for Mary was still only about twenty-
four.

By the summer of 1381, when the great revolt took place,
John of Gaunt had become the best hated man in England. By

[1] Mary was probably born in 1369 or 1370. At the inquisitions after the death
of her father (16 January 1373) her age was variously given as 2, 3 or 4:
Cal. I.P.M., vol. xiii, pp. 130–46. She proved her age (14) on 22 December
1384: *G.E.C.* under Hereford, vol. vi, p. 477. Cf. Wylie *H. IV*, vol. iv, pp.
132–3 and note: *Gaunt's reg. 1379–83,* vol. i, pp. 179–80, shows that the marriage had taken place by March 1381
[2] *Gaunt's reg. 1379–83,* vol. i, pp. xl, 210, 309. Cf. Rymer, *Foedera,* vol. vii,
p. 343; *Cal. Pat.* (1381–5), p. 95
[3] Somerville, *Dy of Lancaster,* vol. i, p. 68

birth and nature he was an aristocrat more likely to scorn the feelings of the people than to court popularity. The failure of his military expeditions, and his behaviour in living openly with his daughters' governess, Katherine Swynford, did not make him popular: his political actions aroused bitter resentment. When the so-called 'Good Parliament' was meeting in the summer of 1376, the King being old and infirm, the Prince of Wales dying, and their heir Richard barely ten years old, the leadership of the Government fell perforce upon him. He was falsely accused of disloyalty and of trying to secure the succession to himself. The Commons attacked the King's ministers, and more strongly and more justly his mistress. After the dissolution of the Parliament Gaunt reacted brusquely; he imprisoned Peter de la Mare, leader of the Commons, and deprived William of Wykeham of his temporalities as Bishop of Winchester. The Parliament of the next year, 1377, was more favourably inclined towards Gaunt, but he widened his quarrel with the bishops, forcibly preventing them from trying Wycliff for heresy, and aroused the wrath of the citizens of London, who supposed that he was about to suspend their charters and take away their liberties. During the next three years Gaunt was held responsible for the unpopular acts of the Government, notably the poll-taxes, whilst at the same time accused of trying to supplant his nephew. Consequently it was to be expected that both rebellious peasants and rioting citizens of London would look first for the property and perhaps the family of the Duke of Lancaster when they began to burn and pillage.

As soon as the rebellion began Henry took refuge with King Richard in the Tower; but whilst Richard rode to Mile End to parley with the rebels on 14 June, the mob broke into the Tower where most of the court had remained, carelessness or treachery having left the doors unguarded. Simon Sudbury, Archbishop of Canterbury, Robert Hales the treasurer, and a number of others were beheaded by the rebels; but Henry's life was saved by a certain John Ferrour of Southwark. Twenty years later Henry was able to repay this service. Ferrour was tried with others for treason at Oxford Castle in 1400. Whilst the others were executed Ferrour was granted a free pardon for having saved the King's life in 1381. John of Gaunt himself meanwhile was fortunate enough to be away on the northern border treating with the

Scots, and when he heard that he might be in danger if he returned south, even took refuge in Scotland for a short time. When he did return all was over, but his great palace of the Savoy beside the Thames between London and Westminster was no more. On that the rebels had turned their hatred and their anger. His wines were consumed, his furnishings, his treasures and his records were burnt with the palace itself.

During the summer of the next year, 1382, both Gaunt and his son Henry were present at Lincoln at the trial before the Bishop of William Swinderby, a Lollard commonly known as 'the hermit';[1] Gaunt's Lollard sympathies, if he ever had any, being already forgotten. By this time the young Earl of Derby had his own house in Fleet Street, and a wardrobe in Coleman Street in London. Hugh Waterton was still his treasurer, and his household included a yeoman of the chamber, two clerks and esquires, and a keeper of the palfreys. Hugh Waterton's account as Henry's receiver for the year 1381–2 has survived. It shows Henry, now fifteen or sixteen, leading the normal life of a nobleman with an itinerant household, and his own council, distinct from his father's council of the duchy. In the course of twelve months he visited Pontefract, Leicester, Lincoln, Kenilworth, Tutbury and a number of other places, ranging from York in the north to Windsor and London in the south. If he stayed longer at one place than any other it was at Hertford Castle, which was to remain a favourite, perhaps *the* favourite, residence after his accession to the throne. Most of the places where he stayed were of course Lancastrian castles or manor houses.[2]

The only life known to Henry and those of his rank and age was that of the itinerant household. Whether as young nobleman, as adventurer, pilgrim or exile overseas, as duke or king at home, he was continually on the move. His rank made him the leader of a body of companions and servants, comparatively small in peace, swollen to an army in war, which travelled on from place to place, visiting tenants, friends or subjects. Usually there would be an advance party perhaps with heralds, seeking out and preparing lodgings, then the main cavalcade, and finally a string of carts laden with baggage of all kinds. Not only did the lack of sanitation make frequent moves desirable for a large

[1] McFarlane, *Wycliffe*, p. 113
[2] P.R.O., D.L. 28/1/1

party, but also it was necessary for a lord to be seen by his tenants, and a king by his subjects. Moreover if a lord had many castles and manors growing food for his followers and their horses, it might be easier to take men and horses to their food rather than to bring food to them. That was in time of peace. War differed from peace mainly in the urgency of the marches, the size of the following, and the problems of supply. For Henry life tended to be one long campaign, with seasonal moves to various places, and an accompanying household growing with his own importance.

With all this travelling it is hardly surprising to find that in 1381–2 'horses' was the heaviest item in Waterton's account of expenses, £113 out of £237, or almost half of the total. Several small sums were spent on play – presumably Henry was gambling with his followers – and others on gifts and religious offerings. Two more names of those who were to go forward in the company of the Duke and King appear, Thomas Totty as yeoman of the chamber, and William Loveney as the Earl's clerk. A similar account for five years later introduces Simon Bache, another of the band, as treasurer of the household. Waterton remained chamberlain and receiver-general. A councillor and an attorney in the exchequer, Thomas Paufrey and Richard Gascoigne, were named, and Henry's London house was described as St. David's in Fleet Street.[1]

By the 'nineties there was a complete household administration with chamberlain, steward of the estates, clerk of the great wardrobe, and a steward, a treasurer, and a controller of the household, together with a receiver-general and auditors. Though itinerant the household was most often to be found at Peterborough or in London. The council included the chamberlain and the estates steward, with two serjeants at law, three apprentices and three attornies, one in each of the three principal courts. The serjeants, William Gascoigne and John Markham, both of whom were to become judges in Henry's reign, had a fee of 20s. each, the apprentices 40s. or 13s. 4d.[2]

The household accounts also reveal a close relationship between Henry and Geoffrey Chaucer, both of whom were in-

[1] P.R.O., D.L. 28/1/1 and 28/1/2
[2] Somerville, *Dy of Lancaster*, vol. i, pp. 131–3, 385–7. The last group of pages contains a list of Henry's officers

debted to Gilbert Mawfield, a London merchant banker in 1392. In 1395 William Loveney as clerk of the wardrobe bought 101 civet skins from Robert Markeley of London for the considerable sum of £8 8s. 4d. in order to provide a scarlet gown for the poet at Henry's expense, and shortly afterwards Chaucer delivered £10 from Loveney into Henry's hands in London. On 19 February in the next year Henry was admitted to the fraternity of Lincoln Cathedral, and was thus enabled to share the spiritual benefits of the masses celebrated there. There were many lay members of the fraternity, including his own father, admitted in 1343. Most of the people admitted to the order with Henry on this occasion belonged to the family circle, being relatives of his father's new wife, Katherine Swynford, and may indeed have been gathered at Lincoln for the wedding, which had been celebrated there shortly beforehand. They included Sir Thomas Swynford, Katherine's son by her first husband, Sir John Beaufort, her eldest son by her new husband, John of Gaunt, Robert Ferrers, the husband of her daughter Joan Beaufort, and Philippa Chaucer, her sister and the poet's wife.[1]

Twelve years earlier in December and January 1383–4 Henry was put on a commission with his father to negotiate with Flanders and went to Calais for that purpose,[2] his first journey overseas so far as is known. In 1384 he accompanied John of Gaunt on his expedition against the Scots, and from September 1385 he was summoned to successive Parliaments as Earl of Derby, although it is not until 1387 that there is definite evidence of his attendance. By this time Henry was twenty-one; his boyhood was far behind, and he was at last ready to play a distinctive part of his own in the affairs of the kingdom.

As boys the cousins Richard and Henry may have been much together, but apart from their ages they had little in common. If Richard had taste and imagination, Henry was more conventional, ready to accept the values which his world offered, and not inclined to look beyond them. He took his part in knightly exercises and was soon to distinguish himself in the lists, as his father and uncles had done before him. Richard, who was not physically strong enough for such sport, must have envied him his prowess, whilst the exaggerated respect which as king he

[1] *Chaucer Life-Records*, pp. 91–2, 275, 501–2
[2] Rymer, *Foedera*, vol. vii, pp. 412–13

developed for his own regality was not calculated to appeal to one who, like Henry, was so near and yet so far from the throne. The contrast between Richard's state and his own, between the royal council which ruled a kingdom, and the duchy council which merely administered estates, was a natural source of jealousy. A prince who preferred the camp had but little sympathy for one who preferred the court. Even so, Henry's opposition to Richard was moderate and of slow growth, only becoming complete when Richard's mistrust and treachery drove him to seek revenge.

It was John of Gaunt's absence from the kingdom which created the occasion for his son's first period of opposition. Edmund of Langley, afterwards Duke of York, Gaunt's younger brother, had been sent to Portugal in 1381 to conquer Castile for Gaunt. Towards the end of the following year he returned to England completely unsuccessful. Indeed he left Portugal temporarily at peace with the Trastamara Government of Castile, which he had been sent to overthrow. This peace did not last very long, and in 1386 Gaunt decided that his turn had come. In July he set sail from Plymouth, determined to land an army in Spain and make good his fifteen-year-old claim to Castile and Leon. Henry went to Plymouth to see his father, stepmother, and sisters depart, for John of Gaunt was taking his family with him; if war should fail he would try to conquer by way of marriage. Whilst at Plymouth, on 16 June 1386, in the palace of John of Gaunt in the house of the friars Carmelites Henry gave evidence in the famous heraldic dispute between Richard, Lord Scrope of Bolton, and Robert Grosvenor of Hulme, who were both claiming the right to use the same arms. In giving his evidence Henry said that he was young and had borne arms for but a short time.[1]

After King Richard's expedition to Scotland in 1385 he made his two youngest uncles dukes. Edmund of Langley became Duke of York and Thomas of Woodstock, Duke of Gloucester. York, as he had proved in Portugal, was singularly lacking both in character and ability. Though by nature a nonentity, he remained throughout his life, owing to his outstanding birth and rank, something of an embarrassment to all parties. With Gaunt away overseas the middle or moderate party, which he had led,

[1] Nicholas, *Scrope and Grosvenor*, vol. i, p. 50; vol. ii, pp. 163, 165–6

broke up, and Thomas, Duke of Gloucester, the King's youngest uncle, was left leading a group of magnates who wished to control both the King and the kingdom. Gloucester was still only thirty-one years of age and possessed neither common sense nor the respect for the King's estate which had been shown by his brother, John of Gaunt. When the Parliament, always known to history though not perhaps to contemporaries, as the Wonderful Parliament, met in October 1386, Richard II provoked the opposition by creating his favourite, Robert de Vere, already Marquess of Dublin, Duke of Ireland. The parliamentary opposition then asked for the removal of the King's chancellor and treasurer, Michael de la Pole, newly created Earl of Suffolk, and John Fordham, Bishop of Durham. After withdrawing from Westminster to Eltham Richard finally gave way. Thomas Arundel, Bishop of Ely, became chancellor, and John Gilbert, Bishop of Hereford, treasurer; whilst Parliament set up an executive commission to rule the country for one year. This included the two royal Dukes and the Earl of Arundel, who like his brother, the new chancellor, was a supporter of Gloucester. The ex-chancellor, de la Pole, was then impeached, convicted and heavily fined.

Richard had already shown himself completely lacking in all those qualities of tact and statesmanship that were required of a king, and it was only the advantage of possession combined with the strength of his subjects' reverence for 'such divinity' as 'doth hedge a king', which kept him on the throne for another twelve years. His uncontrolled outbursts of temper were not compatible with the 'political dominion' of the Kings of England, which Sir John Fortescue was to contrast with the absolute rule of other kings.[1] Now deprived of all power he withdrew from London, and in 1387 twice formally consulted the judges as to the validity of the appointment of the parliamentary commission. They pronounced it illegal, giving him the answer which he wanted, whereupon he returned to London in November and summoned Gloucester and Arundel to his presence. After joining forces with the Earl of Warwick in Essex, however, these two finally came to Westminster, and there appealed, or accused, five of the King's supporters of treason. Richard replied by referring their cases to Parliament which was to meet in the following February.

[1] Fortescue, *Governance*, pp. 109–10 etc.

Four of his five accused supporters fled, including de Vere, who went north to Cheshire, and there raised an army.

So far Henry had kept himself somewhat in the background. His eldest son, the future Henry V, was born at Monmouth in August 1387, and Henry himself was perhaps in the marches of Wales during the autumn. His closest associate at this time was Thomas Mowbray, Earl of Nottingham, and afterwards Duke of Norfolk. A list of John of Gaunt's followers shows Henry's name first, followed by that of Mowbray.[1] He was a few days older than Henry, and was now married to Elizabeth, the daughter of the Earl of Arundel, who was himself a cousin of Henry's mother, being the son of Eleanor of Lancaster. The two Earls had therefore several close ties with the three opposition lords, Gloucester, Arundel and Warwick, and with Arundel's brother, Thomas, now chancellor and Bishop of Ely; but it was not until December 1387 that they joined forces, and even after that Derby and Nottingham seem to have been on the side of moderation.

De Vere having raised an army in Cheshire set out for London, but, hearing that the forces of the now united five lords were blocking his path at Northampton, marched southwards through Stow-on-the-Wold. Derby then advanced to prevent his crossing the Thames, whilst the other lords by occupying the Cotswold towns behind him forced him into a trap at Radcot Bridge in Oxfordshire. Henry had part of the bridge demolished and placed a guard of men-at-arms and archers on it. There was some fighting when de Vere reached the bridge, but when he discovered that Gloucester's forces were coming up behind him, he abandoned his army and tried to swim his horse across the Thames. He escaped to make his way to join the King at Windsor, whilst his deserted followers were quickly dispersed by the five lords and their men.[2] Thereupon Richard sought refuge in the Tower of London, all power remaining in the hands of his enemies. Adam of Usk, the chronicler, then a law student at Oxford, 'saw the host of the five lords march through the city on their way to London from the battlefield; whereof the Earls of Warwick and Derby led the van, the Duke of Gloucester

---

[1] *Gaunt's reg. 1379–83*, vol. i, p. 6
[2] J. N. L. Myres, 'The campaign of Radcot Bridge in December 1387', *E.H.R.*, vol. xlii (1927), pp. 20–33

the main body, and the Earls of Arundel and Nottingham the rear.'[1]

By 27 December the army of the appellants was encamped at Clerkenwell, and Richard was in the Tower little more than a mile away, his possible escape routes cut off. The events of the next few days are very obscure; the deposition of Richard had already been discussed before Radcot Bridge but opposed by the Earl of Warwick. Now it may well be that Richard was actually deposed, and that for the last three days of 1387 England had no king. But who was to succeed? Gloucester and Derby representing two separate branches of the royal house could not agree. So failing to find a successor they replaced Richard and hushed up his deposition. If this is a true account of what took place, and it has been most convincingly argued,[2] it helps to explain the distrust of both Norfolk and Derby, which Richard was to display at Coventry eleven years later. It may also have served as a rehearsal for the events of 1399, with Henry already one of the principal actors, if not yet able to take the lead as he did in the later years. Even if Richard was not deposed his cousin was at the centre of events able to see how a throne might be lost or won, and in defeating de Vere at Radcot Bridge almost without bloodshed he had shown his tactical ability. Richard, whether he had been temporarily deposed or not, was humiliated, and still in the power of the five lords when Parliament met on 3 February 1388. The fact that he was made to renew his coronation oath at the end of the session may indicate either that the lords felt he had broken it, or perhaps that they had weakened it by deposing him.

By its treatment of the King's friends this Parliament earned for itself the name of the Merciless Parliament. The five appellants entered the assembly arm-in-arm, a rough and overbearing display of their power. All the King's supporters were condemned even though the Queen went down on her knees to plead for the life of Simon Burley, Richard's tutor, and Henry himself is said to have wished to spare Burley's life. For three weeks Richard tried to save him, but finally in order so keep his throne he gave way, and Burley was beheaded on 5 May. The Parliament ended in June and another met at Cambridge in September.

[1] *Usk*, p. 145
[2] Clarke, *Fourteenth Cent. Studies*, pp. 91–5

Everything went as the magnates wished until May in the next year, 1389. Then Richard suddenly took the initiative. In a great council at Westminster he announced that he was old enough to rule of his own, and dismissed the officers appointed by the appellants. A moderate chancellor and treasurer were named in the persons of the Bishops of Winchester and Exeter, William of Wykeham and Thomas Brantingham. Richard, regarding Nottingham and Derby as the more moderate appellants, attempted to win them over. Nottingham was confirmed in office as Warden of the East March towards Scotland, whilst Henry remained a councillor, and was present in the council on 13 September.

Two months later on 19 November John of Gaunt landed in England once more. Militarily his expedition had been as much of a fiasco as that of his brother Edmund; his force had simply melted away without a battle. But diplomatically it had not been unsuccessful; he had triumphed by way of marriage. His eldest daughter Philippa was married to the King of Portugal, and Katherine, the daughter of his second marriage with Constance, to Henry, son of John I of Castile. To John, the son and heir of Henry of Trastamara, Gaunt sold his wife's claim to the throne of Castile, after prolonged negotiations, for a capital sum of £100,000 and a yearly pension of £6,600.[1] On 10 December 1389, he, Gloucester and Arundel were all present at a council at Reading. Now that he was free to devote himself once more to English affairs, there was a chance that more moderate counsels might prevail; and for Henry, his son, there was a lessening of responsibility, a withdrawal from the foreground of politics.

His sister, Philippa, and his half-sister, Katherine, Henry was never to see again. He had been brought up with Philippa and their sister, Elizabeth, and it is possible that had his exile lasted longer in 1399 he would have gone to Lisbon to see her. Certainly their relationship remained as close as the distance would allow. Philippa continued to correspond with him, and interceded with him on behalf of her friends. Elizabeth, the thrice-married younger sister, was evidently the least serious member of the family.

[1] Russell, *Eng. Intervention*, pp. 505–6

Chapter 3

Crusader and pilgrim, 1390–3

JOHN of Gaunt's return from his expedition to Spain left his son free to escape from the discords of Richard's court. Henry, a married man with three sons, was now twenty-three years of age. Most of those years he had spent journeying slowly across the north and the midlands of England, as far south as London, and sometimes into the marches of Wales. In the company of his father he had fought on the Scottish border, and been on a diplomatic mission to Calais. Left on his own he had become a leader in the skirmish at Radcot Bridge, had borne arms against the King's friends, and had played his part in the conflicts which disturbed Richard's Parliaments and councils; but compared with many contemporary princes and noblemen he had seen little of either war or foreign travel. The next ten years were to be very different, to widen his experience, and include all the foreign travel, if not all the fighting, of his life.

In 1390 his family was probably at Kenilworth or one of the other Lancastrian strongholds on the Welsh border. In January and February he attended the Parliament at Westminster. However, that was over by the beginning of March, and he was able to look for another occupation. At this moment there came a challenge from three French knights, led by Jean de Boucicaut, afterwards Marshal of France, a redoubtable young warrior of exactly the same age as Henry himself. The three knights, prevented by the truce from fighting their traditional enemies, offered to joust for the honour of France, undertaking to hold the field at St. Inglevert, half-way between Boulogne and Calais, against all comers for thirty days from 1 March. The challenge was carried all over Europe, and perhaps brought to England by John of Gaunt's own Lancaster herald. The place chosen, lying as it did on the borders of the English pale at Calais, was in itself a provocation to the knights of England; and they, bored like their French counterparts by a truce which deprived them of their natural occupation, were not slow to respond. Amongst

28

the first challengers were the Earl of Huntingdon, the Earl Marshal, the Lords Beaumont and Clifford and Sir Peter Courtenay. Other knights came from Bohemia, Germany and northern Europe. Henry was not far behind. He arrived towards the middle of the month with nine other knights, including John Beaufort, his half-brother, Thomas Swynford, the son of his father's mistress, Katherine Swynford, by her first husband, and Henry Percy, better known to history as Hotspur. 'These foreigners', we are told, 'were recognised as the bravest of all the challengers.' The tournaments went on from day to day, probably lasting well into April, and Henry had ample opportunity to meet many of the leaders of the chivalry of Europe.[1]

Boucicaut, campaigning from the age of twelve, was almost as experienced and well-travelled as Chaucer's gentle knight. He had already served in Normandy, in Guyenne and in Castile, as well as at the battle of Roosebecke, where he was knighted. Latterly he had been in the East, to Hungary, and then by way of Venice to Damascus, Cairo and Palestine. Now he was doubtless talking about the war which the Teutonic knights were waging in the lands by the Baltic, and in which he was himself to take part in the following year.[2] Also he was perhaps boasting about the successes which the French would soon be having against the heathen on the Barbary coast of North Africa. Both these minor wars, which offered employment to idle knights and soldiers of fortune from all over Christendom, could, since the enemy were not Christians, be dignified with the name of crusade. Henry, a simple orthodox churchman, was anxious all his life to serve the church by leading a crusade against the infidels, and now he determined to embark on both crusades.

He returned to London, and on 6 May appointed Richard Kingston, Archdeacon of Hereford since 1379, to be his treasurer for wars for the journeys which he said he was about to make both into Barbary and into Prussia.[3] Horses and stores were purchased in London, and Henry immediately returned to Calais, following the old Dover Road, which was always busy with

[1] *Religieux de Saint-Denys*, vol. i, pp. 673–83. *Chronographie Regum Francorum*, vol. iii, p. 97; Boucicaut, pp. 583–5
[2] *Dict. Biog. Franc.*, vol. vi, art. Boucicaut
[3] The remainder of this chapter is based, unless otherwise indicated, on Smith, *Expeditions*

pilgrims, soldiers, merchants and diplomats, making their way
to Dover by way of Rochester and Canterbury, and thence
across the Channel. From 9 to 31 May he had a number of men-at-
arms and archers in his pay at Calais, apparently waiting to go
on the expedition to the Barbary coast. Two of his followers, Sir
William Elmham and John Stokes esquire, were sent to Paris
to ask the French King for a safe-conduct for his party. Whether
this was refused or not is not known, but certainly Henry soon
abandoned the idea, and no more is heard of his going to the
Barbary coast. At the end of May he began to send his men home,
and on 5 June crossed back to England with his personal following. Meanwhile, however, John Beaufort, his half-brother,
with twenty-four English knights and a hundred archers did
apparently join the Barbary crusade.

Henry had decided to go to Prussia instead. Active preparations
for this expedition were at once begun. Richard Kingston as
treasurer received 1,000 marks from Hugh Waterton, who was
still Henry's chamberlain, and small sums from Simon Bache,
the treasurer of his household, and John Leventhorp, his receiver-
general; but the main cost of the journey, amounting to more than
£4,000 in all, was paid by John of Gaunt, out of the money which
he had brought back from Spain after selling his claim to the
throne of Castile. Within little more than a month of returning
from Calais Henry visited Hertford and Berkhamstead to see his
father and his children, made offerings in Lincoln Cathedral
with his wife, and collected his men and stores at Boston. By
8 July vessels had been hired at Boston – three were needed to
transport the expedition – and carpenters were being employed
to build cabins for Henry and his knights. They sailed on the
19th, and arrived in Prussia after a voyage of three weeks.

Eleven knights or squires, Peter Bukton, John Clifton,
Thomas Erpyngham, Richard Goldsburgh, John Loudeham,
John Loveyn, John Norbury, Thomas Rempston, Thomas
Swynford, Hugh Waterton and William Willoughby, son and
heir of Lord Willoughby, accompanied Henry, but strangely
enough, Swynford seems to be the only one of them who had
been in his company at St. Inglevert. Of the others Erpyngham
and Waterton had of course already been in Henry's service for
some years, and a number were to hold high office after he came
to the throne. These eleven had at least seven archers in their

company. Henry had four household officers, eighteen other squires – including Thomas Totty in his service since 1383 – twenty-five yeomen or grooms and six minstrels, making a known total of just over seventy who travelled from England; but the real total must have been a good deal larger, perhaps more than double, since many servants were not separately paid or named. After arriving in Prussia the party was increased by the employment of a large number of Germans to perform the more menial tasks. Even so it is unlikely that the total was much more than 300 men, the lowest figure suggested by the chroniclers.

The ships touched at various places to obtain water and provisions; fish for example was bought at Stralsund. Leba on the coast of Pomerania was reached on 8 August, and there Robert Waterton, Thomas Totty and John Payne were landed as an advance party. Henry himself landed at Rixhöft (Rozewie), where bread, beer, mead, fish and firewood were bought, to prepare the first meal on land. The party proceeded in, or with, three carts to Putzig (Puck), where a horse and saddle were bought for their leader. The night of the 9th was spent at a mill by the road, and on the 10th they reached Danzig (Gdánsk), where they stayed until 13 August, in the house of the 'Lord de Burser', possibly Bourchier. Here it was learnt that Engelhard Rabe, the marshal of the Teutonic knights, had already started his campaign, and Henry lost no time. Lancaster herald was sent forward with letters from John of Gaunt to the Grand Master of the knights at Marienburg (Malbork). The stores and horses brought with the expedition were unloaded at Danzig and additional ones bought. Thirteen carts with their horses and carters were hired, as well as shallow boats to take all the heavy baggage and some of the horses to Königsberg (Kaliningrad) by water.

Crossing the Vistula without staying at Marienburg Henry's party spent the night of the 14th at Elbing (Elblag). The next day they rode through Braunsberg (Braniewo) and Brandenburg, and arrived on the 16th at Königsberg. From there the heavy baggage was carted to Insterburg (Chernyakhovsk) Castle to be left in store for the duration of the campaign. Two tents and a horse to carry them were hired, and another twenty-two carts, with four horses each, were employed in carrying the stores and provisions on the expedition itself.

Two German knights were appointed by the Grand Master to accompany Henry, who set off again on 18 August, slept at Kremitten, passed through Tapiau and Norkitten, and on the 21st entered the forest on the borders of Lithuania. This forest was too dense for the carts to get through, and some of the provisions had then to be transferred to packhorses. On the next day the English contingent came up with the main army under Marshal Rabe, probably near Ragnit, and by the 24th they had reached and crossed the Memel (Neman) river. Henry received a warm welcome. Musicians were provided by the Master of Livland, who had joined the army, and presents of horses, an ox, sheep and peacocks were received from the marshal and his knights. Near Trappöhnen on the Memel news was received of the death of the Grand Master of the knights, Konrad Zölner von Rotenstein, but this was not allowed to hold up the operations. It was learnt at the same time that the enemy commander, Skirgal, with a strong force was beside the Memel at its confluence with the Vilnya. An immediate surprise attack was launched. On 25 August the combined army lay before Georgenburg (Jurbakas). Marching through the forest towards Kovno (Kaunas) they forced the Vilnya, attacked and defeated Skirgal, captured three dukes and eleven boyars, as well as two hundred horses, and continued their advance. Sir John Loudeham was killed, whilst fording the river, and his body was taken to Königsberg.

The victory was won on Sunday, 28 August. On 4 September the outerworks of Vilnya, the strongly fortified capital of Lithuania, were captured, thanks largely, as it was said, to the efforts of Henry and his followers, one of whom first planted his flag on the walls. Many prisoners were taken, many people slaughtered, and many homes burnt. The army then laid siege to the two forts which defended the hill city, but after five weeks, was forced by sickness and shortage of stores to abandon the attempt to capture them. The army split up, the different contingents returning to their homes. Henry and his party set off to return to Königsberg, taking with them a number of captive Lithuanians, who had been converted to Christianity.

The return journey followed much the same route as the outward one. The English party passed near the junction of the Vilnya and the Memel, through Insterburg and the forest to Tapiau, whence Henry sent his man, John Gylder, with letters o England. On 20 October Königsberg was reached once more. One knight had been killed and two captured during the campaign. Henry attempted to persuade the Poles to intercede for the release of the two captives – Derby herald was twice sent to King Jagello on their behalf – but it is not known whether they were ever set free. At Königsberg on 1 November Henry learnt the news of the birth of his fourth and last son, Humphrey, who for no obvious reason was to be remembered in succeeding centuries as 'the good Duke'.

Soon after this Henry must have decided not to return home until the spring. The ports may have been frozen, or the risks of bad weather considered too great for the whole party in winter. On 4 December he gave letters of attorney for one year to eight of his councillors in England, presumably because he expected to be away for some time. About four months including Christmas and the New Year were spent at Königsberg. Tournaments and hunting parties were doubtless the normal amusements of his hosts, and additional ones were perhaps arranged for his entertainment. He was repeatedly presented with gifts of horses and hawks, deer, three young bears, a wild bull, perhaps an elk. Some animals were no doubt intended as food, others for use, or as curiosities. The party left Königsberg on 15 February, and were then at Danzig until 31 March. At least sixty persons were still on the payroll, including Sir Peter Bukton, steward, John Dyndon, valet of the wardrobe, Hugh Waterton, chamberlain, Richard Kingston, treasurer, Robert Waterton, marshal, Hugh Herle, chaplain, John, Derby herald, William Pomfreit, chief clerk of the kitchen, John Payne, butler, and John Dounton, armourer, Erpyngham, Swynford and Dalyngrigg, knights, Norbury, Malet and fourteen other squires, twenty-five yeomen or valets, and six minstrels. Besides this permanent band of six many other musicians of various kinds were constantly arriving to entertain the English party. Fur dresses for many members of the household to enable them to endure the Baltic winter figure in the accounts.

On 9 February the household began to move from Königsberg and by the 15th they were at Danzig. Here Henry was temporarily housed in the home of a burgess called Klaus Gottesknicht, whilst the greater part of his retinue moved into the castle of the Bishop of Leslau. This was evidently in a ruinous state, but was quickly made habitable, whereupon Henry rejoined his followers in it. At Danzig he made a seven-day pilgrimage visiting four churches each day, probably during Easter week. Meanwhile two ships were hired with Prussian masters and English pilots from Boston. Carpenters set to work once again erecting cabins for the knights and squires, and stables and cages for the livestock; for besides the gifts which he had received Henry had bought a number of birds and animals of various species. Quantities of stores were collected. Easter Sunday, 26 March, was spent in festivities and offerings in the churches. Finally about 31 March the ships sailed for home. The party disembarked at Hull, probably at the end of April. Some of the baggage was sent in coastal vessels to Boston, some ferried across the Humber to Barton, and thence taken southwards to Bolingbroke. At Barton food and other necessaries were bought for 'Bewford' – perhaps John Beaufort if he had come to meet the party on their return – Thomas Swynford and others, white bread, wine, beer, fish, milk, starch, saffron, butter, salt, firewood, fodder and horseshoes. Henry followed the same route, eating a hasty supper at Caistor on the way. From Bolingbroke he made a pilgrimage to Bridlington, presumably to give thanks for his success and safe return, going by way of Horncastle, Louth, Caistor, Barton-upon-Humber, Beverley and Watton.

In November 1391 he attended Parliament and was appointed a trier of petitions. He was at Peterborough, where minstrels were paid for his entertainment in October, at Hertford in January and London in February and April,[1] but otherwise his activities have left no record for almost a year.

The next journey was a diplomatic one. John of Gaunt had undertaken to visit the French King in an attempt to convert the existing truce into a firm peace between the two countries. His retinue was an imposing one. With him he took his brother, the Duke of York, his son, Henry Earl of Derby, the Earl of Huntingdon and Sir Thomas Percy. The party landed at Calais early in March 1392. From the boundary of the Calais pale the Duke of Lancaster and his party, numbering, it is said, a thousand horsemen, were escorted by the Count of St. Pol to St. Riquier and Doullens. On Monday, 25 March the King of France, Charles VI, made a state entry into Amiens, accompanied by his

[1] P.R.O., D.L. 28/1/3

lords, knights and men-at-arms. At the same time Gaunt rode in from Doullens escorted by the princes of France. Before going to his lodging he insisted on visiting the King, who was at the Archbishop's palace. The English were housed at Malmaison, and were royally entertained with banquets, but although both sides were anxious for peace there was a great deal of difference of opinion as to what would constitute an acceptable settlement. The French would have liked to see the surrender of Calais, the English a return of the peace of Bretigny, both absurdly impractical claims at that time. No progress was in fact made, and the existing truce was simply prolonged for another year. In April the party returned to England to report the results of their mission to the King and council.[1]

By this time Henry was already thinking of another expedition to Prussia. At the beginning of July 1392 Kingston was again asked to act as treasurer, and set out from Hereford, where he was archdeacon, for Lynn. He arrived on 15 July and was formally appointed treasurer of war. On 1 July John of Gaunt had granted his son 2,000 marks a year to be paid quarterly from the revenues of Tutbury and Bolingbroke. On the 19th he advanced the 2,000 for the first year and made a gift of a further 1,000, so that in addition to his own revenues he had (the mark being 13s. 4d.) £2,000 to begin with. In all he was to spend nearly £5,000 before he saw England again, and probably most of it came from his father as before. Stores were bought in London and Lynn, and some baggage was brought there from Peterborough. Three ships were prepared for the voyage and the party sailed from Heacham, on the Wash, on 24 July.

This time Henry's more important followers included Otto Granson, a distinguished Burgundian knight, William Willoughby, Hugh Waterton, Peter Bukton, Ralph Rochford, Richard Kingston and Hugh Herle. Sir Thomas Erpyngham joined them later at Schöneck (Skarszewy) near Danzig. The fifteen squires, of whom eleven had been on the previous journey, included Thomas Totty, John Payne, and Robert and John Waterton. There were also two heralds, Master William Cook, William Pomfreit, clerk of the kitchen, John Fisher the baker, forty-nine yeomen, seven minstrels and two 'henksmen', or grooms. At least twenty-four out of the last group of fifty-eight had served on the previous

[1] *Religieux de Saint-Denys*, vol. i, pp. 737–43; Froissart, Bk. iv, chap. 27

expedition. Altogether the party may well have comprised upwards of two hundred persons, nearly half of whom had probably accompanied Henry before.

Making a quicker journey than on the previous occasion the party landed at Putzig and Danzig on 10 August, and stayed there for a fortnight, occupying three houses. On the 25th Henry set out, passing through Dirschau to Elbing, where he made offerings at the Augustinian abbey on the 29th. On the 31st he was at Braunsberg, and at Königsberg on 2 September. There he evidently found a much less warm welcome than two years earlier. This was perhaps simply because there was for the moment no campaign in which he could be employed, and not, as has been stated, because one of his followers had killed someone at Danzig, but there is no real clue to the reasons for his change of plan. At all events, although his services were not required, the Teutonic order did pay him £400 towards his expenses in coming to their aid, or perhaps to buy him off. He only stayed one or two nights at Königsberg, and was back at Danzig by 7 September, having now decided on a pilgrimage to the Holy Land instead.

Whatever the reason for this sudden turn round, it necessitated some changes in his retinue. On 3 October one ship was sent back to England with Robert and John Waterton and four other squires, about six minstrels, twenty-four yeomen, and William Pomfreit. Meanwhile on 22 September Henry left Danzig with the main party, including seven officers and knights, about ten squires, two heralds, upwards of thirty yeomen and servants, the trumpeter and a hired guide, that is to say about fifty altogether without mentioning personal servants, and others employed temporarily during the journey. Others joined them by the way, Peter Seinlatour for example, and at Venice an Austrian knight, Ralph de Vienna; and some others no doubt dropped out so that the numbers were always fluctuating.[1] From Danzig they went to Schöneck, where, as has been said, Sir Thomas Erpyngham joined them. From there they went through Hammerstein (Czarne), Poleschken (Polczyn), Schievelbein (Swidwin), Dramburgh (Dransko), Arnswalde (Choszczno), Landsberg (Gorzow Wielkopolski) and Drossen (Osno), following the Oder up-

---

[1] Richard II asked the King of France and the Duke of Burgundy to give Henry safe conducts for up to 200 persons. *Anglo-Norman Letters*, pp. 139–40

stream to Frankfurt by 4 October; then up the Neisse by Gubin to Görlitz and so to Prague on the 13th. Here at the court of King Wenceslas of Bohemia, whose sister Anne was married to Richard II, Henry stayed for eleven days, spending three days at the country residence at Zebrak near Pilsen, visiting Hradschin Castle and making offerings in Karlstein Castle.

In Prague cloth and clothing for Henry himself and for some of his followers, jewelry, altars for his chapel, and heraldic paintings of his arms were bought. On 26 October he went on to Brod, and on the 29th he was at Brno. Then he made a detour, crossing the river March at Göding and going to Weisekirch near Olmutz (Olomouc). On 4 November he reached Vienna, where he met the Duke of Austria, Albert of Hapsburg, who sent letters, with Henry's own to Venice, asking the Senate to let him have shipping to take him to Palestine. The envoys were joined by John Redington, the Prior of St. John of Jerusalem in England. On 18 November they reached an agreement with the Venetian authorities for the hire of a galley. This was to be fitted out for sea, but Henry was responsible for all stores and provisions, including the furnishing of the cabins. He was not allowed to carry any merchandise or any passengers, apart from his own retinue. For the galley and for the journey to Jaffa and back, he was to pay 2,785 ducats.

Whilst in Vienna – he only stayed four days – Henry was in touch with Sigismund, King of Hungary and brother of Wenceslas of Bohemia. Albert, Duke of Austria, paid for his stay in Vienna, and sent a squire to accompany the party to Venice. They proceeded by way of Neunkirchen, Leoben and Knittelfeld, Freisach, St. Veit, Feldkirchen, Klagenfurt and Villach (on 17 November) into Friuli; then by Venzone, San Daniele and Spilimbergo, Sacile to Conegliano on the 21st. Treviso was reached on the next day, and there a stop of two days was made. The baggage was sent on to Portogruaro, where Henry established his headquarters. Wilbram and Totty were left there in charge of a sort of base camp throughout the winter. Barges and boats were hired several times to carry men and stores from Portogruaro to Venice. Henry himself went on to Venice on 1 December to prepare for his voyage, and stayed on the Island of St. George for three weeks. On 30 November 360 golden ducats from the treasury of the Republic were voted to give him a public reception.[1] He was received by the Doge, in whose company he made offerings at St. Mark's on more than one occasion. He also visited a number of other Venetian churches. Money was received both from John Redington, the Prior of St. John, and from the merchant bankers, the Albertini, before the party finally left Venice. Doubtless John of Gaunt or his agents had paid it in at Clerkenwell, and the London office of the Albertini, for his son to drawn upon. Beds were hired at Portogruaro. Salted meat, wine, spices, bread and poultry were bought there, and coals, fish, poultry, roes, fruit, spices, meat, bread and wine at Venice.

For the voyage itself provisions were bought in the surrounding country: 2,250 eggs, with live poultry, cheese, oil, fish, vegetables, spices, 2,000 dates, 1,000 lb of almonds, sweets, sugar, wines, bread and biscuits, fruits, butter and fuel, also a mattress, a featherbed, warm clothing, bowls, cups, wooden and earthenware vessels. Eight or ten of the party were left at Portogruaro. The remainder sailed with Henry about 22 December. They included Granson, Seinlatour, Prior Redington, Erpyngham, Willoughby, Mowbray herald, squires and yeomen. On Christmas day they were at Zara (Zadar) on the Dalmatian coast. From there they sailed by way of Corfu and the Morea to Rhodes, the headquarters of the knights hospitallers of St. John. Here whilst Henry visited the Grand Master of the Order, fresh supplies were bought, his armour and the ship's rudder were repaired. Then they went on to Jaffa.

Bukton, Kingston and perhaps Chelmeswyke, a squire, Henry the henchman, a guide Antonio, Mowbray herald, a servant and a yeoman, are all who are known to have accompanied Henry on the final stage of his pilgrimage from Jaffa to Jerusalem. Fish was bought at Jaffa and an ass hired to carry food to Ramla, where more was bought, but no animals seem to have been bought or hired except to carry food, so the journey of thirty miles or so was probably made on foot. At Jerusalem wax candles were bought, and Henry made offerings apparently at the Holy Sepulchre and the Mount of Olives. No details are known, even the exact dates, but the visit was certainly brief. Henry quickly returned to Jaffa and sailed for Famagusta.

At Famagusta he was lodged in the castle, and sent his principal followers as ambassadors to James I of Lusignan, King of Cyprus.

[1] *Cal. S. P. Venice*, vol. i, pp. 33–4

A leopard which was acquired at this time, may well have been a gift from the King. At Nicosia or at Rhodes repairs were made to the galley, and a cage built for the leopard. By this time falcons and a parrot had also been obtained, probably as gifts from one or another of Henry's hosts by the way. He also had a converted Turk, who travelled with Herle the chaplain, and the baggage, and eventually reached Peterborough. At Rhodes offerings were made in the churches, gifts of wine received, and more food and wine bought for the return journey. Venice was reached about 20 March by the same route as on the outward journey.

Once again Henry spent about three weeks on the island of St. George, staying in Venice over Easter, which fell on 6 April in this year. One hundred ducats were voted to be spent in honour of his return visit. Offerings were again made in the churches, shields of his arms hung in St. Mark's, food bought, and gifts made to the poor. Preparations for the homeward journey then began. The party from Portogruaro moved with horses and stores to Treviso, where the friars' convent was made ready for Henry to lodge in. Carts and horses were hired for his baggage, and he arrived there by way of Mestre. A fortnight was spent there by the main party, whilst preparations were made for the long overland journey to Calais. Harness was repaired. A goldsmith came from Venice to sell collars of silver and gold, and a cage was bought for the parrot. Meanwhile Kingston stayed behind in Venice, probably receiving money and settling accounts. Finally on 28 April the whole party set off with carts and horses by way of Padua, Vicenza and Verona. Mowbray herald, who went in advance to announce their coming, and perhaps to find lodgings, reached Milan on 11 May.

Henry stayed in Milan for a few days. His uncle, Lionel Duke of Clarence had married the sister of Gian Galeazzo Visconti, Duke of Milan, and then promptly died there. Visconti now entertained Henry, taking him to see his uncle's tomb as well as those of St. Augustine and Boethius. More jewelry and some velvet was bought, and before he left Henry was able to arbitrate in a dispute between the Duke and a house of Austin friars. Proceeding on the 17th he went through Vercelli and Chivasso, where still more silver collars were bought, and reached Turin, where he gave alms at St. Anthony's, on the 21st, Rivoli on the

22nd and Avigliano on the same day. From there three mules laden with baggage were sent over the mountains to Troyes and Champagne, whence it was probably carted to Paris. Otto Granson must have left the company some weeks before, and perhaps reached Burgundy by another route from Venice. Approaching the Alps Henry appears to have remained at Susa for three days, 23 to 25 May. He then crossed by the Mont Cenis pass, was at Lanslebourg (Savoie) on the 26th and reached Chambéry on the 31st. On the next day he was at Yenne on the Rhône. From Susa onwards he gave frequent alms to the poor and others as he passed them, to the lepers on the mount near Susa, and now to a hermit on Mont du Chat near Yenne. Crossing the Rhône he rested at Rossillon (Ain) on 2 June, St. Rambert (Ain) on the 3rd and reached Macon on the 6th. He then crossed the Sâone into Burgundy and so made his way to Paris by the 22nd.

From Chalon-sur-Sâone he sent forward Walter Inteburgh, who had already carried a message to Granson in Burgundy, with some household officers to Paris to make ready for his coming there. At Troyes he visited the church of St. Anthony and was at Provins (Seine-et-Marne) on 18 June. It was from here that Hugh Herle, two other clerks and the converted Turk, with a falcon and some of the baggage, were sent down the Seine and to Calais by water, and so to Peterborough. In Paris Henry only stopped for two nights, perhaps he was not so warmly welcomed as he had expected. At all events he only stayed long enough to have his harness repaired, to buy some clothes and a ring with a ruby. On 24 June he was making oblations at Amiens, four days later he was at Calais, and crossed thence to Dover. Four boats were needed to carry men, baggage and the leopard. He was at Sittingbourne on 1 July, Rochester on the 2nd, Dartford on the 3rd and London by the 5th. He had been away for only ten days short of a year, travelling almost continuously, apart from three weeks in Venice coming and going.

Chapter 4

Exile and return, 1393-9

THE five years which elapsed between Henry's return from the Holy Land and his banishment by Richard II in 1398 were not altogether happy ones for him or his father, the male members of the house of Lancaster, providing but little scope for their warlike energies or political ambition. Gaunt's hope of carving out a kingdom for himself had been finally disappointed, and his nephew, the King, now approaching thirty years of age, no longer needed his tutelage. For Henry there was even less prospect of active employment. A member of the baronial class, whose business was war, he was by both birth and training a natural warrior, a leader of men. At twenty-seven he was already a prince of European renown, at the zenith of his physical strength, proved both in the lists and in battle; and as he travelled across Europe his hosts had been impressed by his handsome appearance, his courtesy and his generosity. Where in England could he exercise his talents? Certainly not at his cousin's court. Whilst he had been abroad the political situation had changed, if at all, for the worse. When he returned to England in the summer of 1393 his father and his uncle, the Duke of Gloucester, had been sent north by the King to pacify their tenants in Yorkshire and Cheshire.[1] Disturbances there had become so widespread as to suggest organised insurrection, and the Earl of Arundel who had taken no active steps to restore order was suspected of complicity.

In the Parliament of January 1394, which Henry attended, Arundel attempted to forestall accusations of treason by an attack on John of Gaunt, who, he said, showed undue familiarity towards the King by walking arm-in-arm with him, whilst the King wore Gaunt's livery. He also suggested that the grant of the duchy of Aquitaine to one who, like Gaunt, had spent so much of his country's resources of men and money in his expedition to Spain, was against the interests of the kingdom. The

[1] *Cal. Close.* (1392-6), pp. 140-1

King in reply said that he treated his other uncles in the same way, and defended both his uncle and himself. Arundel was made to apologise to Gaunt before the King and Lords in Parliament, and had to retire from the council, but no more was heard of his alleged complicity in the northern disorders.[1] John of Gaunt then went back to France to continue his negotiations for peace, and at last met with some success, securing an extension of the truce for four years.

Before attending this Parliament Henry had given and received the customary New Year presents. The lists of people with whom he thus exchanged gifts are interesting as an indication of the society in which he moved, the Lancastrian section of the court and the nobility. At the beginning of 1394 gifts, mainly jewels, gold and silver, were made to the King, the Duchess of Gloucester who was both his sister-in-law and his aunt by marriage, the Countess of Hereford (his mother-in-law), the Queen, Katherine Swynford, Katherine Waterton, the Countess of Norfolk, Thomas Mowbray, Earl Marshal and grandson of the last-named, Thomas Erpyngham, John Bussy (soon to be chief steward of the duchy of Lancaster as well as a royal councillor), Richard Abberbury, Elizabeth Ashford, and, no doubt, many others. The cost of the presents ranged from £9 10s. spent on the King and the Duchess to 8s. 4d. for Elizabeth Ashford. Amongst those who gave Henry presents in return were the King and Queen, his father and stepmother, the Duke and Duchess of Gloucester, the Countess of Hereford, John Waltham, the Bishop of Salisbury, the Earl Marshal, the Countess of Norfolk and Lady Audley.[2]

The year 1394 was however to be one of royal bereavements, and a number of those who were thus exchanging presents did not live to see another New Year. Gaunt's second wife, Constance of Castile, the excuse for all his adventures in Spain, died on 24 March. Anne of Bohemia, Richard's queen, died on 7 June, and Mary Bohun, Henry's wife, a few weeks later. In 1396 John of Gaunt scandalised the court by marrying Katherine Swynford, who had been the governess of his two eldest daughters, for

[1] *Rot. Parl.*, vol. iii, p. 313; Walsingham, *Hist. Angl.*, vol. ii, p. 214; *Annales R. II*, 159–62, 166
[2] P.R.O., D.L. 28/1/4. Account of William Loveney 30 June 1393 to 15 February 1394

many years his mistress, and the mother of his third family, the Beauforts. Arundel's rudeness in arriving late for the Queen's funeral provoked Richard to a personal assault. This action and the order for the partial destruction of the manor house at Sheen, where Anne had died, showed the extent of Richard's grief. There can be little doubt that he felt his loss more deeply than his uncle and his cousin did theirs. The counsellors of his youth like Simon Burley, Michael de la Pole and many lesser men had been killed or exiled by the appellants; his one real friend of his own age, Robert de Vere, had died in exile, and Richard had come to rely the more on his wife Anne, who unlike his friends was also generally popular. Deprived of this last support he was driven back on his personal conception of kingship, and on his own judgment, which was always optimistic and usually wrong.

How far Henry felt the loss of his wife, who in some ten years of married life had given him six children, there is no means of knowing; nor is there any evidence that he followed his father's amorous example either before or after Mary's death. His children were now in the care of noble ladies or trusty retainers, and he himself appeared to be settling down to play a part in domestic politics befitting his rank, if ill-suited to his abilities. In the Parliament of 1395 and the two Parliaments of 1397, the last three Parliaments as it happened of the reign, he was again a trier of petitions. In September 1394 whilst Gaunt set off to establish himself in Guyenne as duke and King's lieutenant, and Richard went to Ireland in an attempt to pacify that most unruly dominion. Henry, who might well have been expected to assist either one or the other with his counsel or his sword, stayed behind as a member of the council which ruled England in the King's absence. In 1396 he was invited by William of Hainault, his second cousin,[1] to join him in the war which he was

[1] The relationship with Hainault may be shown thus:

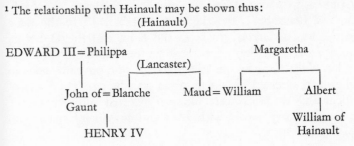

then waging against Friesland, but he was forbidden to go, it is said, by his father. The latter having achieved very little in Guyenne returned home after about a year. Instead of warlike expeditions father and son now both together attended the ceremonial meeting between Richard and Charles VI of France, which took place between Guines and Ardres outside Calais on 26 October 1396 and the following days. Beside the Duke of Lancaster and the Earl of Derby, the Duke of Gloucester, the Earls of Rutland (York's son), Nottingham and Northumberland, and many other lords and knights accompanied Richard, who had arranged to strengthen the peace between the two countries with a marriage alliance. At this meeting accordingly Isabel, the younger daughter of Charles VI, was handed over to the English King to become his second wife, a child bride, not yet eight years of age.

In the Parliament of January 1397 Henry's half-brothers and sister, the Beaufort family, were declared legitimate, and the eldest of them, John, Henry's comrade in arms, was created Earl of Somerset. Richard had been quietly building up his own party, and effective opposition was, as always in the presence of Gaunt, impossible. The Duke of Gloucester seems however to have been determined to make trouble for the King. At a royal banquet in the summer, at which some of its former garrison were present, he upbraided the King for the surrender of Brest. Pledged to the English in 1378, this town had now been redeemed, so that Richard could not in honesty do anything but give it up. Then in July according to the author of the *Traïson et Mort*, who began his story of the fall of Richard at this point, Gloucester and the Prior of Westminster were guests of the Abbot at St. Albans, and after dinner a treasonable plot was conceived. The meeting was adjourned for a fortnight to another dinner party at Arundel, to which Gloucester also invited Henry, the Archbishop of Canterbury and the Earl Marshal. There the main proposal was apparently to seize the King and the Dukes of Lancaster and York and imprison them for life; but the plot was revealed to the King by the Earl Marshal, who promptly rode to Pleshey and arrested his uncle in his own home.[1] The Earls of Arundel and Warwick were likewise arrested and sent to the Tower. The story is told with great and convincing detail, and

[1] *Traïson et Mort*, pp. 3–7, 122–9

44

there is no doubt about the arrest of Gloucester, who was sent to the Tower, and thence in the care of Mowbray, the Earl Marshal, to Calais; but that Henry was privy to a plot to imprison for life his father, with whom he always appears to have been on good terms, is more difficult to believe. Henry apart, however, it does form a possible prelude to the September Parliament.

This, the second Parliament of 1397, met at Westminster, surrounded, or guarded, by a body of those Cheshire men, who were long held to be the surest archers in England, and had now been collected by the King into a private army. Richard at last had his revenge for the Merciless Parliament of 1388. The pardon granted to Archbishop Thomas Arundel who had been translated from York to Canterbury only one year before, was revoked and he was banished from the kingdom, shortly to be replaced by a new archbishop. Then the three original appellants, Arundel, Warwick and Gloucester, were themselves appealed of treason. The Earl of Arundel, Thomas's brother, was promptly sentenced to death and executed on Tower Hill. Henry took part against him, Gaunt whom he had attacked in 1394 presided over the trial, and his other old colleague Thomas Mowbray, Earl of Nottingham, led him to execution. Then Nottingham, the Earl Marshal, was called upon as Captain of Calais to produce the Duke of Gloucester, who had been imprisoned there. But Gloucester could not be produced, for he was already mysteriously dead at Calais, probably murdered. He could only be sentenced after death. Finally Thomas, Earl of Warwick, having made some sort of confession, was banished to the Isle of Man.

This Parliament saw Richard's triumph, but he did not, or would not, realise that suspicion, violence and revenge call by their own nature for more suspicion, violence and revenge. He was adding to his enemies in exile and alarming those who now seemed his friends. Moreover he was soon to show that he was not easily contented even in victory. On 29 September 1397 the Parliament was adjourned from Westminster to meet again at Shrewsbury at the end of January. To end the session Richard created five new dukes, a marquess and four earls. Henry became Duke of Hereford; Thomas Mowbray, Earl of Nottingham, Duke of Norfolk; John Holland and Thomas Holland, nephew and cousin of the King on his mother's side, Dukes of Exeter and Surrey; Edward, Earl of Rutland, son of the Duke of

York, was made Duke of Aumerle; John Beaufort, recently created Earl of Somerset, became Marquess of Dorset; and Thomas Despenser, Ralph Neville, Thomas Percy and William Scrope or Lescrope became Earls respectively of Gloucester, Westmorland, Worcester and Wiltshire. Never before had honours been so lavishly bestowed by an English king, and never again were five dukes to be created at one time. The traitors had now been punished, the loyal and moderate men rewarded with new honours.

The King had indulged his love of pageantry with his new creations, and outwardly all was peace and concord, but at least one of the new dukes, Thomas Mowbray of Norfolk, felt neither happy nor secure. Close relationships existed between his family and Henry's. Mowbray herald had accompanied Henry on his travels. At least one of Henry's children, John the third son, was at Framlingham, in the care of Mowbray's grandmother, the Dowager Countess of Norfolk, who to keep up with her grandson had just been made a duchess in her own right. On New Year's Day 1398 in recognition of the care which had been taken of his eight-year-old son, Henry gave presents not only to members of the Norfolk family, but also to the treasurer, chaplain and damsels of the Duchess.[1] But in spite of this apparent harmony a violent quarrel broke out between Henry and Thomas Mowbray. Since Mowbray left no account of his side of the affair the whole story of the dispute can never be known. The official version,[2] which was based on Henry's own account, may however be supplemented from the chronicles, especially the *Traïson et Mort*. This tells the story in some detail, confirming the main outline of the official version, making some notable additions, and occasionally contradicting or muddling minor points. According to Henry the trouble began when the two newly-created Dukes were riding together from Brentford to London in December 1397. Norfolk then remarked that they were both about to be undone. Whereupon Henry, now Duke of Hereford, asked why, and Norfolk replied, because of Radcot Bridge. Hereford pointed out that they had been pardoned for that episode, but Norfolk said that nevertheless Richard would deal with them as he had already dealt with the others. He went on to remark somewhat enigmatically that this world was a marvellous one and a false.

[1] P.R.O., D.L. 28/1/6
[2] *Rot. Parl.*, vol. iii, pp. 360, 382–4

Further he said that there was a plot to kill Henry and his father at Windsor after the Parliament, and that four lords who were close to the King (Thomas Holland, Duke of Surrey, William Scrope, Earl of Wiltshire, Thomas Montagu, Earl of Salisbury, and Thomas le Despenser, Earl of Gloucester) were aiming to destroy the four Dukes of Lancaster, Hereford, Aumerle and Exeter, the Marquess of Dorset, and Mowbray himself, the Duke of Norfolk. If they could not accomplish their purpose immediately, they would be prepared to wait ten years to destroy them in their houses, but destroy them they would.[1]

The inclusion of Richard's half-brother, John Holland, Duke of Exeter, along with Henry, his father, his half-brother, his cousin and Mowbray seems rather odd, especially as Exeter's nephew, Thomas Holland, was included amongst the opposing group of King's friends. It is not impossible that the Duke of York, Gaunt's only surviving brother, was intended. With this proviso it may well be that Norfolk was right, that Richard could not forgive any of those who had contributed to his earlier humiliation, and that he was only awaiting the opportunity to destroy them along with his surviving uncles. If so Henry, by denouncing Norfolk, himself created the opportunity for the destruction of either or both of them.

Norfolk's words were perhaps treasonable, but being part of a private conversation, which apparently he alone had heard, there was no obvious need for Henry to betray a confidence by mentioning them to anyone. If that was all that was said he might well have kept silence and waited for further evidence. But clearly the official account does not tell us all. Mowbray's earlier conduct, especially his dubious relations with Gloucester, was not calculated to give anyone much confidence in him. If rumours of his treasonable behaviour, and of quarrels with Gaunt, were already current, Henry could not well ignore these words. What in fact he did was to report them to his father, who in turn conveyed them to the King, thus making the breach between the two Dukes irreparable and finally alienating Norfolk from the King. Henry was summoned to the King's presence, and Richard asked him to repeat the whole conversation. It was then arranged that he should accuse Norfolk of treason when the Parliament, which had been adjourned from London, reassembled at Shrews-

[1] *Traïson et Mort*, pp. 12–22

bury. Accordingly he produced a schedule or written account of the affair in full Parliament on 30 January 1398. Norfolk was not present, and the matter was referred to a special committee of eighteen which the Parliament set up.

The two Dukes were brought face to face in the King's presence at Oswestry on 23 February where Henry called Norfolk 'a false traitor, disloyal to your royal majesty, your crown, the lords, and all the people of your Kingdom.'[1] Norfolk merely replied that this was a lie. There were no witnesses. Each Duke's words stood unsupported against the other's. Richard adopted delaying tactics towards the two Dukes until finally they were indeed 'both undone', as Norfolk had suggested and the King may well have foreseen. Norfolk was imprisoned in the King's wardrobe in London in charge of the mayor,[2] whilst four dukes stood sureties for Henry. On 28 April they appeared before a court of chivalry at Windsor, and it was perhaps here that Henry brought further charges, not directly mentioned in the official account, against Norfolk. He suggested that Mowbray as Captain of Calais had misappropriated several thousand pounds which had been entrusted to him for the payment of the garrison, and also that he had been implicated in the murder of Thomas of Woodstock, Duke of Gloucester.[3] The latter charge was one which Richard would not perhaps wish to have fully investigated. To the former Norfolk replied that Calais was now as well guarded as ever it had been, and that he had never received any payment for the expenses he had incurred on various embassies in the King's service. It was true, he said, that he had once laid an ambush for the Duke of Lancaster, but that had long since been forgiven him. Now he asked for trial by battle. Both Dukes having refused the King's request to be reconciled it was ordered that such a trial should take place in the lists at Coventry on 16 September.

Elaborate preparations were made for this encounter. The two Dukes arrived in Coventry on the day before and each went to pay his respects to the King. A number of distinguished foreigners, including the Count of St. Pol – bringing, it has been suggested, advice from the French King to Richard not to

[1] *Traïson et Mort*, p. 12
[2] Rymer, *Foedera*, vol. vii, p. 36; *Anglo-Norman Letters*, p. 104
[3] *Traïson et Mort*, pp. 14–15

permit the contest to take place – came over specially for the occasion, and Richard was accompanied by all the nobility of England. Then came the dramatic anti-climax. As soon as both contestants had completed all the formalities and were ready for the fray, the King forbade it. After some delay his decisions were announced. By finding both parties guilty he appeared to confirm Norfolk's suggestion that he wished to destroy them both, and to be manifestly unjust to at least one of them. Henry was banished for ten years, Norfolk for life. Part of Norfolk's revenues were to be devoted to paying his debt for Calais, a proviso which seemed almost to confirm one of Henry's charges against him. Both Dukes were made to swear to observe their sentences, and not to meet whilst abroad, or even to live in the same country. Henry also swore not to have any correspondence with Thomas Arundel, the exiled Archbishop of Canterbury. There would soon be insufficient countries in Europe to house all the exiles whom Richard fondly hoped to keep apart. Norfolk set out through Germany to make a pilgrimage to Jerusalem. He returned from there to Venice, where he died of the plague on 22 September 1399, a few days before his opponent of Coventry became king.

Richard, in response to the urgent pleading of John of Gaunt, reduced Henry's term of banishment from ten years to six. It was unlikely to make much difference to Gaunt since he was hardly expected to live so long. Henry himself did not waste much time. Within a fortnight he was in London. On 3 October the faithful Thomas Totty was ordered to find ships for his passage beyond the seas, and on the same day Richard gave him permission to spend one month in Calais with a retinue of twelve persons, and six weeks in the nearby castle of Sangatte. On the 8th Henry appointed his attornies in England, who were empowered to receive his inheritance, if his father should die whilst he was in exile. On the 6, 9, and 10 October he confirmed letters patent of his father,[1] and on the 12th his followers had letters of protection to go overseas and appointed their attornies in England. These followers were his loyal servants, Thomas Rempston, John Dabrichecourt, Thomas Erpyngham, John Tochet, knights, John Norbury, Henry Bowet clerk, William

[1] *Cal. Pat.* (1396–9), pp. 440, 470, 499, 534, 537; Rymer, *Foedera*, vol. viii, pp. 48–50; *Rot. Parl.* vol. iii, p. 372.; P.R.O., C 76/83

Loveney, Thomas Totty and Robert Challoners.[1] It was probably the next morning that Henry set out from London on the first stage of his journey. According to Froissart vast crowds turned out to see him go, the mayor and leading citizens escorting him as far as Dartford. If this was indeed the case it was a startling tribute to the son of one who had been so well hated but seventeen years before, and a resounding public rebuke to the King. Unfortunately Froissart the fullest chronicler of these events is also the least reliable. Now over sixty years of age he had not been in England for thirty years, apart from a brief visit to the court at Eltham in 1395,[2] and was somewhat out of touch with English affairs. Most of the now discredited stories of this period were originally told on Froissart's authority. Even so some story of popular support for Henry must have reached him probably from a member of Henry's own party when they reached France. Such a demonstration would doubtless increase Henry's awareness of the injustice with which he had been treated, and show him the potential strength of his cause, both moral and physical. He would remember it when a return to England came to be discussed.

In 1396 John of Gaunt had granted his house at Calais to his retainer Reynold Curteys to hold for life rent-free on condition that he provided accommodation for the Duke and his family whenever they should be in Calais.[3] But Henry did not stay there long. Declining a new invitation to join the expedition to Friesland, he went directly to Paris, where he was received as a person of royal rank, and assigned the Hotel Clisson for his residence. Negotiations for his marriage to the daughter of the Duke of Berri were begun, but very soon the warmth of his first reception was allowed to cool. The Earl of Salisbury and the Bishop of Carlisle were at this time in Paris trying to secure a dowry for Isabel, now Richard's queen, and they are said to have protested against the friendliness shown to Henry. However, the Bishop left London on 19 October and was back there forty-one days later on 28 November,[4] so that he may well have witnessed

---

[1] P.R.O., C 76/83 m. 11

[2] Margaret Galwey, 'Froissart in England', *University of Birmingham Historical Journal*, vol. vii, (1959) pp. 18–35

[3] *Cal. Pat.* (1396–9), p. 513

[4] Rymer, *Foedera*, vol. viii, p. 52; P.R.O. E 364/32E

Henry's arrival in Paris but had in fact very little time to make protests about the ensuing marriage negotiations.

The Shrewsbury Parliament had been dissolved on 31 January 1398, the day after Henry's accusation of Norfolk. Before dispersing, the Parliament set up a standing committee of eighteen, twelve lords and six knights of the shire, to deal with outstanding petitions and also to settle the dispute between Hereford and Norfolk. The petitions were dealt with at Bristol in March 1398, and the sentences pronounced on the two Dukes at Coventry were given the authority of this committee. Its work therefore appeared to be done. Early in 1399, however, a new copy of the Parliament Roll was made, and in this copy the words 'and other things' were added after the petitions, which the committee was empowered to determine,[1] thus apparently giving unlimited parliamentary authority to a body favourable to the King, and Richard soon found work for it to do.

When Henry went into exile in 1398 his father, Gaunt, was approaching sixty, quite an advanced age for the fourteenth century. Shakespeare's 'aged Gaunt, time-honoured Lancaster' was not perhaps so wild an exaggeration as at first sight appears. Probably Gaunt was already failing, and Henry, beginning a six-year exile, could hardly expect to see his father again. As it happened John of Gaunt died on 3 February 1399, and his death started the chain of events which made the year for ever memorable. The beneficiaries under his will, made exactly one year before, included the King, all the members of his family, and many religious houses. They all received gold and silver vessels and jewels, rich furnishings and tapestries, as well as gifts of money. The King especially was liberally provided both with gold vessels and with money,[2] but he had much larger ideas. On 18 March he used the parliamentary committee to announce that Henry's sentence amounted to perpetual banishment, that the licence given to the attornies to receive the inheritance of the Duke of Hereford was revoked, and that all the possessions of the house of Lancaster were forfeited to the Crown.[3] On 23 April Henry Bowet, who had either stayed behind or come back

[1] J. G. Edwards, 'The Parliamentary Committee of 1398', *E.H.R.*, vol. xl (1925), pp. 321-33
[2] The will is printed in Armitage-Smith, *Gaunt*, pp. 420-36
[3] *Rot. Parl.*, vol. iii, p. 372

to act as Henry's attorney, was pronounced a traitor by th
committee, whilst all the estates were kept in the King's hands
By their seizure Richard had given Henry a grievance which ever
landholder in England would immediately understand, and Henr
now faced the King able to act on his own, unrestrained by hi
father; for Gaunt so long as he lived not only stood betwee
his son and any claim to the crown, but also always counselle
moderation.

Disastrous as it proved, the confiscation must have seemed a
obvious move to the King, since it both completed his reveng
and provided him with funds. He stood in immediate need o
money, if possible without recourse to Parliament, for anothe
expedition to Ireland, where new measures were urgently neede
to restore his authority. After Richard's first expedition t
Ireland in 1395 Roger Mortimer, Earl of March, recognised a
heir presumptive to the throne, had served as his lieutenan
there, but on 20 July 1398 Roger was killed in an ambush. A
heir to himself, and perhaps to Richard, he left a seven-year-ol
son, Edmund; in Ireland he left revolt and defeat.

So Richard resolved to make a second expedition there him
self. Before setting out he endeavoured to secure the loyalty o
his people at home by making them swear special oaths o
allegiance, and by threatening penalties for failure to observ
them. At the same time he exacted the notorious 'blank charters',
the destruction of which in the next reign, whilst it proves tha
they really did exist and were not just an invention of the chroniclers, has unfortunately left their exact nature something of a
mystery. It appears that leading men in each county were compelled or persuaded to set their seals to these 'charters', which were
then sent to London, to be held there as an undefined and unlimited pledge, no man knowing what the King might choose to
put on his own 'charter'.[1] Far from ensuring loyalty no measure
could have been better calculated to arouse opposition. Having
thus created antagonism at home, and provoked Henry in France,
Richard could hardly have chosen a worse moment to absent
himself from the kingdom. Moreover having decided to go

---

[1] J. G. Dickinson, ' "Blanks" and "Blank Charters" in the 14th and 15th
centuries', *E.H.R.*, vol. lxvi (1951), p. 384. M. V. Clarke and N. Denholm-
Young, 'The Kirkstall Chronicle', *Bull. J.R.L.*, vol. xv, no. 1 (1931),
reprinted in Clarke, *Fourteenth Cent. Studies*, pp. 99–115

overseas he could hardly have found a worse lieutenant to leave behind than his one surviving uncle, that Edmund, Duke of York, who had so often proved his ineptness. Edmund was appointed to this office on 18 May 1399. To assist him Richard left his treasurer, William Scrope, Earl of Wiltshire, and his already unpopular servants, John Bussy or Bushey, Henry Green and William Bagot. Bussy, Speaker in the Parliaments of 1394 and 1397, had owed allegiance to both the King and John of Gaunt, but had now chosen the wrong side, and was shortly to suffer for his choice. On 29 May the King sailed to Waterford, with a large force including most of his leading supporters. He also took with him, perhaps as hostages, the young Humphrey, son of the murdered Duke of Gloucester, and Henry's eldest son, Henry of Monmouth, afterwards Henry V.

Once again Henry was quick to act. Despite his oath, the Arundels, Thomas, the Archbishop, who had been in exile in Cologne, and Thomas, the Earl, came to him in Paris. They were the brother and son of Henry's old colleague the appellant Earl, and they were also Henry's cousins, the old Earl and Archbishop being sons of Eleanor of Lancaster. Froissart's story that the Archbishop had come straight from London with an invitation from the Londoners to come and set them free from the tyranny of Richard cannot be true, because the Archbishop had been in exile for two years; but it is not impossible that his nephew had brought some such message, or that he himself had it at second hand. During his travels Arundel had visited the Roman court, and afterwards in January 1398 wrote to the Prior of Canterbury from 'an earthly paradise near Florence'.[1] At forty-six the Archbishop was a most experienced politician. He had become a bishop at twenty-one, and before being deprived of his see and banished by Richard he had been an archbishop for nine years, eight at York, and one at Canterbury. For eight of the King's twenty-two troubled years he had served as chancellor, but he had begun to wield the great seal on behalf of the opposition, and was never really Richard's man. Now it was clear enough that he had very little chance of being restored to the primacy so long as Richard remained effectively King. In short he had need of Henry, and Henry was soon to prove that he had need of the Archbishop. For the rest of his life he leaned heavily

[1] *Lit. Cant.*, vol. iii, pp. 70–2

on Arundel, and it was to be Arundel who provided some of the forceful leadership and adroit statesmanship, which was later to be so constantly needed and so rarely forthcoming from Henry himself.

On 17 June 1399 Henry made a treaty of friendship with the Duke of Orleans,[1] the French King's brother. It is said to have been witnessed by his three faithful servants, Thomas Erpyngham, Thomas Rempston and John Norbury. Froissart has a detailed account of how Henry took leave of the King of France and went from Paris to Nantes where he conferred with the Duke of Brittany, before embarking for England, and landing at Plymouth.[2] Had he done this he would also have met the Duchess, Joan, whom he was to marry three years later. As however less than three weeks elapsed between Henry's leaving Paris and his landing in England, it is more likely that he proceeded to Boulogne and embarked there, and he certainly did not land at Plymouth.

The Duke of York and his councillors learning of Henry's movements did indeed expect him to land in the south, and small sums were spent on the defence of Rochester and Queenborough Castles. But Henry sailed on up the east coast, landing briefly for provisions, and putting to sea again. Many of his own Lancastrian estates lay in Yorkshire, and perhaps he already had an understanding with the northern earls, who had excused themselves from accompanying Richard to Ireland. Certainly his own party, carried in three small ships, was hardly of a size to conquer a kingdom. Adam of Usk put it at 'scarce three hundred followers'[3] and it can hardly have been larger than that, probably no bigger than the forces he had led in Prussia. When they did eventually land, it was at Ravenspur north of the Humber at the southeastern tip of Yorkshire. The date was probably 4 July.[4]

The next three weeks were spent in a triumphal ride from stronghold to stronghold, many of them Lancastrian castles. From Ravenspur Henry went to Pickering, thence to Knares-

[1] Douët d'Arcq, *Pièces inédites*, vol. i, pp. 157–60. No witnesses. Also *Report on Foedera*, D 145 from Archives Nationales, K 55 pièce 2
[2] Froissart, Bk. iv, chaps. 72, 73
[3] *Usk*, pp. 25, 174
[4] Various dates are given by the chroniclers, *Usk* gives 28 June, but this seems to fit the known timetable best.

borough, and so on to Pontefract. 'He was first met by Robert
Waterton accompanied by two hundred foresters, perhaps from
Knaresborough, and trusty John Leventhorpe also joined him.'[1]
These were old servants, Lancaster men, and now the lord of
Lancaster had come home. The castles were taken with no great
difficulty, and Lancastrian custodians, like Sir David Roucliffe,
John of Gaunt's Constable of Pickering, were installed. Ponte-
fract was about a week's journey, so he would be there about
11 or 12 July, and there he was joined by many more knights
and squires from the Lancastrian estates in Lancashire and
Yorkshire.

From Pontefract Castle he is said to have sent out circular letters
putting his case against Richard to all the towns and nobility of
England,[2] but even so he hardly halted on his march. From Pontefract it is only a few miles to Doncaster, and at Doncaster he received strong reinforcements. There he met Henry Percy, Earl of
Northumberland, and Henry Percy his son, one of the knights
of St. Inglevert, also their cousin and rival in the marches of
Scotland, Ralph Neville, Earl of Westmorland, and William,
Lord Willoughby, who had succeeded to his father's barony
since the expedition to Prussia. Each of these and many others
had a large following, and each of them was no doubt discontented with Richard's rule, but there is no real clue to their intentions
when they joined Henry at Doncaster. Yet their adherence
converted Henry's following from a personal band of retainers
into a political movement, and some statement of policy may
well have been thought necessary. According to the story later
put out by the Percies this statement took the form of a solemn
oath sworn by Henry in the presence of his new-found army at
Doncaster. According to this story he swore that he had only
come to claim his own inheritance and that of his late wife.
Richard was to remain king for the rest of his life, ruled by
the good counsel of the lords spiritual and temporal; or in another
version of the story, the boy Earl of March was to be the nominal
King. Henry, without looking very far ahead, may have envisaged
himself as the chief councillor of the titular King. On the other
hand the story of the oath may have been invented by the Percies
in partial justification of their revolt, four years later, when it

[1] Somerville, *Dy of Lancaster*, vol. i, p. 137
[2] *Traïson et Mort*, pp. 34–5, 180–2

was certainly put into circulation. Its truth cannot be tested now, but many people who were present at Doncaster were certainl still about in 1403, and it is difficult to believe that the stor was pure invention. Probably Henry, still without a clear ide of his own intentions, was obliged to take some such oath i order to give varied elements amongst his followers the basi of a common programme. He had arrived at a moment wher Richard's policy had become so unpopular that many were look ing for a banner of revolt, and rebellion once begun had ; momentum of its own. Henry was rushed forward by his owr success, too fast for a careful formulation of plans or policy.

This meeting at Doncaster must have taken place on or abou Sunday, 13 July. It transformed Henry from a rebellious lorc at the head of his own tenants into the commander of an army of national proportions. Hardly conscious perhaps of his nev role and power, he moved on without waste of time. The growing army was led across the whole breadth of England by way of Derby, Leicester, Kenilworth and Evesham to Berkeley Castle near the Severn in Gloucestershire, which was reached by 27 July. Since landing, Henry and his followers had averaged thirteen or fourteen miles a day, despite the time taken in meeting the northern lords and other contingents, and in recovering and garrisoning the Lancastrian castles, no small achievement with an army which grew day by day as it advanced.

Meanwhile the Duke of York and his council had also attempted to collect an army, but without any great measure of success. It appears from the payments made that the total strength of his forces was about 700 men-at-arms and 2,400 archers. This cost him £1,800 to raise, but it was not lack of funds which restricted his recruiting, because there was still a balance of £2,303 left in cash at the exchequer when the office was closed for the summer vacation on 12 July.[2] There can have been very few fighting men left in the south of England, and some of these may well have been reluctant to serve under so bad a leader as York, in a cause so unpopular as the King's. The net result was that only three peers, John Beaufort, Marquess of Dorset, Henry's half-brother, Michael de la Pole, Earl of Suffolk, and Robert, Lord Ferrers of Chartley, were found to join the Duke. The Queen's household

[1] Bean, 'H. IV and the Percies'
[2] P.R.O., E 403/562–3

was already at Wallingford, when York's council decided that the King's unpopularity made London unsafe for them also. They left Westminster on 12 July, were at Aylesbury on the 14th, Oxford on the 16th and Wallingford on the 20th. There part of the administration, probably the privy seal office, remained; but York with his council and army thought it better to move westwards in the hope of being able to join forces with the King on his return from Ireland. York went as far as Berkeley Castle; Lescrope, Bussy and Green were all at Bristol on 27 July. Bagot went off to Ireland to take the bad news to Richard.

It was at Berkeley Castle on 27 July, therefore, that Henry and his uncle, the Duke of York, met, and there York simply united his forces with those of his nephew. He was in no position to resist, as some of his small force probably sympathised with Henry. The victory was not altogether bloodless, for on the following day Sir Peter Courtenay surrendered Bristol, handing over William Scrope, Earl of Wiltshire, Bussy and Green. These three were executed forthwith, their heads being sent to decorate the gates of London, York and Bristol. Thus without even a battle or a skirmish Richard's supporters in England were added to his enemies.

Richard himself had landed at Waterford with his army on 1 June. After some hesitation he marched to Dublin and back again, skirmishing with the Irish, but failing to bring them to a decisive battle. Bad weather delayed the news of Henry's landing, which should have reached him early in July, and when he did receive it he was persuaded, against his own judgment and that of many of his councillors, not to return to England at once. Instead he sent the Earl of Salisbury with an army to land in North Wales, whilst he collected as many armed men as he could. His delay was probably due to the advice of York's son, Edward, Duke of Aumerle, advice given with the secret intention of helping Henry. It certainly contributed to Richard's failure. He probably did not leave Waterford until 27 July, the day on which the treachery or incompetence of Edward's father, York, destroyed the royal army in England at Berkeley Castle. From Waterford the King crossed to South Wales, only to find that his second army was breaking up. Whilst his cousin, Aumerle, and Thomas Percy, Earl of Worcester, the steward of his household and the Earl of Northumberland's brother, deserted to

Henry, Richard hastened northwards with only a few followers. He was making for Conway whither he had sent the Earl of Salisbury with his force. Richard probably left South Wales in the first few days of August, and covered the 160 miles to Conway by the 12th. He was just too late. His third and last army had got tired of waiting there, uncertain of his fate, and had melted away. The position was now desperate, although Conway was a strong fortress, Richard had hardly enough men to hold it. Certainly not enough to advance against his enemies. One way of escape was offered by the shipping in the harbour, but Richard, still optimistic, would not go into exile, or, as some advised, to Bordeaux.[1]

Henry had learnt or guessed that Richard would advance northwards, and himself set off in the same direction. He was at Bristol on 29 July, at Berkeley on the 30th, and proceeded thence by way of Gloucester, Ross, Hereford, Leominster, Ludlow and Shrewsbury, where he spent two days, to Chester. He had arrived there by 9 August, thus covering 160 miles in ten days.[2] At Chester he waited until he heard of Richard's arrival at Conway.

Now each side sent envoys to the other. To Richard at Conway Henry sent the Earl of Northumberland, accompanied perhaps by Archbishop Arundel. Northumberland asked Richard to restore Henry to his rightful place as Duke of Lancaster and himself come before Parliament as King. Deposition was not hinted at, and may not have been in Northumberland's mind, although by this time it was perhaps in Henry's. Richard, remembering that he had turned the tables before, agreed, and set out for Flint. On the way he was ambushed by Northumberland's men, and by the time he reached Flint, where Henry came to meet him, it must have been clear to Richard that he was a prisoner. He had been captured by a ruse, in which Northumberland, who had sworn that he should remain king, was the leading agent. The Earl may not have been aware that he was being used to deceive Richard, and if that was the case, it would explain his later oppo-

[1] The chronology of Richard's journey from Ireland to Chester, and the dating of events at Conway and Chester, are much disputed. For another view see E. J. Jones, *Speculum*, vol. xv (1940), pp. 460–77.
[2] *Usk*, pp. 25–6, gives: Hereford 2 Aug., Leominster 3 Aug., Ludlow 4 Aug., two days at Shrewsbury. He was with Henry at this time.

sition to Henry as king, but his whole career suggests that he would not be over-scrupulous about betraying either his friends or his enemies.[1] From Flint Richard accompanied Henry to Chester, still formally king, but in fact a prisoner. In little more than a month Henry had transformed himself from an exile into the master of both king and kingdom, a position from which he could not withdraw, but a position which posed several well-nigh insoluble problems.

[1] For Northumberland's part see: B. Wilkinson, 'The deposition of Richard II and the accession of Henry IV', *E.H.R.*, vol. liv (1939), pp. 215–39; Bean, 'H. IV and the Percies', pp. 212–17

Chapter 5

The making of the King, 16 August–13 October 1399

THE week from 9 to 16 August 1399 saw a complete break in the administration of the kingdom. Letters under the Great Seal were dated from Wallingford, where the Duke of York must have left one of the royal seals, up to 8 August. After that the next orders to be issued in the King's name were dated from Chester on the 16th, probably the day on which Richard was brought there as a prisoner. In the meanwhile Henry had been receiving petitions,[1] and issuing his own letters, in which although styling himself Duke of Lancaster and Steward of England, and using the seal of the duchy, he seemed to be assuming some of the prerogatives of kingship. A grant to John Norbury was dated at Leominster on 31 July, letters patent dated at Gloucester on 1 August in response to a petition ordered the delivery of a barge to a merchant of Bayonne, the Earl of Northumberland had an appointment as keeper of the West March towards Scotland dating from the next day, and the Prior of Beauvale had a safe-conduct dated the 10th.[2]

The possession of the King's person, however, enabled the use of legal forms to be resumed. From 16 to 20 August orders were issued from Chester in the King's name.[3] The first one appointed Bishop Trevor of St. Asaph Chamberlain of Chester and North Wales. John Trevor had been one of Richard's closest friends, and may have changed his allegiance at this moment. It has even been suggested that he was the eyewitness who wrote

[1] Two petitions from merchants of Bayonne, Piers Deucasses and Piers de Conties. (P.R.O., C 81/1539). It is possible that the petition addressed to the Duke of Lancaster in *Anglo-Norman Letters*, pp. 5–6, really dated from this period.
[2] B.M., Add. Chart. 5829; *Cal. Pat.* (1399–1401), p. 243; E 404/15/108, R. L. Storey, in *E.H.R.*, vol. lxxii, p. 603; Madox, *Formulare*, p. 327, E 327/577, seal of the duchy
[3] *Cal. Pat.* (1396–9), pp. 586–97

of the *Deposition and death of Richard II*.[1] The second order which appointed as Abbot of Shrewsbury Richard Prestbury, a strong opponent of Richard, is much more easy to understand. On the 19th summonses were sent out for a Parliament to meet at Westminster on 30 September, the day after Michaelmas, and on the same and following days some appointments of officers for Calais were made. On the 20th also writs were issued in the King's name 'by advice of Thomas Archbishop of Canterbury, Henry, Duke of Lancaster, the Earls of Northumberland and Westmorland, and other great men of the realm', ordering that the King's peace should be maintained; and on the same day an order was issued simply on the authority of King and council. After some fumbling a formula had been found, and for the next six weeks the fiction was maintained that the King was governing 'by the advice' of his council; or in other words Henry, Arundel and Northumberland ruled England by 'advising' the King. Arundel's deprivation of his see, and the position of his successor, Roger Walden, were, like Henry's banishment, ignored.

On 21 August Richard was taken by his captors to Nantwich, and from there letters were issued appointing that staunch Lancastrian knight, Thomas Erpyngham to be Constable of Dover Castle, thus securing to Henry one of the doors of the kingdom. Now the King and his self-appointed councillors moved rapidly towards London, by Stafford and Lichfield, where the privy seal office perhaps joined them on the 23rd, Coventry and Daventry. At Lichfield or Coventry Richard made some attempt to escape, or some Welsh or Cheshire men tried to rescue him.[2] The only result was that he was more securely guarded and more harshly treated henceforth. Somewhere on the road also – different accounts say at Chester, at Coventry, or at Lichfield – a deputation of three aldermen from London came to express their support for Henry, and to renounce their allegiance to Richard. They said that the citizens had arrested Archbishop Roger Walden and two other clerical supporters of Richard, who were being kept in custody until they could be tried before Parliament.[3]

Dunstable was reached on the 30th and St. Albans on the 31st.

[1] E. J. Jones, *Speculum*, vol. xv (1940), pp. 460–77
[2] *Traïson et Mort*, pp. 61, 211–12; *Annales R. II et H. IV*, pp. 250–1
[3] *Usk*, pp. 28, 179; *Hist. du roy Richard*, p. 176; *Traïson et Mort*, pp. 62, 212

Finally on 1 September, after two months of marching across England from north to south and back again, Henry entered London in triumph, with Richard as his captive, 'having gloriously' said Usk 'within fifty days, conquered both king and kingdom.'[1] Humiliated and exposed to the jeers of the mob, the King was led to the Tower. The army which Henry had collected fought no battles and suffered no casualties, but the country had not altogether escaped the ravages of war. Adam of Usk himself described how the army on the Welsh border pillaged all the country around, robbing houses and churches, and another chronicler said that all the rogues and robbers had joined Henry's banner and made havoc in the county of Chester.[2] Law and order were easily thrust aside, for it was a quarrelsome time and men were wont to rely on their own swords, but now at the beginning of September, as the knights were being chosen to go to Westminster for the Parliament, the whole country was waiting. What would happen next?

In the closing days of that month lords, bishops and abbots together with knights, squires and burgesses from thirty-seven counties and eighty-six boroughs, were riding towards Westminster. They would be aware that the Parliament to which they had been summoned in the name of King Richard was going to be no ordinary meeting, for the country was unquiet and anxious. Rumours and stories followed the messengers, as they brought the royal writs to the sheriffs in each county, commanding them to hold elections. Many travellers were on the roads, stewards and receivers going from manor to manor for the yearly audit, merchants and carriers with their goods, friars preaching and begging from village to village and town to town. With so many to carry it news travelled fast. Despite the smallness of the population, perhaps two and a half million people, spread lightly over a land so large that at least eight days of hard riding were needed to reach the capital from the most distant shires, there was no great distance between village and village. Most of the land was cultivated, and mainly undisturbed by the rapid marches of Henry's army, the harvest would be coming in, the people getting ready to slaughter their surplus cattle and face the hardships of

---

[1] *Usk*, pp. 28, 179
[2] *Usk*, p. 26; Clarke, *Fourteenth Cent. Studies*, p. 62. cf. *Rot. Parl.*, vol. iii, p. 433

inter. Even if the climate was a little milder than that of twentieth-century Britain, winter inevitably brought darkness, wet and cold, and for many the threat of hunger.

Now there was much discontent and some disorder. The recent strange acts of the King, and the coming of the Duke, were only the culmination of an unsettled reign. After the wars of Edward III violence had come home. For a few days in 1381 the ruling lords and gentry had found themselves faced with disaster, their authority challenged, and even for the moment overthrown, by a mob of townsmen and peasants. The danger passed as quickly as it had come, but their world had trembled and memories of the shock remained. Afterwards the country had seen the clash of the King and his lords. The law was still respected, but every man went armed, and those who could kept bands of armed retainers ready to defend and enforce their rights, as they themselves saw them. On the outskirts of the kingdom, on the Scottish March, in Ireland, Aquitaine and the Channel, there was almost constant strife; and in the centre, London, was the struggle of gilds against gilds. Between the extremes, in the shires, the King's peace was generally maintained, but it was far from secure. And in the background, far and wide, was the unsettling talk of the Lollards. Starting from theological disputes between clerks at Oxford the Lollard movement changed as it grew, challenging both the accepted doctrines of the church and its worldly goods. Ranging amongst the laity from labourers and craftsmen to the gentry, and even affecting one or two lords, it was diluted as it spread across the country into a vague anti-clerical sentiment, rather than a doctrine, a resistance to the claims of the clergy combined with a jealousy of their great wealth. More numerous than the Lollard preachers were the friars, also moving about the country with many stories true and false. They were often unpopular and sometimes suspected of sorcery.

The members of the Parliament would therefore be prepared for strange events, but hardly perhaps to witness the deposition of a king, whom they were not even allowed to see. For no one doubted that Richard, whatever his failings, was the rightful King, the son of Edward the Black Prince and the grandson of Edward the King. It was seventy years since a crowned and anointed king had been deposed, and then only to make way for his son and heir.

Hence the problem which faced Henry was no easy one t resolve. Having taken Richard to the Tower, he withdrev to Hertford to consider the next step. He had almost the whol month of September for consultation and decision before th Parliament met. Somewhere between Doncaster and Londor during those two months on the march, he had probably mad up his mind to be king, even if it did mean breaking a solem oath sworn at Doncaster. As his strength grew and he felt th reality of power, his ambitions grew too. By this time the ide of being chief councillor no longer satisfied him. A settlemer such as is said to have been suggested at Conway would alway have left the way open for Richard to recover his authority, an take his revenge as he had done before. If Richard remaine king neither Henry nor any of his leading supporters coul ever feel safe. Moreover no councillors ruling in the name of powerless king could hope to give the country the strong govern ance which was its greatest need. Richard must therefore b deposed. But what next? Roger Mortimer, Earl of March recognised as the next heir had been killed in Ireland. His so was eight years old, and like Richard could now be no more tha a nominal king for some years, with Henry as chief councillor The obvious answer for Henry was to become king himself but having made up his mind to seize the throne, he came u against the real problem – how to justify that seizure. First h must satisfy his own conscience, not perhaps the easiest task Then how far would his own followers be prepared to accep him, and how far the other magnates and knights, whom h would soon be meeting in Parliament?

Orders were sent out to all the leading abbeys and priories t despatch their chronicles to Westminster, so that they migh be searched for precedents and evidence of Henry's right to th throne; a committee of bishops and doctors being set up t study and report on them. The name of only one member of thi committee is known to us, and that is Adam of Usk, who wa now bustling with his own importance. On 21 September h was allowed to visit Richard in the Tower, where he found hin bemoaning his fate and muttering 'sad stories of the death o kings',[1] for by this time he must have realised that his reign wa at an end.

[1] Shakespeare, *Richard II*, Act 3 scene ii; *Usk*, pp. 30, 182

Chronicle evidence brought before the committee overwhelmingly refuted Henry's claim – first said to have been mooted by his father – that his ancestor, Edmund of Lancaster, and not Edward I, was the elder son of Henry III, with the result that when he came to claim the throne Henry did not venture to assert, but merely hinted at, this strange theory. The fact that the committee could suggest no clear-cut claim is shown by the somewhat ambiguous words which Henry eventually used. Their negative findings cannot have endeared them to Henry, and even less would have been heard of them but for Adam. For it is clear that Adam had a tendency to say too much. Although he was a Lancastrian supporter the detail which he relates sometimes contradicts the official version of events, which tells us what Henry's supporters would have believed, rather than what actually happened. The collapse of the claim to succeed to the Crown by right of birth left Henry with two alternatives, to claim by parliamentary election, or by right of conquest. The former would have made his position weaker, if possible, than it was, since what Parliament had given, Parliament might be supposed able to take away. The claim by conquest on the other hand would be a negation of all law, and might be held to place all rights and properties at his disposal. So if Henry was reluctant to accept a parliamentary election from his supporters, they were fearful of admitting a claim by conquest from him, and some kind of vague compromise was inevitable. In the King's own mind this left doubts and a struggle of conscience which probably pursued him right through to his dying day. In the minds of his subjects, with their inborn prejudice in favour of heredity, his title to the throne was never firmly established, so that they were never able to give him the formal respect and unquestioning loyalty which an obviously rightful king might expect. Rebellion could be very easily justified.

Whilst he was thus waiting for Parliament to assemble, balancing the possibilities, and considering how to cover his usurpation with an acceptable suggestion of legality, Henry set up an administration of his own. John Norbury, his constant companion, who had ridden by his side not only all the way from Paris, but also for most of the last ten years, was appointed treasurer of England on 3 September in place of the murdered Earl of Wiltshire. The appointment of a humble squire to the second most important office in the kingdom, usually held by a bishop or a peer, is at first sight surprising, but besides his close friendship with Henry Norbury seems to have had some influence in the City of London, which was already an important force in financial matters, and his daughter Joan was married to William Parker, alderman and mercer of the City.[1] On appointment he was granted the castle of Leeds in Kent for life. Two days later John Scarle, a chancery clerk, who had been keeper of the rolls and clerk to the Parliament was appointed chancellor, another comparatively humble occupant of high office, Scarle did the routine work of the office and had his formal place in the royal council, but it was Archbishop Arundel who preached the opening sermon of the Parliament, and acted as the leading adviser to Henry; and it has often been asserted that he held the great seal for a time during August 1399, although there is no record evidence of this.

By the appointment of Erpyngham as Constable of Dover Castle Henry had already made sure of that port. All the key offices of Calais were also given to his supporters: Sir Peter Courtenay became captain; Nicholas Usk, a servant of John of Gaunt, treasurer, William Caston, controller, John Norbury, Captain of Guines; and Thomas Totty, still usher of the chamber to Henry, keeper of the Tower by the port.[2] Most of these offices were in the normal course exercised through deputies, but the control was none the less effective. Henry was securing the outposts of his kingdom.

Some time in August or September he was also joined by his eldest son, Henry of Monmouth, now twelve years old. The younger Henry had been taken to Ireland with his cousin, Humphrey of Gloucester, by Richard, perhaps as a hostage. In Ireland Richard is said to have knighted him, but on returning to Wales left both the cousins as prisoners in the castle of Trim. As soon as he learned this Henry ordered them to be brought to England. A special ship was sent from Chester to fetch them and the furnishings of Richard's chapel.[3] The younger Henry reached Chester by sea and thence his father, but Humphrey died on the journey.

[1] *Anglo-Norman Letters*, p. 422
[2] P.R.O., C 76/83
[3] P.R.O., E 403/569 under 5 March

On 30 September archbishops and bishops, abbots and priors, dukes and earls, barons and judges, knights and squires, citizens and burgesses, all duly assembled in Westminster Hall; but one person essential to a full meeting of Parliament was lacking; there was no king. The throne remained vacant, covered, it is said, with a gold cloth. Many historians have regarded this meeting as a Parliament, but since Richard II, the King who had summoned it, was said to have renounced the throne the day before it met, its claim to the title of Parliament must remain for ever in dispute.[1] In the official Lancastrian view it was not a Parliament, although it was, perhaps inadvertently, called Parliament in the Coronation Roll.[2] Sir William Thirning who had been Chief Justice of the Common Bench since 1396, played such a prominent part in the official parleys that he may be regarded as Henry's spokesman. He described the persons who gathered on 30 September as 'the estates' and this seems to have been the Lancastrian view of their status. It was probably the normal word used to describe both Lords and Commons together.[3] The meeting was not therefore officially a Parliament, and no separate Parliament Roll was made of its proceedings; but since a record was needed, an account of them was enrolled, by way of exemplification, with the proceedings of the first Parliament of Henry IV.[4] This official account is the main surviving evidence for what happened at that meeting, for the Lancastrian chroniclers did little more than summarise the official account, and the only hostile chroniclers were the French ones, who were too far

[1] Concerning the status of this meeting in particular, and the deposition of Richard II in general, see especially: S. B. Chrimes, *English Constitutional ideas in the 15th cent.*, pp. 106–16; M. V. Clarke and V. H. Galbraith, 'The deposition of Richard II', *Bull. J.R.L.,* vol. xiv, pp. 125–55, reprinted in *Fourteenth Cent. Studies*, pp. 125–81; G. T. Lapsley, 'The Parliamentary title of Henry IV', *E.H.R.*, vol. xlix, pp. 423–49, 579–606, and 'Richard II's "Last Parliament"', *E.H.R.*, vol. liii, pp. 53–79, reprinted in *Crown, Community and Parl.*; H. G. Richardson, 'Richard II's last Parliament', *E.H.R.*, vol. lii, pp. 39–47; A. B. Steel, *R. II*, pp. 260–8; Stubbs, *Constit. Hist.*, vol. ii, 532–3; Bertie Wilkinson, 'The deposition of Richard II and the accession of Henry IV', *E.H.R.*, vol. liv, pp. 215–39; and *Constit. Hist.*, vol. ii, pp. 284–327; H. G. Wright, 'The Protestation of Richard II in the Tower in September 1399'. *Bull. of J.R.L.*, vol. xxiii, pp. 151–66
[2] Rymer, *Foedera*, vol. viii, p. 90; P.R.O., C 57/2
[3] e.g. *Rot. Parl.*, vol. iii, p. 549 'and alle Estates thynken the same'
[4] *Rot. Parl.*, vol. iii, pp. 416–24

away to be trustworthy witnesses. What is known therefore about the proceedings of 30 September, and indeed of all the events of 1399, is in the main what the Lancastrian official wished to have remembered. Their account of the meeting was written not simply as a record of proceedings, but also, and primarily, as an explanation and defence of the Lancastrian succession to the throne. If Richard II had set the example of 'editing' the Parliament Roll, others could follow it. By having the chronicles searched Henry had also given them recognition as evidence in constitutional matters, and if they were to be so considered in the future, it was reasonable to ensure that their evidence would be favourable.

The assembled 'estates' were told that on the previous morning, Monday, 29 September, certain magnates had met at Westminster in the room where the council was wont to meet. They were the Archbishop of York, the Bishop of Hereford, the Earls of Northumberland and Westmorland, Hugh, Lord Burnell and Thomas, Lord Berkeley, Sir William Thirning and John Markham, justices, Thomas Stowe and John Burbache, doctors of law, Thomas Erpyngham and Thomas Grey, knights, and William Feriby and Denis Lopham, notaries public; that is two bishops, two earls, two barons, two judges, two lawyers and two knights, with two notaries. These personages then proceeded to the Tower to see Richard, and there reminded him of a promise which he was said to have made at Conway to the Earl of Northumberland and Archbishop Arundel, to give up his throne. It is in fact most unlikely that he made any such promise at Conway. If he made it at all it was probably at some time during his imprisonment in the Tower. However, the official story goes on to say that Richard then asked to see the Duke of Lancaster and Archbishop Arundel. They came, and the Lords Roos and Willoughby also joined the deputation. Then the King agreed to a renunciation, saying that had it been in his power to decide he would have liked Henry to succeed him; and to Henry he gave his signet ring.

Richard's renunciation was produced in Westminster Hall and read aloud both in Latin and in English. Then thirty-two articles reciting the misdeeds which the Lancastrian lords attributed to him were also read. These charges went back to 1387, and included both specific wrongs done to individuals, especially the Duke of

Joust at St. Inglevert, near Calais, attended by Henry of Bolingbroke in 1390

Lancaster, Archbishop Arundel and the murdered Duke of
Gloucester, and other examples of misgovernance and uncon-
titutional behaviour. Taken together the articles formed a
history of Richard's reign as seen by his enemies and victims,
and an indictment of his conduct as king. According to the official account he had accepted his abdication in the Tower with a
cheerful face, but if so his mood had changed considerably
from that reported by Adam of Usk, who had seen him a week
earlier. Moreover if he was so willing to abdicate, why could he
not have been brought before the 'estates' to tell them so? It
is more likely that if he had been brought before them, he would
have attempted to answer the charges against him, as he probably
hoped and expected to do. But the opportunity was not given
him. Another possible explanation, that the shock of his capture
had upset his mental balance, that the cheerful grin was that of a
madman, and that he was in no state to be produced in public,
is supported by neither evidence nor probability.

In the course of the proceedings Thomas Merks, Bishop of
Carlisle, still loyal, stood up alone and spoke for his king; but
no support for Richard, no suggestion that he should be heard in
his own defence, was put on the record. Instead the Roll says
that it was agreed by acclamation that his renunciation of the
throne should be accepted. But this in itself was not enough, it
left the way open for a change of mind should circumstances
change. Commissioners were appointed to carry out a formal
deposition, still in the absence of the King. Once again each of
the estates was represented; there was one bishop, St. Asaph,
one abbot, Glastonbury, one earl, Gloucester, and one baron,
Berkeley, with two knights, again Erpyngham and Grey, and
Sir William Thirning, the chief justice, according to whom
Erpyngham represented the 'bachelors and commons of the
land' in the south, and Grey the same in the north. Standing
before the empty throne these commissioners proceeded to
depose Richard, thus making it vacant in theory as well as in
fact.

Henry's opportunity had now come. He had been summoned
to the meeting by a writ addressed to the Duke of Lancaster as
the first of the peers, and he was now seated in his place amongst
them. He stood up, made the sign of the Cross, and spoke in
English:

F

In the name of Fadir, Son and Holy Gost, I, Henry of Lancastre chalenge this Rewme of Yngland, and the Corone, with all the membres and appurtenances als I that am disendit be right lyne of the blode comyng fro the gude lorde Kyng Henry therde and thorghe that ryght that God of his grace hath sent me, with helpe of my kyn and of my frendes to recover it; the whiche Rewme was in poynt to be undone for defaut of governance and undoyng of the gode lawes.[1]

Thereupon all the lords and estates being asked both individually and together to judge his claim declared that Henry should be king, and he showed them the signet ring which Richard had given him the day before. Archbishop Arundel then led the new King to his throne and preached a short sermon, taking out of their context the words with which the Lord had appointed Saul to rule *vir dominabitur populo*, and by stressing the word *man* implying that Richard and other possible candidates were but children. Finally Henry made another brief speech:

Sires, I thank God, and zowe, spirituel and temporel, and all the astates of the lond, and do yow to wyte it es noght my wil that noman thynk that be waye of conquest I wold disherit any man of his heritage, franches, or other ryghtes that hym aght to have, no put hym out of that that he has and has had by the gude lawes and custumes of the Rewme except thos persons that has ben agayn the gude purpose and the commune profyt of the Rewme.[2]

Henry thus left the exact nature of his claim to the throne carefully undefined. He mentioned descent from Henry III, in spite of the disproof of the story of the seniority of the Lancastrian line, but this could be interpreted as no more than an assertion of his family's royal origins, and a pious reference to the last bearer of his own name to occupy the throne. His words were deliberately vague. He mentioned but did not insist on his hereditary claim, and at the same time skilfully avoided committing himself to being elected or appointed by Parliament. Finally, without disclaiming the right by conquest, he was careful to state that he would deprive no man of his rights, a statement which shows how much his followers were in need of reassurance

[1] *Rot. Parl.*, vol. iii, pp. 422–3
[2] *Rot. Parl.*, vol. iii, p. 423

on this point. By suggesting all three titles he ensured that no one of them predominated. The kingdom needed a man to give it governance, and he was that man. That was the simple answer, and the later fifteenth century, not uninfluenced perhaps by his example, was to show that possession was the only valid title to the throne. But Henry himself never escaped from the implications of his weak title. Not only did it make rebellion easy for the consciences of his subjects, but it was also a great handicap in his dealings with the Commons in Parliament, and perhaps even with his own council. The Percies, who had been his strongest supporters in arms, may have felt that they had been outmanœuvred by Henry, who had secured the throne without conditions, or apparent dependence on any man; but if so they were content to bide their time. The King still needed them and they gave no sign, so far as is known, of any reluctance to support him.

Having been recognised as king, Henry IV issued writs for a new Parliament to meet on Monday, 6 October. Since these could not reach the more distant counties in time, and since the members were already at Westminster, this was mainly a matter of form; a precaution to ensure that, unlike the assembly of 30 September, the Parliament of 6 October should be legally constituted. At the same time the date of the coronation was fixed for the Monday after, 13 October. Meanwhile on the 1st Thirning accompanied by his colleague, John Markham, went to the Tower to inform Richard of his deposition by the 'estates'. Richard is reported merely to have said that he hoped his cousin would be 'a good lord to him'. There was little more that he could say, but the mood of resignation to his fate, which this suggests, does not accord well with his character as it is known to us, unless, as suggested above, he had already fallen into a state of depression bordering on madness.

The new King proceeded to establish his Government, and in doing so naturally rewarded his friends and supporters. Scarle and Norbury, recently appointed chancellor and treasurer in Richard's name, were formally reappointed. The two northern Earls, Northumberland and Westmorland, were appointed respectively Constable and Marshal of England. From the moment of Henry's landing they always appeared in court or council together. They could have been close friends and allies, but were almost certainly jealous rivals, each afraid that in his own absence the other might gain some advantage. Richard Clifford, who had been keeper of the privy seal to Richard, was continued in office, and all the judges and lesser officials were reappointed, a striking continuity of personnel in such circumstances. In the royal household Sir Thomas Erpyngham was made chamberlain, and Sir Thomas Rempston, another comrade in arms from the Prussian campaign, became steward on 10 October. Rempston was also entrusted with the office of Constable of the Tower of London, and Thomas Tutbury, sometime treasurer of the household of John of Gaunt, became treasurer of the royal household. The King's second son, Thomas, was appointed Steward of England, and on 4 October in the White Hall at Westminster he held a court to determine the claims of those who would take part in the coronation. On account of his youth Thomas Percy, Earl of Worcester and recently steward of Richard's household, acted as his deputy for part of the proceedings.[1]

All those who had been present on 30 September duly reassembled in Westminster Hall on 6 October, in response to the writs issued after the earlier sitting. This time there was a king on the throne, and none could dispute that this was a proper Parliament. Proceedings were opened with another sermon from Archbishop Arundel, who declared that it was the will of the new King to be guided by the advice of the honourable, wise and discreet persons of his kingdom. He promised that law and justice would prevail, and that the liberties of the church, and all other persons and bodies would be respected. He then proposed that the session should be adjourned until the Tuesday of the following week, the day after the coronation. The Earl of Northumberland, as Constable, asked the Lords whether they agreed to this, which they did. Receivers and triers of petitions were appointed and the meeting ended.

Two days later the charters of Westminster Abbey were confirmed, and the list of witnesses probably provides a good indication of the leading personalities of Henry's court in the first days of his reign. These witnesses were the two Archbishops, the Bishops of London, Exeter and Ely (Robert Braybrook, Edmund Stafford and John Fordham), the Duke of York, the King's uncle, the Earls of Warwick, Westmorland and Northumberland, the Lords Roos, Willoughby and Cobham, and the officers, the

[1] P.R.O., C 57/2

chancellor (John Scarle), the treasurer (John Norbury), the keeper of the privy seal (Richard Clifford), the King's chamberlain (Thomas Erpyngham) and the steward of his household (Thomas Rempston). The Lords Roos and Willoughby had been among the first to join Henry after his landing, whilst the veteran Thomas Beauchamp, Earl of Warwick, Henry's old associate as one of the 'five lords' of 1386, had been imprisoned by Richard in the Isle of Man, whence Henry had released him.

On Sunday, 12 October Henry was at the Tower, where he knighted his three younger sons and a large number of other young nobles. The new knights then rode to Westminster with the King, bareheaded in spite of the autumn rain, in readiness for the coronation. This took place on Monday, the feast of the translation of Edward the Confessor, and also the anniversary of Henry's leaving London to go into banishment. The traditional form was followed in all its details. The sword of justice, which Henry had borne as his father's deputy at the coronation of Richard II, was carried by his son, Henry. The sword which he himself had worn when he landed at Ravenspur was now given the name of Lancaster sword and carried by the Earl of Northumberland in virtue of his new lordship of the Isle of Man, which had been taken from the Earl of Wiltshire. The other special feature of the coronation was the use of the miraculous phial of oil, which was said to have been presented to St. Thomas Becket by the Virgin Mary, and afterwards hidden at Poitiers, to be found there by Henry's grandfather, the Duke of Lancaster. He gave it to the Prince of Wales who left it in the Tower of London where it lay forgotten until Richard II found it too late for his own anointing. It was duly used for Henry, and it was no doubt hoped that the story attached to it would give additional sanctity to the ceremony. He took the same oath as his predecessors, swearing to keep and guard the laws and rightful customs of the realm, and to defend them with all his power. The coronation ceremony was followed by the usual banquet, at which the Constable, the Marshal and the King's champion, Sir Thomas Dymock, were all present in the hall on horseback. Dymock offered to do battle with anyone who challenged the King's title, whereupon the King assured him that if necessary he would defend his crown in his own person; as very shortly he was obliged to do.

So just three months after landing with his small party Henry was a crowned and anointed king, but his position was clearly not a strong one. His troubles were not over, rather they were about to begin. Richard's behaviour had weakened the monarchy, his overthrow had brought it into disrepute. Succeeding him with a doubtful title Henry was very soon made aware of his dependence on the support of the great lords, and on the forbearance of his Parliaments. The fact that some may have believed that in taking the crown he had broken his solemn oath did not help, and many were the taunts that could be flung at him whenever his actions became unpopular. The power of the monarchy had in fact reached a very low ebb, and the speed with which Richard's deposition, and Henry's accession, coronation and Parliament were made to follow each other shows that his advisers were not unaware of the dangers of a hiatus in the kingship. The later years of Edward III, no less than the twenty-two years of Richard II, had witnessed a weak monarchy and the growing power of Parliaments. As a subject Henry may well have believed, like all subjects, that the King should live of his own, that is without raising taxation whether in the form of tenths and fifteenths, or in experimental ways, such as by the disastrous poll-taxes. As a king he was soon to learn how necessary such taxation was. But the Commons in Parliament were beginning to realise their power, to see that this need for their grants of money gave them the chance to interfere in the governance of the realm and to make their grievances heard. Moreover the lords and magnates, who were his ministers, had themselves no desire to submit to a strong king, shared the Commons' dislike of taxation and other grievances, and gave him but little support. Henry not only had a weak title, he also seemed to lack the strength of character needed to control his council and his Parliaments. Betrayed perhaps by his own conviction that he was a usurper he was never able to secure that position of unquestioned dominance in the kingdom, which by virtue of his strength and ability as a leader seemed to come naturally to him in the field. In consequence he was kept short of money. Shortage of money restricted his freedom of action, and the thirteen and a half years of his reign did not prove very happy ones.

Chapter 6

_____

Parliament and council, October–December 1399

ON 6 October 1399, the same day as Parliament, the convocation of the province of Canterbury met in St. Paul's Cathedral. The two Earls of Northumberland and Westmorland together with Sir Thomas Erpyngham attended to explain the King's wishes. Henry had already given evidence of his orthodoxy by issuing proclamations against heresy on the very day of his accession, and now further pleased the clergy by refraining from asking for a grant of clerical taxation. Unlike Parliament, convocation did not get in the way of preparations for the coronation, and was able to go on meeting up to Saturday, 11 October. On the 8th all the bishops of the southern province except Ralph Erghum of Bath and Wells were present. As Erghum died on 10 April in the following year it was no doubt ill-health which kept him away. Of the northern bishops, the Archbishop of York and the Bishop of Durham were almost certainly in London; whilst Thomas Merks, Richard's faithful Bishop of Carlisle, was in protective custody, in the care of the Abbot of St. Albans.

Once the coronation was over, however, Parliament was able to get down to business on Tuesday, 14 October, and the work of convocation was overshadowed if not forgotten. Summonses had gone out to two archbishops, eighteen bishops, twenty-five abbots and priors, sixteen dukes and earls, and thirty-four barons. Of these all are known to have attended except three bishops, sixteen abbots and priors, the Earls of Devon and Oxford and eleven barons. 'Out of those ninety-seven summoned there were no fewer than sixty-three ... certainly in attendance ... the overwhelming preponderance of absentees being among the regular clergy. Never again perhaps was Henry IV to see so many of his prelates and magnates gathered together in either parliament or great council.'[1] All the seventy-four knights of the shire appear to have been present, since all claimed their expenses.

[1] J. S. Roskell, 'The problem of the attendance of the lords in medieval parliaments', *Bull. I.H.R.*, vol. xxix, p. 178

About two-thirds of them are known to have sat in one o
more of the Parliaments of Richard II's reign, though not sur
prisingly only three can be found who had sat in the last on
in 1397–8. The citizens and burgesses seem to have played ;
rather lesser part at this time. Only 32 out of 174 received writ
for their expenses, but this of course does not prove that the other
failed to attend.

The Commons immediately presented as their Speaker Si
John Cheyne, one of the members for Gloucestershire, bu
Cheyne was known to have Lollard sympathies and Archbishor
Arundel had already warned the clergy in convocation that the}
must count Cheyne amongst their enemies. On the next day
Wednesday, he asked to be excused from the office on the grounds
of ill-health and weakness. He was so weak, he said, that he coulc
not make his voice heard.[1] John Doreward, an Essex squire whc
had entered Henry's service one month before, and was perhaps
a protégé of the Archbishop, took his place. As for Cheyne,
neither ill-health nor unorthodox views were to prevent his
later employment in the King's service. The usual subsidy on
the export of wool, 50s. on each sack from English merchants,
and 60s. from foreign merchants, was granted to the King for
three years from Michaelmas 1399. No new grants of tenths and
fifteenths were made, and the half tenth and fifteenth due to be
collected at Michaelmas was cancelled. All that Henry was allowed
to do was to collect the arrears of earlier grants made to his
predecessors. A grant may have been refused, but it is more
likely either that Henry, determined to be a model king unlike
his predecessor, declined to ask, or that his council did not feel
that their position was strong enough to allow them to do so.
Whatever the reason they were certainly soon to regret the consequent lack of revenue. Taxation was not however their immediate concern, or the major business of this session.

All the measures which had been passed by Richard's Parliament of 1397 at Westminster and Shrewsbury were at once
repealed, and those of the Merciless Parliament of 1388, at least
seven of whose members were now present in the Commons,
were reinstated. On the same day, Wednesday, 15 October, the
King's eldest son, Henry of Monmouth, was created Prince of
Wales, Duke of Cornwall and Earl of Chester, and recognised as

[1] *Annales R. II et H. IV*, pp. 290, 302

heir apparent, a recognition which implied the acceptance of the house of Lancaster as the rightful royal line and could hardly be withheld once Henry was recognised as king. A week later the Prince was also made Duke of Aquitaine, and on 10 November he was given the title of Duke of Lancaster, but the estates of the duchy were ordered to be kept forever separate from the other possessions of the Crown; and so they have been, although the title of duke has since 1413 always been borne by the reigning sovereign, and never by a subject however near to the throne.

Whilst dukedoms were being showered upon the future King, Parliament was also concerning itself with the fate of the former one, and with the dukes whom he had created. A proposal made on 21 October that Richard should be brought before Parliament for trial found no favour with Henry, who was evidently still anxious not to give Richard the opportunity to defend himself. Two days later it was agreed that the ex-King should be kept in safe and secret ward, none of his former counsellors or servants being allowed to see him. So important was this decision considered that the unusual step was taken of recording on the Parliament Roll the names of all those who agreed to it. They were the two Archbishops, thirteen bishops, seven abbots, the Prince of Wales, the Duke of York, six earls, twenty-four other lords, and Henry Percy, Thomas Erpyngham and Mathew Gournay, knights. On the following Monday Henry himself came before Parliament to pronounce the sentence of perpetual banishment on Richard, to which all the lords had assented. Shortly afterwards the ex-King was removed by night from the Tower, taken to Leeds Castle in Kent, and from there to Henry's own castle of Pontefract in Yorkshire.

An even more difficult problem than the disposal of Richard was the treatment of his followers. To punish anyone for obeying the rightful king would create an unfortunate precedent, and the obvious policy for Henry was to make as little disturbance as possible, but some action had to be taken against Richard's supporters if only to justify the change of king. Sir William Bagot, who had carried the news of Henry's landing to Ireland, was now the only survivor of Richard's close advisers, but the peerage promotions of 1397, and some of Richard's grants of lands, must also have been bitterly resented by other lords.

Bagot was brought before Parliament, and in defending himself accused the Duke of Aumerle of being one of Richard's evil counsellors. Aumerle, the son of the Duke of York, had been Earl of Rutland before 1397. He was now accused of complicity in the death of the Duke of Gloucester, and a certain John Hall, described as a servant of Thomas, Duke of Norfolk, was brought from Newgate to bear witness against him. This led to the kind of situation which Henry must have been most anxious to avoid, if any sort of peaceful settlement was to be assured. The Dukes of Surrey and Exeter were also accused, other lords joined in, both for and against, and challenges were thrown down in the Parliament chamber on more than one occasion, until in the end the King was forced to intervene to preserve the peace.

Hall, having given his evidence, was executed. On 20 October Aumerle was committed to Windsor Castle, Exeter to Hertford Castle, and Surrey with the Earls of Gloucester and Salisbury to the Tower. On the 29th they were all brought before Parliament for trial, and with them Thomas Merks, Bishop of Carlisle. Finally on 3 November the judgment of the King and Lords was pronounced by Chief Justice Thirning, acting once more as Henry's mouthpiece. The three Dukes, Aumerle, Surrey and Exeter, lost the titles conferred in 1397, and returned to being Earls of Rutland, Kent and Huntingdon. The Marquess of Dorset, who was John Beaufort, the King's eldest half-brother, reverted to his former title of Earl of Somerset. Five days later the King's favour was shown in his appointment as Chamberlain of England. The Earl of Gloucester returned to being Lord Despenser, and all estates conferred on these lords since 1397 had to be given up. Thomas Merks was deprived of his bishopric of Carlisle, but allowed to live in retirement in St. Albans Abbey, and William Bagot went to live in peace on his Warwickshire estate. The Earl of Salisbury also suffered no punishment. On 30 October the King agreed that the Archbishop of Canterbury should be able to recover damage to his temporalities against Roger Walden, who was deprived but not punished. No real evidence had been produced against any of the accused, but nonetheless Henry's clemency, soon to be rewarded with rebellion, was surely unparalleled in medieval Europe.

The legislative business of Henry's first Parliament, though not unimportant, was less immediately controversial. On 31 October here was a consultation between the Lords and Commons, not recorded on the Parliament Roll, about ten points to which they wanted the King's agreement.[1] The first point to which the King did later agree was that the Commons should not be parties to judgments, or recorded as such in the rolls of Parliament. The other matters concerned the Prince of Wales, the judges, sheriffs, the defences of the realm, and the claim of the Duke of Brittany to the earldom of Richmond. Some of these were granted amongst the petitions of the Commons. Others seem to have been lost or left unrecorded. The earldom of Richmond had already been granted by the King to the Earl of Westmorland, and Henry now evaded a direct answer. The most important statute of the session restricted the giving of liveries and badges by the magnates to their followers. The law of treason was limited by a return of the statute of Edward III, the delegation of the powers of Parliament, and appeals in Parliament were both forbidden, the King and his council were empowered to moderate the Statute of Provisors, sheriffs were to be allowed some adjustment by the exchequer of the farm of their shires, the chancellor was to have general authority to confirm charters of liberties, and some regulations were made about the packing of cloths, and the subsidy on them. The blank charters exacted by Richard II were declared null and void, and in November it was ordered that they should be publicly destroyed.

Parliament was dissolved on 19 November. A large number of petitions were dealt with, apart from those relating to the matters already mentioned, and altogether the King might well be satisfied with the volume of business transacted in the first seven weeks of his reign. Before the dissolution he himself announced in Parliament his intention of waging war against the Scots in person. For the moment he might feel secure, and it was only now that he released a large part of the army which had been with him since Doncaster. Two-thirds of this force, which had no doubt served like Richard's archers in 1397, but perhaps less obtrusively, to overawe Parliament, was made up of the retinues of the Earl of Northumberland and Henry Percy, his son. Smaller contingents were commanded by William, Lord Will-

[1] H. G. Richardson and G. O. Sayles, 'Parliamentary documents from formularies', *Bull. I.H.R.*, vol. xi, pp. 155–8; *Anglo-Norman Letters*, pp. 25–6

oughby, William, Lord Roos, the Earl of Westmorland, Si
John Berkeley, Sir Robert Berkeley, and several other knight
and squires. The fact that the followers of the Percies were kep
in the King's pay directly contradicts a statement made by th
chronicler Hardyng in defence of the Percies that Henry sen
them home as soon as he secured control of Richard, so as to b
able to depose him against the will of the Percies.[1]

Whilst establishing himself as king at home, Henry was als
aware of the need for securing recognition abroad. Even befor
becoming king he wrote as Duke of Lancaster and Steward o
England suggesting to the King of the Scots that the truce whic
was due to expire at Michaelmas should be extended. In Franc
the King is said to have been enraged by the deposition of hi
son-in-law, but Henry remained on good terms with the Duke
of Berri, the King's uncle, and Orleans, and some of thei
retainers were present at Westminster for the coronation. On
29 November Walter Skirlaw, Bishop of Durham, and the Earl
of Worcester, were sent to Paris to treat for the continuance o
the truce with France.[2] With other states relations were rather
easier from the start. On 3 October Henry wrote to William,
Duke of Guelders,[3] who had disliked the peace policy of Richard
II and befriended the Earl of Arundel in exile, and on the following day to the Doge of Venice,[4] with whom he had himself
established friendly relations on his way to and from the Holy
Land. With the Queen of Portugal, his sister, and the Queen
of Castile, his half-sister, Henry always seems to have maintained
cordial relations.[5] On 24 October he confirmed the privileges of
the Hanse merchants in London, on condition that English
merchants were given similar privileges in the Hanse towns,[6] and
also that representatives of Lübeck, Wismar, Rostock, Stralsund
and Gripswold should come before the council before midsummer
to answer the charges of English merchants for injuries and make
restitution. To emphasise the importance of these conditions
it was made clear that the King had seen them and himself

[1] Bean, 'H. IV and the Percies' p. 216
[2] Rymer, *Foedera*, vol. viii, p. 118
[3] *R. Letters, H. IV.*, vol. i, p. 33
[4] *Cal. S.P. Venice,* vol. i, p. 39
[5] Russell, *Eng. Intervention*, pp. 544–52
[6] *Cal. Pat.* (1399–1401), p. 57

handed them to Thomas Stanley, keeper of the rolls of chancery for enrolment.

This is one of the earliest references to Henry's council, which had probably not been formally constituted by this time, although the members of the first Parliament clearly showed that they expected the new King to be advised by his council. The Archbishop in his opening speech had promised that the King would be guided by 'honourable, wise and discreet' persons, and whilst one petition asked that the King should make grants only 'by the advice of his council', another suggested that he should appoint good and sufficient captains to his castles 'by the advice of his wise council'. To the second petition the King agreed, and to the first also 'saving always his liberty', a phrase which might mean as much or as little as he pleased. In moderating the Statute of Provisors the King was to have 'the advice of such wise and worthy persons as he was pleased to call to his council'. Thus Parliament, whilst expecting the King to consult his council, seems to have shown no wish to interfere with the free choice of his councillors. Nor did later Parliaments, although anxious to have the councillors named, so that they might know who they were, ever claim the right to name councillors themselves.[1]

But the King's choice, if free in theory, was in practice severely limited. On the one hand there were those whose claim to be of the council was too strong to be ignored, and on the other the number of those who were able and willing to do the routine work of the council was limited. Hence there were two elements, the magnates who not only came to the council when they would but also stayed away when they would, and the officers who were always there making the small decisions of day to day, the working administration of the kingdom. Another limiting factor was the evident feeling that the council should be 'representative' in character. Just as two bishops, two earls, two barons and so on had been sent to Richard in the Tower, and one member of each estate put on the commission to depose him, so the council tended to be made up of so many bishops, earls, barons, knights and squires, in addition to the officers. There were even at one

---

[1] For the council see: J. L. Kirby, 'Council and councillors of Henry IV', *Trans. R.H.S.*, 5th ser., vol. xiv, pp. 35–65, and the sources quoted there; A. L. Brown, 'Commons and the Council in the reign of Henry IV', *E.H.R.*, vol. lxxix, pp. 1–30

time, when their money and financial advice was most needed, three citizens and merchants of London. From 1406 however the magnates took control of the council and commoners were excluded.

Whilst the witnesses to royal charters were not all councillors their names are of some importance, for they were the leading men of the realm, from whom the King must choose the greater part of his council. Those who witnessed the charters of Westminster Abbey have already been named. Other charters granted before Christmas 1399 added a few more names of witnesses. Besides the Bishops of London, Exeter and Ely, those of Durham (Walter Skirlaw), Lincoln (Henry Beaufort, the King's half-brother), and Winchester (the aged William of Wykeham) appear. There were no more earls, apart from Northumberland, Westmorland and Warwick, until 12 November when Somerset, the King's eldest half-brother reduced from the rank of marquess and newly appointed Chamberlain of England, appeared. A few days later Lords Grey of Ruthyn and Lovell came in to join Roos, Willoughby and Cobham. The officers, chancellor, treasurer, privy seal, King's chamberlain and steward of the household, remained unchanged. Some names were omitted from some charters, but there was no significant change until 10 December when charters for Winchester College were witnessed, in addition to those already named, by the three Earls of Rutland, Kent and Huntingdon, and the three rather undistinguished Bishops of Rochester, Hereford and St. Asaph. These were the three earls who had been reduced from the rank of duke in Parliament. The inclusion of their names suggests that they were regarded as members of the King's court, even though it does not imply their actual presence in it, but less than a month later they were in revolt against the King.

Such were the leading people around Henry. The five officers were bound to form the core, if not quite the whole, of the working council. Archbishop Arundel and Henry Percy, Earl of Northumberland, as the two leading supporters of Henry on the road to the throne, occupied a very special position. Arundel remained for many years the principal councillor, although often absent from the daily routine meetings. Northumberland's presence was always jealously balanced by that of Westmorland. Other bishops and lords also attended less regularly than the officers, but often enough to lend the weight of their rank to the decisions of the council. No doubt the council soon began to meet almost every day, but records are very scanty. Some petitions were referred to it by the King, sometimes it asked for his guidance, for he rarely attended himself, and usually the council continued to meet in London or Westminster, whether the King was there or not. Some administrative orders were issued by the King, some by the council, but the more important ones were usually made jointly after consultation. It was the chamberlain's duty to note the King's assent on a petition before passing it to the council or chancellor for action. The King's chamberlain or steward of the household often brought his instructions by word of mouth, but any councillor might serve as an intermediary. From time to time the Archbishop of Canterbury or the Earl of Northumberland did so, more often a trusted squire.

In the list of the 'lords' on the Parliament Roll[1] who agreed on 23 October to the secret imprisonment of Richard II were the names of three who had not been summoned as peers to attend the Parliament, and who had not been returned as members of the Commons. These were Henry Percy, the son of the Earl of Northumberland, better known to us as Hotspur, Sir Thomas Erpyngham, then or soon afterwards the King's chamberlain, and Sir Mathew Gournay. Gournay is reputed to have been present at Sluys, Crécy and Poitiers, and to have been well over ninety when he died in 1406.[2] Like Chaucer's knight he had been at the 'sege . . . of Algezir, and riden in Belmarye', but whether he was 'worthy' and 'wyse . . . meke as is a mayde', who 'no vileinye ne sayde', and a 'verray parfit gentil knight'[3] is more doubtful. These three, Percy, Erpyngham and Gournay, neither lords nor members of the Commons, can only have been present in Parliament as councillors.

That some sort of council, nominally Richard's council, was acting with Henry at least from the time of his arrival at Chester has already been shown.[4] Doubtless the same magnates con-

---

[1] *Rot. Parl.*, vol. iii, pp. 426–7

[2] John Leland (*Itinerary*, vol. i, pp. 159, 297) claims to have seen Gournay's tombstone at Stoke-under-Hamden in Somerset, according to which, as he says, Gournay died on 26 September 1406, aged ninety-six; a story very difficult to believe.

[3] Chaucer, vol. iv, pp. 2–3, 'The Prologue'

[4] Above, chap. 5, p. 20

tinued to act after Henry became king. No record has survived, and probably none was made, of the formal setting up of Henry's council, but it is likely that this took place on 11 November, one week before the end of the parliamentary session. From that day a number of the humbler and more regular members were paid for their services as councillors, and on that day the first recorded meeting of the council was held. At this meeting Archbishop Arundel, the Bishop of Durham, the Earls of Northumberland, Westmorland and Worcester, the chancellor, treasurer, keeper of the privy seal and King's chamberlain, the Lords Cobham and Lovell, and Sir Mathew Gournay were present. Of these only Worcester and Gournay had not appeared in the charter lists of witnesses. The Earl of Worcester was Thomas Percy, brother to the Earl of Northumberland, steward of Richard's household until he deserted to join Henry in July. Before joining his family in another change of sides he was to become steward of Henry's household from 1401 to 1402. At other meetings of the council in November the Bishop of Winchester and the Earl of Warwick appeared, as did also John Prophet, John Doreward and William Brampton. Prophet had been clerk of the council under Richard II and a clerk in the privy seal office. He later became Henry IV's secretary. Doreward was the Speaker of the recent Parliament, and Brampton was a prominent London citizen. These were the kind of working members, not of the magnate class, who might be counted on to assist the officers with the routine business of government.

On 4 December a larger meeting was attended by the Bishops of London, Exeter and Hereford, the old Duke of York, three of the recently reduced peers, Rutland, Huntingdon and Despenser, and Thomas Coggeshale, John Frenyngham and William Rees, in addition to those who have already been named. The last three, like Doreward, came from the class of knights and squires prominent in Parliament. Two more meetings on the 8th and 9th added only the Bishop of Bangor, and Richard Whittington, the famous mayor of London, whose loans to Richard II were being repaid. He may well have been called in as a financial expert. Rutland appeared on the 8th, but the other degraded lords are not known to have come again. It looks as though membership was still somewhat fluid depending on who was in London or at court. Whilst the council was busy hearing petitions and settling

POMFRET CASTLE in *YORKSHIRE*, before it was demolished.

Pontefract Castle

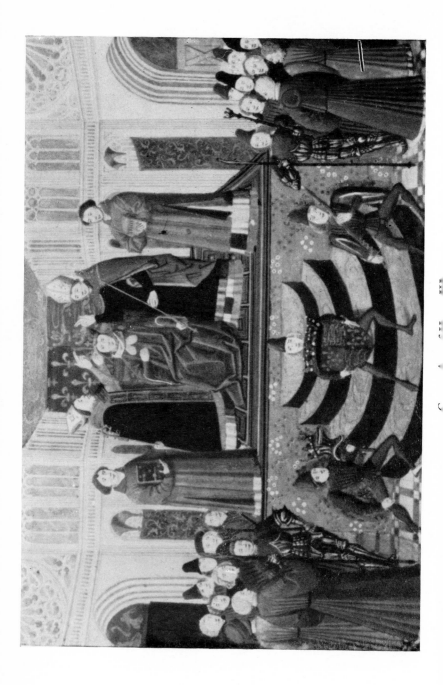

disputes, the chancery was issuing confirmations of all the grants of offices and annuities made by Richard II, so that their holders could apply to the exchequer for their fees and pensions. Until these confirmations had been issued the exchequer was not very busy. Some feudal revenues and customs collections were paid in, but there had been no special grant of taxation; and on the other side of the account money had to be found for the King's household, for the two northern Earls for keeping the Scottish march, and for the treasurer of Calais for the garrison there, whilst the judges and other officers drew their salaries. But all this was routine; there was no call to work overtime at the exchequer, with suppers charged to the royal accounts, during the first term of the reign. The whole administration in fact continued as usual apparently unmoved by the change of king.

About 10 December Henry left Westminster for Kennington across the river, long a manor of the duchy of Cornwall and now vested in his son, and after about a week there he went on to Windsor to spend the Christmas holiday in feasting and enjoyment of his new state. It was perhaps about this time that John Norbury wrote to the Earl of Westmorland telling him that the King had recovered from his malady, but that there was no certain news from France, the English ambassadors being still at Calais.[1] The letter was probably written early in the reign, though it is not possible to date it exactly, because English ambassadors were frequently at Calais in these early years. However, it is interesting as one of a number of letters showing Norbury at the King's side sending news of the court to absent councillors. Indeed Norbury was on such good terms with the King that he was able to write letters on his behalf, which had they come from the King himself might have appeared too formal or official. This is also the first suggestion of another difficulty with which Henry had increasingly to contend, his own ill-health.

---

[1] *Anglo-Norman Letters*, pp. 405–6

Chapter 7

The rising of the earls and the death of Richard,
January–July 1400

THE year 1400 not only saw the completion of the Lancastrian revolution, but also brought the new King abruptly face to face with most of the major problems of the reign. In January he survived a sudden and urgent crisis, a crisis in which a few hours' delay might have cost him his throne. In the summer Owen Glendower began a rebellion, which was to become not only a threat to the security of the kingdom, but also a serious drain on its financial resources. The shortage of money was destined to be an ever-pressing problem. How to find enough money to pay for his household, and for the defence of his kingdom, Henry and his council never really discovered. Nor did his reluctant and critical Parliaments give very much help. But first of all the King had to defend his own life.

After the Earls of Rutland, Kent and Huntingdon had been degraded in Parliament, the Abbot of Westminster had become a surety for them, and they had been lodged in the abbey. The sympathies of the Abbot, William Colchester, were strongly on the side of Richard II, and he allowed his abbey, at the very centre of the administration of the kingdom, to become the headquarters of rebellion. According to the French chroniclers these three earls, who were apparently newly reconciled with Henry, appearing in his council and witnessing his charters, dined with the Abbot at Westminster on 17 December. Also present at this remarkable entertainment were the Earl of Salisbury, Lord Despenser, Thomas Merks ousted from the see of Carlisle, Roger Walden who had been intruded into Arundel's archbishopric of Canterbury by Richard II and since displaced, a certain Master Pol, sometime Richard's physician, Richard Maudelyn a former clerk of Richard whose physical appearance greatly resembled his master's, and Sir Thomas Blount, a knight loyal to Richard.[1] Such a gathering of all the leading supporters of the

[1] *Traïson et Mort*, pp. 77, 229

ex-King could hardly have been accidental, indeed the story is not altogether easy to believe. The outcome and evident purpose was a plot to kill Henry and restore Richard, and the plot was real enough, even if the dinner is a little hard to swallow. Maudelyn was to be used to impersonate the former King until he could be freed to act for himself. A tournament, or a 'mommynge', which was to be held at Windsor on Twelfth Night, would serve as a cover for bringing in armed men to seize the castle and kill Henry and his sons.

Whilst the court was at Windsor the King had been ill, and there were stories of attempts to poison him, and also the Prince of Wales and Henry Hotspur. The King himself talking carelessly with his courtiers is said to have remarked casually that he wished Richard were dead, but afterwards said that only if there were a rising would Richard die. Certainly the air was full of rumours, and with so many plotters in the secret, some news of what was afoot was bound to leak out. One chronicler told how the secret of the plot was revealed by a prostitute to a member of Henry's court,[1] but the French chroniclers whose detailed accounts are the fullest, said that it was the Earl of Rutland who betrayed it,[2] through his father the Duke of York, in much the same way as Henry himself had betrayed Norfolk, through his father, John of Gaunt, two years before.

Whoever was his informant, it is clear that on 4 January Henry discovered that his life was in imminent danger. This was the sort of situation demanding quick action in which he was always at his best. Collecting his sons, he rode with them in all haste to London, and there summoned the citizens to his aid. London was still his, and he did not call in vain. The conspirators meanwhile were but a few hours too late. They seized Windsor, and finding that the King had gone, rode on to Sonning, near Reading, where Richard's child-queen, Isabel, was still living. They tore off the Lancaster badges worn by her servants and guards, and having thus wasted precious hours began to advance on London; but Henry collected an army composed mainly of Londoners and rode towards Hounslow Heath. The rebels, informed of his strength, which was doubtless exaggerated by rumour, hesitated and began to withdraw. After a skirmish at Maidenhead their

[1] *Eulogium*, vol. iii, p. 385
[2] *Traïson et Mort*, pp. 80, 233

withdrawal became a retreat, and they passed quickly through Wallingford and Faringdon to Cirencester. By the time that they reached the last-named town the army which they had raised was discreetly dispersing itself. On arrival however the leaders found lodgings in the town.

John Norbury, who was still apparently at the King's side, wrote a short letter to inform Archbishop Arundel of the position.[1] He said that on the way to Cirencester the Earl of Kent had met Sir Walter Hungerford, the son of Sir Thomas Hungerford, sometime Speaker of the Commons in Parliament and steward of the duchy of Lancaster, and forced him to accompany the rebels. Once arrived in the town Hungerford managed quietly to warn the bailiffs of the circumstances, whereupon the townspeople arrested the rebel leaders. Norbury himself was going with Lord Botiller to fetch them to Oxford on the following Thursday, probably 14 January, to be tried before the King. Before this could happen there was a fire in the town followed by a riot in which the Earls of Kent and Salisbury together with Lord Lumley fell into the hands of the mob and were straightway beheaded. Eighty other rebels were taken in arms and brought to trial at Oxford in the presence of the King. Some were dismissed as being too insignificant to punish, and others received short terms of imprisonment, but nearly thirty, including at least one knight, Sir Thomas Blount, were executed. Their bodies were cut up and taken to London partly in sacks and partly slung on poles between men's shoulders, and afterwards salted.[2] The Earl of Huntingdon was captured at Pleshey in Essex and beheaded by the local people, and Lord Despenser suffered a similar fate at Bristol. It was perhaps fortunate for Hungerford that Norbury, the King's most trusted servant, believed in his loyalty, for it was otherwise with the jurors of Gloucestershire, who on 26 January found him guilty of joining the traitors, and ordered his possessions in the county to be sequestrated;[3] but no further action was taken against him. There must have been many whose main object was to come out of a confused situation on the winning side.

Meanwhile on 10 January Archbishop Arundel wrote from

[1] *Anglo-Norman Letters*, pp. 116–17
[2] *Usk*, pp. 42, 198
[3] *Cal. of Inquisitions Miscellaneous* (1399–1422), p. 30

his London house to tell the monks of his cathedral church at Canterbury of his own adventures.[1] He had left Croydon in order to visit the King at Windsor, and intended to pass the night at Kingston-on-Thames on Sunday, 4 January, but when he arrived there he found the town full of rebel soldiers. Happily he was able to escape unrecognised despite the fact that the Earl of Kent had tried to trap him. He was now rejoicing over the death of the Earl, who was his own nephew, the son of his sister Alice, and describing the Cirencester mob who beheaded him and his allies as the *sancta rusticitas*. In so small a society as that of the English nobility most members were bound to be fairly closely related, but their enmities were made no less bitter thereby.

The other conspirators were tried in London and more formally punished. Sir Bernard Brocas, Sir Thomas Shelley and Richard Maudelyn were executed. Roger Walden and the Abbot of Westminster were confined in the Tower but soon released. Thomas Merks, the same Bishop of Carlisle, who had dared to raise his single voice in opposition to Henry from the first day of his reign, was kept in the Tower for six months, and then handed over to the custody of his ally, the Abbot of Westminster. Finally in the following November he received a full pardon, but was never restored to his see. Henry was still prepared to be lenient at least with clerics.

Another magnate and bishop who was suspected of complicity with the plot was Henry Despenser of Norwich. Younger brother of the executed Thomas, Lord Despenser he had been Bishop of Norwich for thirty years and was now verging on sixty. He had won notoriety by the vigour with which he had attacked and suppressed the rebels of 1381, and two years later had been chosen by Pope Urban VI to lead a disastrous 'crusade' in the Low Countries against the supporters of the rival Pope. Thereafter he had been a strong supporter of Richard II. He was however on good terms with Philippa, Queen of Portugal, Henry's sister, and shortly before Henry became king Philippa wrote to Archbishop Arundel asking him to make peace between the Bishop and the King. The Bishop was in friendly correspondence with her, sending presents to remind her of her former home.[2]

[1] *Lit. Cant.*, vol. iii, pp. 73–5

[2] *Anglo-Norman Letters*, pp. 360-2, 372-3

He appeared in Henry's first Parliament and was amongst those who agreed that Richard should be kept in close confinement. Now he wrote to a nephew saying that he knew nothing of the rebellion until it was over, having had no communication with the rebels since the last Parliament apart from a verbal message from the Earl of Huntingdon. He had not left South Elmham except to attend the funeral of a servant. However he thought it better to say nothing unless he was formally accused.[1] Apparently no formal charge was brought, but his relations with the King remained strained, and he seems to have spent the remaining six years of his life in minor squabbles with his neighbours.

As the plotters had no doubt foreseen, the northern earls and other peers had retired to their own estates for Christmas, too far away to help the King in his need. Hotspur, too, if he had indeed been with the court at Christmas, must have quickly departed. The revolt nonetheless was a fiasco. Henry survived with apparent ease, but both he and his council had been seriously alarmed for the moment. His Government was only three months old, and therein lay part of its strength. The plotters should have given him more time to become unpopular, for the treatment of Richard's adherents showed that it was still against him that popular feeling could be roused. The near panic of the council was reflected in the orders which it issued forbidding anyone to leave the country. This was largely rescinded on 18 January, but an attack from France was still feared. Orders were issued to take ships and to prepare Southampton against invasion. On 30 January a new governor of that town was named. At Frome, in Somerset, and in Lancashire and Cheshire rioting either took place, or was feared by the council. For the rest of the winter, and indeed well on into the summer, they were busy issuing orders to enquire into and collect the money and goods of the various rebels. Even such a comparatively minor source of revenue was not to be despised by the ministers of Henry IV.

The revolt of the earls was a sharp reminder, if one were needed, of the weakness of Henry's Government. This weakness was already emphasised by shortage of money, the first Parliament, as already observed, not having made any grant apart from the usual subsidy on wools for three years. The convoca-

[1] *Anglo-Norman Letters*, pp. 113-15

on of Canterbury had similarly made no new grant, and had like
arliament cancelled the half tenth already granted to Richard
nd due to be collected at Martinmas 1399. All that was left to
Ienry was the arrears of earlier tenths and fifteenths granted by
arliament, and of tenths granted by the clergy. These amounted
o no great sum, and like most old debts would not be easily
ollected.

During the first three months of the reign the exchequer had
eceived in cash £20,700 and paid out £20,500. Another £29,000
lue to creditors had been paid by giving them assignments on
uture revenue. On the surface this appears a satisfactory if
ot exactly a favourable position, but the real situation was very
lifferent. The largest item in the cash receipts, nearly £15,000,
onsisted of the dowry of Isabel of France, Richard's second
vife. This sum has been known to historians as Richard's hoard,
nd in a sense so it was, for Richard had managed to hoard the
lowry in the shape of the very French crowns in which it had
een received. Whoever was now entitled to it, it was certainly
ot Henry, but it had fallen into his hands, and being the only
neans of keeping his exchequer solvent, he had used it. Another
um of £14,000 had been borrowed, so that of the £20,700
only a little over £4,000 was in fact genuine revenue. Moreover
quite a number of assignments were unsuccessful, the revenues
on which they had been made proving insufficient, at least for
he moment, to pay the creditors.[1]

Henry was barely able to cover his current expenses, and he
was anxious to do much more than that. Having suppressed
he January rebellion, he wished to prove both to his subjects
and to his neighbours that he was indeed a king, by displaying
his strength in a punitive expedition against the Scots. He had
told the convocation of Canterbury that he would not ask for a
grant from the clergy except in emergency, and he was no doubt
reluctant to call another Parliament only three months after the last
one. He and the officials of his council – the magnates were still
far away in their fastnesses – decided to summon a great council.

A great council may be regarded either as an enlarged meeting
of the council, or as an informal Parliament. Its meeting involved
like that of Parliament the presence of the King, and it might
contain most or all of the other elements of Parliament, since

[1] P.R.O., E 401/617–18; E 403/564–5

its composition depended upon the King himself. He coul
summon as many or as few as he wished. It lacked the forma
membership and procedure of Parliament, it lacked also th
authority of Parliament, and most important the power to mak
grants of money. Like the ordinary council, it could merel
advise the King. Henry IV must nonetheless have felt that sucl
advice was useful or necessary for the strengthening of his ow
position, since he had quite frequent recourse to great council
during his reign. Perhaps its most important function was to be
told of the King's difficulties, his wishes and his intentions
and so like Parliament to keep the most important elements of the
kingdom informed of these things. It was probably when the
councillors felt that they needed extra advice and authority, and
needed to explain their difficulties, whilst conscious that a Par
liament would be critical and unhelpful in the matter of supply
that they advised the King to call together other magnates and
knights to support their policy or discuss their difficulties
Being informal meetings, and not courts of record like the Parlia
ments, great councils have left no regular accounts of their
proceedings so that often we know very little about them, and
indeed some great councils probably met without leaving any
trace at all.

The first great council of Henry IV met at Westminster on 9
February 1400.[1] The two Archbishops were present, and eleven
bishops. One bishopric was vacant, two bishops were probably
sick, and the Bishop of Durham had gone to Calais with the
Earl of Worcester on an embassy for the King. The other absentees were the Bishops of Worcester and St. Asaph, perhaps
also on embassies abroad, and Bishop Despenser of Norwich,
now apparently reluctant to leave his diocese and meet the King.
There were also present five earls, Northumberland, Westmorland, Warwick, Stafford and Suffolk, and fourteen other lords.
This was the first recorded appearance in the council since
Christmas of any of the magnates. The most notable lay absentees
were the old Duke of York, and his unhappy son, Rutland.
York, who continued to be named as a witness to royal charters
almost until his death on 1 August 1402, may have been too old
to take a more active part in affairs; and Rutland soon recovered
the royal favour, if he had ever lost it, and was appointed the

[1] Nicolas, *P.C.*, vol. i, pp. 102–5

King's lieutenant in Aquitaine. These lords, spiritual and lay, were no doubt reinforced by the officers and other members of the ordinary council, although these were not mentioned.

Considering his great needs and to avoid summoning a Parliament, which would have had to tax the common people, these lords agreed to give aid to the King. The bishops undertook to grant a tenth on condition that if in the future convocation should grant a tenth for the same purpose they should be exempt. It was also agreed that letters should be sent to the abbots and priors of all the more important houses in England, not one of whom was present, asking them to make a similar grant. The lay lords on the other hand agreed to serve the King for three months with varying numbers of men, but without pay. The Earls of Westmorland and Northumberland were each to provide 40 men-at-arms and 120 archers, and the other lords lesser numbers down to the Lords Scales and Bardolf, who simply agreed to serve in their own persons. The total force promised amounted to 148 men-at-arms and 352 archers on land, and 9½ ships, with 190 men-at-arms, 380 archers and the necessary complement of mariners to serve at sea.

The council also ordered that the forfeited lordships should be used to pay for the support of the King's household, since if a Parliament were summoned it might well point out that all these lordships ought to suffice for such payments, and for the defence of the realm. Assignments were to be made on the wool customs to pay for the defence of the Scottish march.

The other important business was the security of the King and kingdom. Here the first suggestion was that if Richard were still alive, 'as was supposed', he should be well and safely guarded for the safety of the King's estate and of his kingdom. A general pardon was to be issued for offences committed during the recent rising, and thanks sent to all those loyal lieges who had helped to defeat it. Certain castles were to be strongly held, a fleet to be collected at Sandwich, commissions for keeping the peace issued and certain esquires and archers from each county to live for a while at the King's wages outside his household, to guard him by night. The household servants should also be armed for defence. How far, if at all, these precautions were adopted, is not known. One further recommendation was that suitable persons should be appointed to report from time to time on the council's advice to the King, and to take the King's wishes to the council, in order to safeguard the King, and also the councillors who wished to acquit themselves loyally as bound by their oath. As stated above the function of intermediary was usually performed by the King's chamberlain or by one of his squires, like John Norbury. The raising of the matter suggests that some friction may already have arisen over the interpretation of messages between King and council. When much of the communication was by word of mouth it is clear that the messenger's function was a vital and delicate one.

Finally the council discussed foreign relations, and especially the embassies which the King had sent, or was about to send, to announce his accession to the courts of Rome, France, Castile, Portugal and Aragon. Nor were the depredations of the Scots forgotten.

With regard to Richard the council further recommended that if he were no longer alive, his body should be shown to the people in order that rumours of his escape to Scotland should be dispelled; and during February or March his body was in fact brought to London and his face exposed to the public gaze. After a funeral service at St. Paul's he was taken to Langley in Buckinghamshire for burial. It is known that he had died at Pontefract Castle, perhaps on St. Valentine's day, but how he died is still uncertain and likely to remain so. One French story, which much later found its way back to England, was that he had been killed at Henry's order by a knight called Sir Piers Exton. No knight of that name is known to have existed, but it is not unlikely that the name could have arisen from a misreading of that of Peter or Piers Bukton, a Yorkshire knight and a lifelong follower of Henry, who was now his standard-bearer. The official gaoler was another trusted Lancastrian knight who had also served under Henry on his Prussian expeditions, Sir Thomas Swynford. The story had however been generally rejected because Richard's skeleton was later found to show no marks of violence, and because no such story is known to have been current in England. It is generally believed that he died of starvation some time after the January rising, but whether the starvation was due to his own refusal to eat and to his despair, or whether it was due to the deliberate neglect of his gaolers, acting on the orders, or with the connivance of, the King, there

s no means of knowing. Henry's enemies never hesitated to
accuse him of murder; his friends tended to keep silent.[1]

Epidemics and brawls amongst the London apprentices, even
in St. Paul's churchyard, were not unusual occurrences at this
time, but those which occurred in the spring of 1400 were evidently even more violent than usual.[2] To the King however
money remained the most pressing problem. Before Easter
Richard Whittington, the London merchant, lent the exchequer
£666; and John Norbury, the treasurer, with five of the prelates
who had been present at the council some £700 more. Even so
the cash receipts between Christmas and Easter amounted to
only £4,000, which was spent as soon as it was collected. The
King took his court to Eltham, which, lying about eight miles
south-east of the capital, was to become for him, as it had been
for Richard, a favourite residence. There on 9 March the council,
including the Earls of Northumberland and Westmorland, met;
but for the most part the officers and regular members of the
council continued to meet in London. About this time Henry
Bowet, the clerk appointed by Henry to act as his attorney in
1398, and subsequently imprisoned by Richard II, became a
regular member. In the next year (1401) he was advanced to the
bishopric of Bath and Wells, and remained high in Henry's
councils for a number of years.

The records of the collectors of the clerical tenths show that
the bishops were habitually the last to pay, apparently hoping
that if they postponed payment long enough they might avoid
it altogether. The grant of 1400 was not exceptional, at least in
this respect. The rather obscure bishops who were absent,
together with six out of the thirteen who were present, appear to
have made no payment into the exchequer at all. Most notable of
the latter six was Henry Beaufort, Bishop of Lincoln, who
as Bishop of Winchester was to be the great moneylender of
the next two reigns. The remaining seven bishops paid in £1,350
to the exchequer by the end of July. Of this sum nearly £800
was contributed by the aged Bishop of Winchester, William of
Wykeham. In all it made a very poor apology for the promised
tenth. Archbishop Richard Scrope's little offering of 100

---

[1] *Traïson et Mort*, pp. 94–6, 248–50; *Annales R. II et H. IV.*, pp. 330–1; *Usk*,
pp. 42, 198–9; *Eulogium*, vol. iii, p. 387
[2] *Usk*, pp. 45–6, 206–7; *Annales R. II et H. IV*, p. 332

marks (£66 13s. 4d.) was stated to be a gift, and out of Wykeham's £800 only £149 is recorded as having been repaid, but all the rest were ultimately treated as loans and repaid by assignments on the clerical tenth granted in the next year.[1]

The poor showing of the bishops was reflected by the religious houses. In accordance with the great council's decision, four of the King's serjeants-at-arms were duly sent out to all the counties of England except the four northern ones, carrying letters under the privy seal asking the various abbots and priors to grant the King a tenth 'by way of a gift, or in any other way by their agreement and free will.'[2] Simon Blackburn, one of the serjeants, reached Huntingdon on 1 April, and then proceeded by way of Ely, through Norfolk, Suffolk, Essex and Kent, reaching Dover on 3 May and going on into Sussex to Robertsbridge, Battle and Hastings. A few of the replies to the letters which he bore are preserved; the Prior of Huntingdon and many others begged to be excused, and so apparently they were. The Prior of Dunmow, on the other hand, promised to send a tenth as soon as possible.[3] But he was one of a minority.

In April the Prior of Bath and the Abbot of Titchfield subscribed £24 between them; May brought in £649 and June £297. Meanwhile the bishops had paid in £780, making a grand total by the end of June of £1,750.[4] Already it was clear that the appeal had failed. Only forty-two monasteries, perhaps one in four of the moderately prosperous houses, had made any payment; and many of the richer ones had given nothing. But already a new expedient had been tried. On 23 June the serjeants-at-arms were sent out again, eight this time instead of four, and this time their letters asked for straightforward loans, not only from the abbots and priors but also from the bishops and certain secular persons.[5] A figure of £100 each was suggested, but this was not taken very seriously; the loans that were made ranged mostly from £10 to 100 marks.

Money continued to come in slowly from the religious houses,

---

[1] P.R.O., E 401/617, 619
[2] P.R.O., E 403/567 under 7 April
[3] The file of replies is in P.R.O., E 28/26 and E 135/10/20. The itinerary of Blackburn can be partially reconstructed from these replies
[4] All figures from P.R.O., E 401/617, 619
[5] P.R.O., E 403/567, under date 13 July

out how far they were still responding to the first letters, and how far to the second it is not possible to say. The important question for the King and his exchequer was how much money was coming in. The answer was £916 in July, £325 in August and £279 in September, making a total for the religious houses of £2,490 since April, or added to the bishops' contribution, £3,837 from the church as a whole. Altogether seventy-two monasteries, which was certainly less than half of the more prosperous ones, had responded. Meanwhile between February and September the laity had lent £9,500 to the Crown.[1] Of the monasteries' contribution of £2,490, £2,130 was subsequently repaid, mostly by assignment in November and December 1401, on the second and third halves of the next clerical tenth to be granted. The remaining £360 is not known to have been repaid at all. The net result was that altogether the Crown raised a loan of £3,800, two-thirds of which was repaid by assignment, mostly about eighteen months later. When this is compared with the £15,500, which was the normal yield of a clerical tenth (Canterbury £14,000, York £1,500) at this time, it will be seen that the great council's device for raising money was singularly unsuccessful. The lesson for the King and his council, if they were willing to learn, was clear enough. It was evident that the only adequate method of raising money was by a grant from Parliament or convocation. Whether he liked it or not, Henry could do very little without the support of his Parliament.

Another great council had in the meantime been summoned for 3 May. The collectors of customs in all the ports were also ordered to be present, presumably in order to inform the council how much money could be raised from that source, but the result cannot have been very encouraging, for the exchequer had been issuing assignments on the customs collectors' future takings from the very beginning of the reign. Nonetheless the King was clearly determined to find money for a campaign against the Scots. The exchequer did not pay out any cash during the Easter term, that is the summer term beginning after Easter, and so slowly began to build up a small cash balance.

[1] The chief lenders were John Norbury (£1,842), the City of London (£1,222 6s. 8d.) and Richard Whittington (£733 6s. 8d.). Of the remaining £4,400 over £1,000 was contributed by the staffs of chancery and exchequer; P.R.O., E 401/617, 619

During May the King remained near London. He arrived a
St. Albans Abbey on 26 May, and heard mass there the nex
morning, Ascension Day. On 1 June he was back at Westminster
but soon afterwards he set out for the north. Proclamations wer
issued ordering all who were receiving the King's fees or wage
to be at York on Midsummer Day 'furnished and arrayed fo
war'. Henry reached Leicester about 6 June, Clipstone in No
tinghamshire on the 14th, Pontefract on the 21st, and York a
the end of the month, but there he was delayed, no doubt waitin
for his reluctant and dilatory followers to come in, and it wa
more than a month before he reached Newcastle-upon-Tyne
From York the King wrote to his council asking them to sen
letters to all the east coast ports asking for as much wine, flou
wheat, oats and other victuals as possible to be sent to Tyne
mouth for the use of the army.[1] Also whilst the court was a
York it was diverted by jousting between a party of Englis
knights led by Sir John Cornewaille, usually known by th
nickname of 'Green Cornewaille', because he was born at sea,
and some Burgundian knights. Cornewaille's prowess won hin
the heart and hand of the King's sister, Elizabeth. Now aged
thirty-one Elizabeth had been first married to the boy Earl o
Pembroke, then hastily divorced and remarried to John Holland
Richard II's half-brother, who shortly afterwards became Ear
of Huntingdon, and later Duke of Exeter. In 1397 as 'my lady
of Exeter' she won a prize as the best dancer and the best singe
at Richard's court.[3] She was now a widow, her husband having
been beheaded in January for his part in the rebellion against he
brother. On her marriage with Sir John Cornewaille Henry
granted them 1,000 marks yearly for life, and this was only the
first of a series of grants. They both lived on to enjoy them int
the reign of his grandson, Henry VI, surviving their only sor
who was killed at Meaux in 1421.

[1] Nicolas, *P.C.*, vol. i, p. 122; R. *Letters, H. IV*, vol. i., pp. 40–4
[2] Chaucer and others used 'green' to describe the sea, perhaps suggesting
light seen through the waves, and so the rough sea.
[3] *Traïson et Mort*, pp. 11, 140

Chapter 8

Scotland and Wales, July–December 1400

THE King of Scotland in 1399 was Robert III, the second king of the Stuart family. Formerly known as John, Earl of Carrick he had become king on the death of his father in 1390. A tall and knightly figure in spite of a permanent lameness due to the kick of a horse, he was already over fifty years of age and said to be popular with his people; but he showed neither the inclination nor the ability to be king in more than name. His younger brother, Robert, Earl of Fife, had already become the virtual ruler under their father, and so continued until at least 1398. In that year he was created Duke of Albany, but at the same time his nephew, David, the King's son and heir, became Duke of Rothesay. Not content to remain like his father a mere spectator, and now just reaching his majority, David was anxious to oust his uncle from the dominant position which he had held for some sixteen years. When however he was appointed lieutenant of the kingdom for three years in place of Albany in January 1399, he very quickly displayed his complete lack of statesmanlike qualities.

For the last ten years of Richard II's reign the truce between England and Scotland was repeatedly renewed. A number of tournaments between English and Scottish knights were held in both countries, and relations between the two were generally good, although border disputes were always liable to break out into open warfare. The last renewal of the truce on behalf of Richard was made on 14 May 1399, extending it for one year from Michaelmas 1399 to Michaelmas 1400.[1] Even before he became king Henry wrote as Duke of Lancaster to King Robert suggesting a ratification of this truce,[2] and Robert promised to put the matter before his Parliament. Early in October 1399, however, the Percies and Westmorland, guardians of the English border, being in London for the Parliament, the Scots invaded North-

---

[1] *Cal. Docs. Scot.* (1357–1500), p. 110
[2] *R. Letters, H. IV*, vol. i, pp. 8–10

umberland, captured Wark Castle, carried off goods to the value
of 2,000 marks belonging to its keeper, Sir Thomas Grey, put
his children and people to ransom for £1,000, burnt his house
and beat down the castle walls, besides inflicting other damage
near the border. News of this raid reached the King and Parliament at Westminster before the end of the session. The Earl
of Northumberland said that he and Westmorland had been
asked to advise the King on the action he should take, but they
had excused themselves, begging the King to make known his
own wishes. Perhaps they were reluctant to invite him to come
in person into the marches which they regarded as their own
private territory. If so they were disappointed, for he came into
Parliament and said 'with his own voice' that God having sent
him into the kingdom and given him his estate for its salvation,
he proposed to go against the Scots in his own person.

Despite this he wrote a conciliatory reply to a second letter
from Robert III proposing that commissioners should meet at
Kelso on 5 January 1400 to negotiate for peace, and on 10
December appointed Sir Thomas Grey, Master Alan Newark
and Janico d'Artasso, a Gascon squire, as his commissioners.[1]
The letter reached Scotland too late to allow Scottish commissioners to be appointed for that date, and Robert or his advisers
put off replying until 14 March, when, apparently playing for
time, he suggested that it would be better to hold the meeting at
the usual place for such parleys, Haudenstank on the Tweed
between Kelso and Coldstream.

The constant threat of warfare between the two countries
had led on the English side to the appointment of regular wardens
of the marches, whose duties usually included both military
defence and diplomatic negotiation. Prior to the reign of Richard
II the wardens were usually small groups of three or four magnates, barons, knights and at times bishops; whilst the castles of
Carlisle and Berwick, the two ends of the Scottish border, were
entrusted to separate keepers, usually knights, and sometimes
the sheriffs of Cumberland and Northumberland. Under Richard
II the arrangements became more regular. Henceforth there were
normally two wardens, one for the west march, and one for the
east, the former being also the keeper of Carlisle Castle, and the
latter of Berwick. A third and junior partner was often entrusted

[1] *Rot. Scot.*, vol. ii, pp. 152–3; R. *Letters, H. IV*, vol. i, pp. 11–13

with the keeping of Roxburgh Castle in the middle of the marches. The wardens generally served for a term of years making an indenture with the King, by which they undertook to provide for the defence of their section of the border, in return for the payment of an annual sum from the exchequer, the number of men-at-arms and archers being sometimes, but not always, specified. This payment was usually doubled in time of war. The emergence of this regular system coincided with the rise of the house of Percy, in whose favour it might appear to have been created. During the years 1384–99 the Earl of Northumberland and his son, Henry Percy, between them held the wardenship of the east march for eleven years and that of the west march for six years.[1] From 1391 to 1395 they held one wardenship each. Richard may well have realised the danger of giving them a semi-permanent command over the whole of the border, which when added to their own lands and castles amounted almost to an independent domain. Certainly his appointment of the Duke of Aumerle to the command of the west march in 1398, when the younger Percy was holding the east, is said to have been the cause of the Percies' dissatisfaction with him, and of their support for Henry in his successful invasion. Not surprisingly, therefore, one of the first acts of Henry, even before he met Richard, was, as has been said, to appoint on 2 August 1399 the Earl of Northumberland to succeed Aumerle in the west march, thus giving father and son control of the whole border once more. This appointment has been described as 'Northumberland's first prize for his desertion of Richard.'[2] It was confirmed by Henry as King on 23 October, two days after he had reappointed Henry Hotspur to the keepership of the east march with both the castles of Berwick-on-Tweed and Roxburgh.[3] The whole of the marches with their castles then remained in the hands of father and son until the son's rebellion nearly four years later.

In the interim the Duke of Rothesay, acting as lieutenant for his father, King Robert, had given Henry a new ally. He had

---

[1] R. L. Storey, 'Wardens of the Marches of England towards Scotland', *E.H.R.*, vol. lxxii, pp. 593–615. For the earlier period: J. L. Kirby, 'The keeping of Carlisle Castle before 1381', *Trans. of Cumberland and Westmorland Antiq. and Arch. Soc.*, vol. liv, pp. 131–9

[2] R. L. Storey, *E.H.R.*, vol. lxxii, p. 603

[3] *Rot. Scot.*, vol. ii, p. 151

been betrothed to Elizabeth, the daughter of George Dunbar Earl of the March of Scotland, but now rejected her in order to marry the daughter of the Earl of Douglas. Affronted by this the Earl of March threw off his allegiance to the Scottish King and on 18 February 1400 wrote to Henry offering his services. His letter was in English and concluded: 'noble Prince, mervaile yhe nocht that I write my lettres in Englishe, fore that ys mare clere to myne understandyng than Latyne or Fraunche.'[1] Henry, too, in spite of his travels, was more at home in English than in courtly French or scholarly Latin. In March he ordered the Earl to be given a safe-conduct to come to England with one hundred persons and to return. A further safe-conduct for the Earl with a retinue of fifty until Michaelmas was issued at Ponte-fract on 21 June, and on 2 August this was extended to include his whole family and a following of eighty persons until Martinmas (11 November). He very soon entered Henry's service, receiving a number of gifts and grants for himself and his family, including the manor of Clipstone, and the castle of Somerton in Lincoln-shire. He not only gave loyal and valuable service to the English King for eight years, but also, if the chroniclers are to be believed, military advice which directly contributed to the victories of both Homildon Hill and Shrewsbury. At the same time Henry was also in correspondence with the Lord of the Isles and his family, who were never very firm supporters of the Scottish kings. He was not therefore without allies when he reached York in June, but he was short of both money and supplies. His army seems to have numbered about 13,000 of whom more than 11,000 were archers,[2] 500 of them being from Cheshire, some of the famous Cheshire archers, who had served Richard as his own bodyguard.

The council in London was busy securing ships and victuals to be sent to meet the King at Newcastle-upon-Tyne. Records of the submissions of the Kings of Scots to Edward III and Richard II were also brought out of the chancery and sent north for the King's information and use. Several commissioners travelled between Henry and the Scots in attempts to negotiate a settlement, but neither side was sincerely anxious for peace as yet, and Henry's preparations went on.

[1] R. *Letters, H. IV*, vol. i, p. 24
[2] P.R.O., E 101/43/3. Account of John Curson, paymaster

From 25 July to 6 August he was at Newcastle-upon-Tyne, where John Curson, his treasurer of wars for this expedition, received about £6,500 to pay the troops. Before advancing from Newcastle the King issued proclamations requiring both the King of Scotland and his barons to do homage at Edinburgh on 23 August. He then rode northwards through Northumberland and crossed the border on the 14th. On the 18th he reached Leith without encountering any serious opposition. The Scots withdrew before him, not offering to do battle, nor did any come to do homage, and Edinburgh did not fall to the invader. It was defended by the Duke of Rothesay himself and was doubtless too strong for Henry to attack with his limited resources of men and money. There were some desertions and food was running short. He refused Rothesay's offer to settle matters by combat with a select band of 100, 200 or 300 knights on either side, in order to avoid the shedding of Christian blood. Such offers were a favourite medieval device, usually made by the weaker side, and more useful for postponing than for achieving a settlement. Instead Henry held a colloquy with the Scottish representatives at the Cross between Edinburgh and Leith. There the Scots promised to discuss his claim to the overlordship of Scotland, but did not recognise it.

This was evidently the most that he could achieve, and he immediately began to withdraw. Before the end of August King and army had recrossed the border, having achieved nothing at all at considerable cost. Henry was never again to invade Scotland, and indeed this was destined to be the last time that an English king crossed the border at the head of an army. Some skirmishes were fought, and the never-ending negotiations for a truce went on, but already Henry was hurrying away, leaving the border to be defended by the Earl of Northumberland and his son. On 29 September Sir Robert Umfraville defeated a body of Scots in Redesdale. A number of prisoners, including Sir Richard Rutherford and John Turnbull, were taken and sent to London. On 9 November a truce was concluded for six weeks, and on 4 December Sir Gerard Heron, Sir William Fulthorp and John Mitford esquire, were appointed to treat for its prolongation or for a permanent peace.[1]

The King's invasion of Scotland had imposed two tasks on

[1] *Rot. Scot.*, vol. ii, 154-5

his council: in addition to supplying his army with food and money, his councillors had to conduct the routine administration of the kingdom. The forfeiture of the earls after the January rebellion left a crop of problems behind. Joan, Countess of Kent, for example, protested that her share of the manor of Chesterfield in Derbyshire, together with her lands in Lincolnshire and Rutland, had been seized with her husband's lands. Commissions were appointed in June to look into her rights and wrongs.[1] The imprisonment and release of wrongdoers, and the illicit seizure of merchant ships also called for the council's attention. Another small matter, about which the King wrote to the council from Clipstone on 14 June, was the circulation of Venetian halfpennies.[2] Certain merchants of Venice, who had arrived in their galleys in the port of London, were making payments with these coins which were worth only a quarter or a third of their English equivalents. The council ordered that their use should cease and that any which were found should be forfeit to the King. In the following years a number were in fact confiscated both in London, and in Sandwich, another port frequented by the Venetians, and their value paid into the exchequer. Meanwhile another Venetian galley was sheltering in Plymouth, unable to proceed to London for fear of enemy vessels in the Channel. The council was instructed to decide whether it was necessary to fit out a squadron to clear the Channel and enable merchant-men to go about their business.

Most members of the council appear to have gone north and to have been with the King at Newcastle-upon-Tyne in July or August, but by the end of the latter month during which the King had been in and out of Scotland they were meeting again in London. The citizens of Cork in Ireland were asking for a renewal or confirmation of their charters. On 31 August Sir Thomas Erpyngham, the King's chamberlain, arrived with instructions for the council to consider this amongst other matters. The council evidently could not or would not act without consulting Archbishop Arundel. He was at his manor of Otford in Kent, and thither the council sent John Doreward to get the Archbishop's views. Doreward was back in London on 2 September,[3] and an

[1] *Cal. Pat.* (1399–1401), p. 346
[2] Nicolas, *P.C.*, vol. 1, pp. 120–1; *Cal. Close.* (1399–1402), p. 195
[3] P.R.O., E 28/7

inspeximus and confirmation of the charters of Cork was issued, dated Westminster 13 September. Superficially it seems a very small routine matter to require so much consultation, but later in the year the City of Cork was pardoned over £400 in arrears due to the exchequer, and released from paying the farm of the city in the future, because of the great losses sustained at the hands of both English and Irish rebels. All this, which was granted 'on the advice of the council' was no doubt discussed on 31 August.[1]

The exchequer term officially ended on 13 July, but the department was kept busy right through to October, when the next term began. The main business was collecting large loans to pay for the Scottish expedition, which cost nearly £7,000 in soldiers' wages alone, apart from the cost of provisions, and of shipping them to the north. For the first year of the reign the largest item of revenue was the £39,000 which came from the customs and subsidies in the ports, though most of this was assigned to creditors in advance and not collected in cash. The feudal revenues of the Crown, including sums arising from the forfeitures of the rebels brought in about £15,000. This sum was the King's 'own' on which Parliament was always hoping that he might live. Loans and the dowry of Queen Isabel brought the exchequer another £15,000 each. There was no other large item, but a number of smaller ones amounted to something like £10,000 between them. On the expenditure side the biggest sum, about £38,000, was taken by the King's household, including all its dependent departments, and the maintenance of the palaces and buildings. The defence of Calais cost £18,000 and of the Scottish marches, apart from £7,000 spent on the King's expedition, another £12,000. These were the largest items, but there were many other essential expenses, such as annuities paid by the Crown, the salaries of judges and of the staffs of chancery and exchequer, the household of Queen Isabel, and the sending of ambassadors. The payment of those who had accompanied the King on his march through England in the previous summer before he ascended the throne cost £3,500. If the exchequer had weathered the first year of the reign it was only because one third of the revenue had come from loans, from the dowry of Queen Isabel, and from the forfeitures of

[1] *Cal. Pat.* (1399–1401), pp. 330, 400

rebels. In September Norbury as treasurer summoned all the collectors of customs in the ports to come to the exchequer in mid-October with all their records in the hope that money could be found for the wars in Scotland and Wales and for the Emperor of Constantinople, who was appealing for funds.[1]

Very soon after he had begun his journey south from Scotland Henry heard of the trouble in Wales. The Welsh rebellion, which was to prove one of the most difficult of all his problems, was largely provoked by the actions of one of his most loyal supporters, Reynold, Lord Grey of Ruthyn. The lordship of Ruthyn, which his family had held for several generations, lay in the valley of the Clwyd between Denbigh and Flint. It appears that there was already some disorder in North Wales early in 1400, probably as a result of Henry's march to Chester, and pillaging by his army. Lord Grey had been asked both by the King and the Prince of Wales, who was the nominal commander in that area, to help to restore order. In replying and reporting on the difficulties he told the story of his dispute with one Griffith ap David ap Griffith. This man, disappointed at not receiving the office of bailiff of Chirkland and suspecting that there was a plot to kidnap him, had encamped for a time on the lands of Ruthyn, and his men had stolen two of Lord Grey's horses. He wrote to Lord Grey rebutting the charge whereupon Grey sent him a most violent letter ending 'a roope, a ladder, and a ring, heigh on gallowes for to henge, And thus shalle be your endyng . . . and we on our behalfe shalle be welle willyng.' Sending on the correspondence to the Prince he denounced Griffith as the 'strengest theife in Wales'. Such violence of language was not well calculated to restore peace to the troubled countryside.[2]

However, the real trouble arose out of Grey's quarrel with Owen Glendower, a Welsh landowner, who had studied law at Westminster, and may have served under Henry himself. His lands bordered on those of Grey, and the dispute began over the

---

[1] *Anglo-Norman Letters*, pp. 418–19. This is the most likely date for this letter.

[2] See J. E. Lloyd in *Archaeologia Cambrensis*, 7th ser., vol. iii (1923), pp. 204–5; R. I. Jack, 'Owain Glyn Dwr and the lordship of Ruthin', *Welsh History Review*, vol. ii, pp. 303–22. The correspondence is printed in H. Ellis, *Orig. Letters*, 2nd ser., vol. i, pp. 1–9; R. *Letters, H. IV*, vol. i, pp. 35–8

ownership of part of their estates. Owen had apparently petitioned the Parliament of 1399, but probably owing to Grey's influence with the King, nothing had come of the petition. Neither Owen nor Grey was a patient man. One story is that Glendower's summons to join Henry on the Scottish expedition was entrusted to Grey, who held it back by accident or design until it was too late for Glendower to go, and then accused him of treasonable failure to obey the summons. The story may well have been exaggerated or invented, and it cannot now be discovered what really happened, but in some way Grey certainly provoked Glendower into taking actions, which could hardly fail to make him a rebel.[1]

On 16 September 1400 Owen had collected all his relations, retainers and friends. Two days later some 300 of them attacked the town of Ruthyn, set fire to houses and carried off money, utensils and linen. Lord Grey was away, perhaps with the King. Glendower and his friends went on to attack the English at Denbigh, Rhuddlan, Flint, Hawarden and Holt. On the 22nd they ravaged Oswestry and on the next day Welshpool, but the rising was short-lived. On the 24th they were defeated on the banks of the Severn by a hastily raised force under Hugh Burnell. On the 28th ten who had been captured in the raid were executed in Ruthyn Castle. The names of 270 rebels including seven women were eventually recorded in the Ruthyn court rolls.[2] Henry had been at Newcastle-upon-Tyne on the 3rd, and thence marched quickly southwards through Durham, Northallerton, Pontefract, Doncaster and Leicester. On the 19th he was at Northampton and there learned of the rising of Glendower. He immediately turned towards the west and advanced by way of Coventry and Lichfield into Shropshire, summoning the men of ten counties to join his banner as he advanced. Apart from Glendower's own uprising disorders occurred in other parts of Wales, but the King found no enemy to fight. After their defeat Glendower's party withdrew into the hills and woods, only emerging when there was a chance of easy plunder. The King marched by Chester to North Wales, along the coast, and even penetrated into Montgomeryshire without meeting any opposition. The routine of the Welsh war was thus established. In three weeks

[1] see J. E. Lloyd, *Glendower*, pp. 28–34
[2] R. I. Jack, in *Welsh History Review*, vol. ii, pp. 310–11

Henry was back at Shrewsbury, and on 19 October at Evesham on his way back to London. He had thus ridden almost unopposed into Wales as he had done into Scotland. All was apparently quiet again, and he might claim the victory, but in fact in Wales he had accomplished nothing. The summer had not been unsuccessful, but Henry had used up a great deal of money, and he had nothing to show. To establish his prestige as king he needed a spectacular victory, and this he had signally failed to achieve.

In October 1400 Henry had been away from his capital for nearly five months. Towards the end of the month he wrote from Windsor to Archbishop Arundel. He had seen the ambassadors from the Emperor of Constantinople, and a final reply would be given to them by the council. Those from France, who had come to see Queen Isabel, and arrange for her repatriation, he was expecting to see on the next day.[1] Shortly afterwards a letter from John Norbury to Sir Thomas Erpyngham reported that Isabel would shortly be returning to France, once the question of her dowry was settled, and also gave news of the King's movements.[2] He had been at Westminster for a week, and was leaving the next day for Hertford Castle, where he would stay with his children for a while before going to Eltham for Christmas.

By this time the King and council had decided to summon another Parliament. They first called one to meet at Westminster in October, changed it to York in November, and finally put it off to 21 January 1401, to be once more at Westminster. The council meanwhile was meeting regularly. In October the Earl of Worcester, the officers of state, and a number of knights and squires like John Doreward, Thomas Coggeshale and John Cheyne were present. John Doreward was paid for his services as councillor on 5 November, as were Richard Whittington, John Shadworth and William Brampton, three leading Londoners, who, however, are not known to have made many appearances. Before Christmas the council was strengthened by the presence of the Earls of Somerset and Westmorland and the Bishop of Durham. At the same time the return of the royal household to the vicinity of London enabled Sir Thomas Rempston, its steward, and Sir Thomas Erpyngham, the King's chamberlain,

---

[1] *Anglo-Norman Letters*, pp. 465–6. The date assigned by the editor (18 October) is too early as the King was then at Evesham.
[2] ibid. pp. 404–5

to attend. A number of persons were taken into custody, brought before the council and committed to the Tower, probably suspected of complicity either in the rebellion of the earls or in that of Glendower. We are told that the year had been equable and fruitful. The King and his Government could not claim to have achieved very much. No strong hand had emerged, but at least they were still there; for a new dynasty with a weak claim time passed was time gained.

For Christmas Henry had a strange and remarkable guest. After the battle of Nicopolis in 1396 the Turks were pressing nearer to Constantinople. The Emperor Manuel II appealed in desperation to the West for help. Then in 1400 he determined to come in person to seek it. He sailed to Venice and made his way thence to Paris. Deciding to visit London also he wrote for advice to Peter Holt, the Prior of St. John of Jerusalem in Ireland, who replied on 11 July, suggesting that he should postpone his visit as King Henry was then in the north on his way to attack the Scots.[1] So the imperial ambassadors came first, but early in December the Emperor himself was at Calais. The council summoned a number of lords and knights to London in order that they might meet the Emperor and act as his escort. He crossed to Dover and spent a few days at Christ Church, Canterbury.

The King himself met the Emperor Manuel at Blackheath, and on 21 December they entered London together. The King then took his guest to Eltham to spend Christmas with him. The Emperor and his followers stayed two months, being entertained at the King's expense with jousts and sports. Eventually Manuel was given £2,000 from the exchequer on 3 February 1401 towards the relief of Constantinople, and returned to Paris where he stayed for another year before going back to Constantinople, which was saved for another fifty years by the defeat of Sultan Bajazet by Timur at Ankara in July 1402. The Emperor's visit had gained him very little in money and nothing in men, but for Henry at least it provided a brief, if expensive, interlude from the problems of the Scottish march, the unruly Welsh, and the ever-present danger of an attack from the French. For his court it must have provided a strange glimpse of the men and manners of the East.

[1] R. *Letters, H. IV*, pp. 39–40

Chapter 9

The second Parliament and the return of Queen Isabel, January–July 1401

AT THE beginning of the year 1401, John Prophet, who had been secondary of the privy seal and clerk of the council in Richard's reign, and a member of the council since the beginning of the new reign, secured the confirmation of all the charters of Hereford Cathedral. He had been Dean of Hereford since 1393, one of the many dignitaries who were prevented from serving their churches by their employment in the royal service; but this grant shows that he was not altogether forgetful of his deanery, and that an absentee dean might on occasion be a useful friend at court. The council was indeed active very early in the year, the Archbishop, four bishops and two earls being present with the usual officers on 12 January. They were concerned with the building of ships, and the collection of money for the Emperor Manuel, but no doubt the main business which had called them together so soon from their Christmas holidays was the preparation for the second Parliament of the reign. Already the members were on their way to Westminster.

The knights and burgesses duly appeared before the chancellor and the steward of the King's household in Westminster Hall on 20 January and answered their names. Eleven of the shire representatives had sat in the previous Parliament, and eleven more in the last Parliament of Richard II, but nearly thirty are not known to have sat before at all. They were told to appear on the next morning in the painted chamber at ten o'clock. When they did assemble there, it was Sir William Thirning, Chief Justice of the Common Bench, not the chancellor or the Archbishop, who greeted them in the King's name, and explained the reason for their summons. This was of course mainly the King's need for money, but it was well wrapped up rather than baldly stated. It was the King's will, Thirning said, that the church should be maintained as it had been in the past, that all the lords, the cities and the boroughs, should enjoy their liberties, and that the law

hould be observed. These promises were the common opening
or every Parliament, but were not perhaps therefore altogether
vithout meaning. Thirning went on to talk about the great
xpenses of the King, in his coming into the realm, his coronation,
iis suppression of the revolt, his marches into Scotland and into
Wales; and also about the need of money for restoring Queen
sabel to France, for the defence of Calais, of Guyenne, and of the
vars of Scotland and Ireland. Finally the chief justice said that in
he past members had often been concerned more with their own
private business than with the welfare of the realm, and he
commanded them in the King's name to attend each day during
he Parliament. This was Thirning's last appearance on the
political scene. He had played a prominent part in the accession
of Henry to the throne, but from 1401 he seems to have confined himself to the duties of his office, which he retained throughout the reign.

The next day the Commons presented as their Speaker Sir
Arnold Savage,[1] knight of the shire for Kent. Savage, who had
peen a chamber knight of Richard II, had sat in three Parliaments
n 1390 and 1391, but he did not again appear in Parliament until
the session of 1401, and may have been out of favour in Richard's
later years. Although comparatively inexperienced in Parliament
he justified his election to the speakership in this Parliament and
that of 1404 by an eloquence, or long-windedness, which both
added to the stature of the office, and tried the patience of the
King. He began his first speakership with the usual protestation
and then having summarised the points made by the chief justice
in his speech, requested that important matters should not be
put before the Commons at the end of the session when they had
not time to consider their answers properly. The Earl of Worcester, who was about to become steward of the King's household,
assured them that the King had no such intentions. Three days
later Savage secured an assurance from the King that he would not
listen to individual members who might report on the proceedings
of the Commons before they had reached a decision. He would
only take notice of their final resolutions. The Commons then
declared that the three necessities of good government were sense,
humanity and richness. They would not dwell on the King's

[1] For Savage see: J. S. Roskell, 'Sir Arnald Savage of Bobbing', *Archaeologia
Cantiana*, vol. lxx, pp. 68–83; and Roskell, *Speakers*, p. 362 and *passim*

virtues, lest they be accounted flatterers, although this was not a danger into which the Commons seemed very likely to fall during this reign. On 31 January, tired perhaps of listening to Savage, the King asked that all future requests should be put into writing, but this did not stop the flow of either demands or eloquence.

On 26 February the Speaker asked that the business of Parliament should be written up by the clerk of the Parliament before the justices left, and the King agreed. No doubt the Commons were aware that the record of Richard's Parliaments had latterly been compiled to suit the King. They complained that the moderation of the Statute of Provisors agreed in Henry's first Parliament had not been correctly recorded, a charge which was rejected by the Lords and by the King. Were they also perhaps aware or suspecting that the roll of that Parliament might not tell the whole truth in other respects? So far the King had conceded most of the demands of the Commons as expressed by their loquacious Speaker, but when finally they asked that they should have an answer to their petitions before they made a grant of a fifteenth and tenth, the King delayed his reply, saying that he would consult the Lords. This demand, that redress should precede supply, was to echo down the centuries. At the end of the session Henry rejected it. Neither he nor Savage can have been aware of the magnitude of the constitutional issue which lay between them. Finally the Speaker who had already likened the King, Lords and Commons to the Trinity, concluded with a comparison between the session of Parliament and the mass. Arnold Savage seems to have been a worthy, wordy, fussy man, very concerned by the divergences between King and Commons, and soon as a councillor to be perplexed by the conflict between the points of view of the Government and the governed.

On the last Saturday of the Parliament, 5 March, the council appears to have submitted proposals to the King which look like a compromise between the demands of the Commons for the reform of the Government and the desire of the King to retain as much as possible of his freedom of action. The Commons apparently asked (though nothing of this appears on the Parliament Roll) that the King should name his great officers and his councillors, define their duties, and tell the Commons who they were before the end of the Parliament. Moreover once named

hey should not be changed until the next Parliament. The
council advised that all the councillors should take the same oath,
nd not as in the past different ones according to their ranks,
outside Parliament, but in the presence of the King and two or
hree members of the Commons; but it should be made clear
hat this was done out of reverence for the King, and not at the
equest of the Commons. Whether the councillors did so swear
we do not know, but certainly the three new household officers
ook their oaths of office in the presence of the King and two
or three members of the Commons. For drastic changes were in
act made in the administration, presumably to please the Commons.

On 1 March Thomas Percy, Earl of Worcester, brother to the
Earl of Northumberland, became steward of the household in
place of Sir Thomas Rempston. The Earl had held the same position in Richard's household, but was now only to hold it
for a year. On 9 March Thomas More became treasurer of the
household in place of Thomas Tutbury. Sir Thomas Brounflete
became controller. To change all three officers at the same time
was most unusual, but on the same day there was an even more
important change. Edmund Stafford, Bishop of Exeter since
1395, became chancellor in place of the comparatively humble
clerk, John Scarle. Stafford had been the last chancellor of Richard
II, so that his appointment might be interpreted as an attempt to
bridge the gap, restore normality to the administration, and re-
duce perhaps the personal influence of the King. But this was
not the end of the changes. In apparent defiance of the Commons'
suggestion that new appointments should not be made between
Parliaments Richard, Lord Grey of Codnor and Sir Thomas
Rempston were appointed admirals in April in place of the
Earl of Worcester, in Rempston's case an exchange of offices.
Finally on 31 May John Norbury was replaced as treasurer
by Lawrence Allerthorpe, who had been a baron of the exchequer for more than twenty-five years. This last appointment
could have been part of the changes arranged in Parliament,
but it might equally well appear as a gesture of independence by the
King. Its meaning is now lost.[1]

The Parliament had lasted for seven weeks, until 10 March.

[1] A. L. Brown, 'The Commons and the Council in the reign of Henry IV',
E.H.R., vol. lxxix (1964), pp. 3, 5, 29; Chrimes and Brown, pp. 205–6

The King had been obliged to listen patiently to a great deal of talk, not to say lecturing, from Savage, to change some of his Ministers, and to name his councillors, though this was not done as in later years, in full Parliament, and the names were not put on record. But he had yielded only on minor points, retained the right to change his officers at will, and he had got his money. The Commons granted one fifteenth and tenth to be levied, half at Trinity (29 May) and half at All Saints (2 November) following, and the grant of tunnage and poundage was confirmed for a further two years from Easter 1401. The five lords who had taken part in the rebellion of the previous year were declared traitors, and the forfeiture of their lands was confirmed. The Earls of Rutland and Somerset on the other hand were declared loyal, and the aged Bishop of Norwich, Henry Despenser, was formally reconciled with that staunch supporter of the King, Sir Thomas Erpyngham, but it is doubtful whether he ever really accepted Henry as King.

The King had no doubt hoped that his incursion into Wales had ended his troubles there, but the Commons were not convinced that this was the case, pointing out that Welsh scholars had withdrawn from Oxford and Cambridge, and with Welsh labourers from many parts of England, had returned home, which suggested that forces were being collected. The King promised that his council, and that of his son, the Prince, would examine the ordinances and statutes for Wales, to see what amendment was required in order to restore and preserve the peace there. The Commons also asked the King, among many other matters, to use his influence towards healing the schism in the church, and to decide with his council the fate of the remaining non-conventual alien priories. All these things had their own importance, but the most memorable chapter of the statute passed in this Parliament was that *De heretico comburendo*.

An order was issued dated 26 February, whilst the Parliament was in session, 'by the King and council in Parliament' for the burning of William Sawtre as a relapsed heretic. The statute which prescribed burning for relapsed heretics when handed over by the church to the sheriff, may not have introduced any new punishment into English law, but it was reviving one which had not been used for a long time. The King and the Parliament who made the statute, and Archbishop Arundel who headed

he church which demanded it, could not have foreseen the
horrors of the next century, but at least they had prepared the way
or them.

William Sawtre was a priest from Norfolk, who had been ex-
amined by the Bishop of Norwich in 1399, found to be in
error, and renounced his doctrines. He had then removed to
London where he resumed his heretical teaching and preaching.
The convocation of the province of Canterbury met in St. Paul's
on 29 January 1401, when eleven out of the seventeen bishops
were present with the Archbishop. The Earl of Northumberland,
Sir Thomas Erpyngham the King's chamberlain, and John
Norbury the treasurer, represented the King at the first meeting.
On 12 February Sawtre was brought before the Archbishop,
and on the 23rd he was publicly condemned in St. Paul's by the
Archbishop sitting with six other bishops. On 2 March he was
burnt to ashes before a large crowd at Smithfield 'chained standing
to a post in a barrel, packed round with blazing faggots.'[1] The
convocation, unaware of the flames they had started, meanwhile
granted the King a clerical tenth to correspond with the fifteenth
granted by the laity in Parliament.

The fact that Henry was to have ten treasurers in little more
than thirteen years is in itself a sufficient indication of the difficulties of that office. Norbury who held it for twenty months, was
destined to prove the third longest holder of the treasurership up
to 1413. His replacement in May 1401 did not signalise any breach
in his friendship with the King. Indeed on ceasing to be treasurer
he was probably able to spend more time with Henry, and certainly remained his closest friend. For the time being he retained
his office as keeper of the privy wardrobe in the Tower, which
was effectively the King's armoury, and he remained a councillor. Moreover at Easter the King visited Leeds Castle in Kent,
which he had given to Norbury for life, as his guest, and stayed
at least sixteen days.

The dissolution of Parliament and convocation left the King
and his councillors with a great deal of business to transact.
The exchequer term had ended officially on 25 February, but
work went on there until 26 March, the day before Palm Sunday.
The treasurer had needed to raise some £5,000 in loans to get
him through the term from Michaelmas, himself lending £158

[1] *Usk*, pp. 58, 222

on the last day. Some of his officials also made small loans, bu
the biggest lenders had been Richard Whittington, and Henry
old servant Sir Hugh Waterton, both of whom advanced 1,0c
marks. On 8 March the council heard a petition from the burgessc
of Pembroke and on the 11th one from the Percies asking fc
payment of some of the money which was owing to them fc
the keeping of the Scottish march and the conduct of the wa
in Wales. Henry Percy the younger had been appointed justic
of North Wales and of Chester on 29 October 1399, and afte
the King's expedition in the autumn of 1400, it fell to him t
conduct such operations as he could against Glendower. He wa
himself present in the council on 13 March, but must have hurrie
back to Wales, for he was writing to the council from Denbig
on 10 April.

Also in the council on that day were the Bishops of Durhan
and Hereford, the Earls of Northumberland and Worcester, th
treasurer, the keeper of the privy seal, John Scarle, who ha
just ceased to be chancellor but may have been standing in for hi
absent successor, the Lords Lovell and Say, Sir Hugh Waterton
Sir William Sturmy and John Curson. Amongst others wh
appeared in council during the month, apart from the chancello
were the Bishop of Bangor, the Earls of Westmorland an
Rutland, the Lords Berkeley, Abergavenny and Powys, Si
Thomas Erpyngham, Sir Thomas Rempston, John Doreward
the Speaker of the first Parliament, Sir John Cheyne, Joh
Frome and Master John Prophet.

On 17 March the council discussed the dispute which hac
arisen between the abbey and town of Cirencester, but postpone
its hearing of the case until after Easter, when the parties migh
be present. John Doreward and others had earlier in the yea
settled a dispute between Lowestoft and Great Yarmouth o
behalf of the council. It was also decided to send John Curson tc
York, to join the Earl of Northumberland in treating with the
Scots. On the 18th the King was present at a small council a
Coldharbour, the great house in the City of London beside Al
Hallows the Less in the Ropery, which had belonged to the
Black Prince, and was later, in 1410, to be given to the Prince o
Wales. On this occasion only the King, the chancellor, the Earl
of Northumberland and Worcester, Master John Prophet and
the King's secretary were present, to discuss the ordinance

proposed for Wales. But it required a further meeting of the full council, without the King, at Blackfriars on the 22nd before the order to apply the great seal to the ordinances was issued.[1] Meanwhile a general pardon, with certain named exceptions, had been issued for Wales on the last day of the Parliament.

A statute for Wales had been issued but it had not covered all the demands of the Commons, and had perhaps surprised contemporaries by its mildness. The six chapters of the statute limited the rights of Welshmen resident in England, protected Englishmen from Welsh juries, ordered the immediate execution of Welsh felons, and required the marcher barons to garrison and defend their castles.[2] The ordinance laid down that all lords with castles in Wales would forfeit them if they were not safely kept, and similarly that the constables of the Prince of Wales might be replaced if they did not guard his castles properly. Certain offices in North Wales were to be held by Englishmen only. The justices of North Wales were to be charged with keeping the peace and governing the people. Evildoers were to be brought to justice in the lordship where their crimes were committed. The Welsh were to pay murage for the defence of the towns of North Wales, and to contribute towards the garrisons of the castles there for three years or more. Insurrections and meetings were to be suppressed by the lords, and the King's subjects were to be indemnified for any losses caused by such disorders. For three years no Englishman was to be indicted or accused by the Welsh. Welsh bards and vagabonds were to be restricted.

It was at this point that the King went down to Leeds Castle in Kent to spend Easter, but he was not able to enjoy very much respite from official business. Ambassadors were appointed to treat with the Duke of Guelders, and for the marriage of the King's daughter to the son of the King of the Romans. On 5 April Henry summoned the keeper of the privy seal and John Prophet to Leeds, bringing with them copies of all treaties with the Duke of Guelders. But Wales was still the main problem, and plans for a summer expedition there were already afoot.

[1] *Cal. Pat.* (1399–1401), pp. 469–70; Rymer, *Foedera*, vol. viii, p. 184
[2] Lloyd, *Glendower*, p. 36; *Statutes*, 2 Hen. IV, cc. 12, 16–20

On Good Friday a party of Welshmen seized Conway Castle when most of the garrison were in church. It took Henry Percy some months to negotiate the recovery of the castle, which was too strong to be taken by assault. Meanwhile he sent a succession of letters to the council in London. On 10 April he wrote from Denbigh. He had, he said, received the recent ordinances and would do all in his power to further the King's affairs. The Prince was beseiging Conway. At the same time his father, the Earl of Northumberland, had written to the council from the north. William and Rhys ap Tudor who had recently seized Conway Castle were now suing for pardon, which was granted on 20 April. On 4 May he wrote another report from Caernarvon. Things were still going well in Wales, but he reminded the council that his soldiers in Berwick and the east march were suffering great poverty from lack of payment, which he said he had asked for several times. He had in fact been paid over £9,000 for the defence of the east march and Roxburgh Castle since the beginning of the reign, but of this only about £2,000 was in cash, the rest in tallies which he was unable to convert into cash. Some of them were replaced by new tallies during this summer, probably in response to urgent requests. On 17 May he wrote yet again, this time from Denbigh, saying that he could carry on only until the end of the current month, or for three or four days into the next month, if he did not receive some money. On 4 June he sent a further report on the situation saying that he must soon leave Wales, as he could not afford to remain there longer at his own costs, and great perils would arise if he left. Probably he had to wait until July when he got tallies for £1,500 and his father for £2,000.[1] He was now however able to report a victory of John Charlton, Lord of Powys, who had captured some of the servants of Owen Glendower, his armour, and some cloth painted with maidens with red hands, and had just missed catching the rebel leader himself. Some of the cloth was sent to the Prince of Wales, and some to the King.[2]

Meanwhile the King's confessor, Philip Repingdon, was writing Henry a letter, which, if he ever received it, must have provided somewhat unwelcome reading. The letter, which included fifteen quotations from the Scriptures, was long but its

[1] P.R.O., E 401/626
[2] *Anglo-Norman Letters*, pp. 292–3; Nicolas, *P.C.*, vol. i, p. 153

message was bluntly expressed. Repingdon said that the King had asked him to write frankly and this he was doing whatever the danger might be to himself. Law and justice, he said, were now exiles from the realm, robbery, murder, adultery and fornication were rife, violence abounded, and everywhere the poor were oppressed. His hopes at the coming of the King had been disappointed, things were getting worse, and there was a great need for the law to be enforced. He was praying that the King would observe the promises made at his accession, and perform his duty to the people.[1] Repingdon, Abbot of St. Mary's Leicester, was also at this time Chancellor of Oxford University, and three years later he became Bishop of Lincoln, so the letter does not seem to have harmed him, and there is no evidence of its effect, if any, on Henry.

He was for the moment most troubled about Wales and was making his way westwards through Wallingford to Worcester. From there he wrote a long letter to the council on 8 June, reporting on the situation in Wales. Owing to Lord Charlton of Powys's victory this was much improved, and as he was also concerned about the arrangements, now almost complete, for the restoration of Queen Isabel to France, and about troubles in the north and at Calais, he started back to London again. On the 21st he was writing once more from Wallingford. He had hoped to be in Westminster by the following Thursday night, the 23rd, but found that he could only reach Windsor by then. He would spend Friday, the feast of St. John the Baptist, at Windsor, and come to Westminster on Saturday, which was just in time to see Queen Isabel.

Richard II had married the younger daughter of Charles VI of France in 1396, when the truce between the two countries first made at Leulighem in 1389 was renewed until Michaelmas 1426. Isabel was then seven years old. When Henry IV came to the throne relations between the two countries were governed by this truce, which although badly kept, was at least nominally in force for most of the reign. There were few years between 1399 and 1413 in which commissioners of the two kingdoms did not meet at Leulighem to discuss the renewal of the truce and the possibility of converting it into a permanent peace. Although Henry IV had been well received as an exile in Paris, the King

[1] *Bekynton Corres.*, vol. i, p. 151

of France could not easily approve of the deposition of his son-in-law and his daughter, and on the other side the English council thought war more likely than peace. However, both Kings had their own domestic difficulties, and neither was in a position to make war. English commissioners were accordingly appointed to discuss the prolongation of the truce in November 1399. Charles VI confirmed it on 29 January 1400 and Henry IV on 18 May following. Negotiations were then begun for the return of Queen Isabel to her father.

Isabel being still only a child of ten or eleven presented something of a problem to Henry. For one thing he had used the remainder of her dowry to keep his own exchequer solvent. Richard, when he set out on his last expedition to Ireland, had left her at Wallingford. From there she had been taken to Sonning near Reading, where the rebels visited her in January 1400, and afterwards to Havering-atte-Bower in Essex. A plan to marry her to the Prince of Wales was soon abandoned, and Henry then began to discuss sending her back to France. Despite difficulties about the dowry agreement was reached on 27 May 1401 that she should be sent back with all her jewels and other possessions, and preparations for her return were accordingly put in hand. It is possible that a threat to invade Guyenne if negotiations broke down had helped to enforce English concessions.

Isabel's household had cost nearly £3,000 during the first year of the reign, and her restoration to France which was to be made in some state was also a costly business. Towards the end of June, perhaps on the day that the King reached Westminster, a meeting of about twenty temporal peers consulted on the policy to be adopted towards France. They were all in favour of restoring the Queen, as arranged at Leulighem in May, but were somewhat divided on the question of going to war with France, some thinking it better to summon a Parliament before deciding to do so, owing to the obvious need of money for making war.

It was then decided that the Earl of Worcester, as steward of the King's household, should go to Tottenham to meet Isabel, who was already on her way to London, on the following Monday afternoon. The mayor, sheriffs and aldermen of London were to meet her at Stamford Hill, and finally the King's son,

Prince Thomas with the Constable and Marshal of England at Hackney. On the next day, 28 June, she was brought before the King, but the child had been very attached to her husband, and had nothing to say to his successor, who was also, as she had no doubt been told, his murderer. Dressed in mourning she went silently through the streets of London on her way towards Dover. To escort her the council thought it necessary to send the Duchess of Ireland, widow of Richard's favourite Robert de Vere, and the Countess of Hereford, the King's mother-in-law, each with one knight, one lady, three damsels, three squires, two yeomen and a groom. There were also two bishops, Durham and Hereford, two earls, Worcester and Somerset, four lords, the Queen's chamberlain, confessor and secretary, six knights, four ladies, seven damsels and two maids, making a total of fifty-five persons, some of whom would themselves have a large number of attendants. This was estimated to cost about £1,500 for the six weeks which the whole operation was expected to take.

There is also mention of a reward of 1,000 marks for nine damsels, ten clerks, thirty-three squires, sixty-seven yeomen of the chamber, thirty-one yeomen of the stable, thirty-nine boys and thirty pages; making another two hundred persons, even if a few of them had already been included in the list above. It was estimated that she would need ninety-four horses, in addition to those of her escort, who would presumably provide their own. The debts of her household up to the previous 8 November were put at £3,500, and household expenses on the journey were expected to amount to £50 daily, or £1,100 in all. The council was consulted on all these matters and even on the issue of cloth for the clothing of the Queen and her entourage, and on the provision of silver vessels and furnishings for her use on the journey. Someone had to be sent forward to arrange lodgings at Calais, the barons of the Cinque Ports had to be instructed to provide three barges and three balingers for the crossing. Two French lords were to come to Dover to accompany her from there, and see that all the arrangements were satisfactory. Tents had to be sent to Calais, and provision made there not only for the Queen and her escort, but also for any French lords who might come to visit her.

Thomas More, the treasurer of the King's household, was also appointed treasurer of Isabel's household, and furnished not only with sufficient funds to take her to Calais, but also enough to bring the escort home. Finally she herself had to be provided with money so that she could give presents and tips to all who had served her in England. One of the council's biggest problems was the raising of loans to provide all this money, which amounted to about £4,000, apart from £3,500 of household debts.

It is not perhaps altogether surprising to find that it took a month to get all this party in state from London to Calais. It was nearly the end of July before the little Queen reached Calais, and it was on the 31st that she was handed over by the Earl of Worcester to the Count of St. Pol at Leulighem, whence she went back to her parents to start another chapter in her unhappy life. In the following February the English council was anxious to get from her a renunciation of her claims on England, since she had by then reached the legal age of twelve. A few weeks after her return her youngest sister, Catherine, was born, the same Catherine, who nineteen years later was to become Queen of England, by her marriage with Henry V. Isabel was to be married again in 1406 to the Count of Angoulême, two years her junior, who became Duke of Orleans on the murder of his father in 1407. Two years after that she died in childbirth.

Henry had managed to counter suggestions that Isabel's dowry should be repaid with revived demands for the unpaid part of the ransom money of that John, King of France, who had been captured at Poitiers, and had now been dead for nearly forty years. Both France and England remained anxious to avoid a full-scale war, and the truce continued. Agreements to keep it in being were made at Leulighem on 14 August 1402, and again on 27 June 1403.

The beginning of the reign of Charles VI of France was not unlike that of his contemporary Richard II in England. When he succeeded to the throne in 1380 at the age of eleven his kingdom came under the rule of his three uncles, the youngest and most forceful of whom was Philip the Bold, Duke of Burgundy. In 1388 Charles, like Richard, tried to assert his own authority, but four years later he was stricken with insanity, and suffered from intermittent madness for the rest of his life. His younger brother, Louis of Orleans, determined as he grew up to wrest the control of the kingdom from their uncle, Philip of Burgundy.

Philip died in 1404 and was succeeded as Duke of Burgundy by his son, John the Fearless. The struggle between the two parties of Burgundians and Armagnacs went on, repeatedly threatening to engulf the country in civil war.

By 1399 the duchy of Aquitaine, now generally known as Guyenne, was a good deal smaller than it had been 250 years earlier when the marriage of Eleanor of Aquitaine and the future Henry II united it with the English crown. With no natural frontiers, and its extent slowly reduced by the constant attacks of the French, it now consisted of little more than the city of Bordeaux and the surrounding country to a depth varying from fifty to one hundred miles, together with the territory towards the Pyrenees, stretching from Bayonne and Dax to Lourdes. There were some doubts in 1399 as to whether Guyenne would follow England in accepting Henry IV in place of Richard II, but it soon became clear that the men of the duchy would for the most part prefer Henry to the only possible alternative, Charles VI of France. Habit and the strong trade in wines tied them to England. Bordeaux supplied about four-fifths of the English wine trade, and it required upwards of two hundred shiploads each year to get it to the English ports. In return Bordeaux imported cloth, fish and corn from England and northern Europe. By December 1399 Henry had secured the allegiance of the duchy and appointed Gaillard de Durfort, Lord Duras, a local magnate, to be its steward. The steward was the permanent head of the Government, exercising the political judicial and military functions of the Crown, except at such times as the King appointed a special lieutenant to do so. Englishmen were appointed to be constables and mayors of Bordeaux, but on the whole Henry left both city and duchy very much to govern themselves. Indeed his preoccupations in England caused him to neglect both the administration and the defence of the duchy, even when it was hard-pressed by the French.

Certainly several small forces were sent out from England, and late in 1401 the Earl of Rutland, having been appointed lieutenant, was sent out with several hundred men-at-arms and a thousand archers. He stayed for about a year, but such help was far from adequate. In spite of the truce between the two countries the French constantly harassed the duchy with small raids. Early in 1402 the title of Duke of Aquitaine, which Henry had

conferred on his eldest son, the Prince of Wales, was given by
the French to the infant son of Charles VI, and he was made to
do homage to his father for the duchy, an act of extreme provocation to Henry. On 19 May in the same year jousts were held at
Montendre some thirty miles north of Bordeaux, at which a
party of seven English knights led by Robert, Lord Scales was
decisively beaten by a similar number of French knights. This
was followed by a challenge from the Duke of Orleans to Henry
to meet him in person in the lists on the borders of Aquitaine.
After some consideration Henry replied that kings did not
normally accept challenges from those of lower rank, and he
would choose his own time for visiting his domains in Aquitaine.
Other Frenchmen were also eager for war. The Count of St. Pol,
Waleran of Luxemburg, who had married Maud Courtenay, a
half-sister of Richard II, declared that he had a personal war
with Henry, to avenge his half-brother-in-law, and that this was
not restricted by the truce between the two countries. One of his
acts, in addition to raids on the English coasts, was to take a
small fleet to the mouth of the Garonne to intercept the wine
ships bound for England, but he was driven off by English
ships. During 1403 both sides committed many acts of piracy in
the Channel, and in December St. Pol 'sailing towards the Isle of
Wight defeated and captured certain poor fishermen, their nets
and gear, and landing on the said island took certain sheep for
which the people were aggrieved.'[1] So wrote Richard Aston,
lieutenant of Calais to the Duke of Burgundy in March 1404.
In revenge the English attacked the county of St. Pol. Meanwhile
in September 1403 Orleans seems to have abandoned all pretence
of observing the truce in the south, despite the fact that an agreement for its prolongation was signed on the 13th of that month.
He now led a small army through Orleans towards Guyenne,
writing to Henry on his way charging him with treachery and
murder. His army laid siege to Courbefy, a strongly fortified
castle near Chalus on a hillside about a hundred miles from
Bordeaux. After a long siege this castle surrendered and its fall
was followed by the capture of many other places, whereupon
the Duke of Orleans rejoined his army ready to lead it in a victorious march on Bordeaux, but shortage of supplies forced him
to withdraw. By this time Henry and his Government were

[1] R. *Letters, H. IV*, vol. i, pp. 221–2

convinced that the situation really was serious, and during the summer and autumn of 1404 a force of ships and men was collected under Thomas, Lord Berkeley, ready to go to the relief of Bordeaux. At one time Henry considered going himself, but eventually the fleet sailed under Berkeley's command.[1]

---

[1] Nicolas, *P.C.*, vol. i, pp. 280-1. The letter was probably 1404, and not 1405, as dated by the editor

Chapter 10

Royal marriages, Homildon Hill,
July 1401–September 1402

THE King had reached London in time to say his farewells to Isabel on 28 June 1401, but he never stayed long in London or Westminster, and now set off on a visit to Hampshire. On 12 July he was at Farnham in Surrey, on the 19th and the 20th at Selborne, on the 21st at Bishops Sutton, on the 25th at Winchester and on the 26th at Southampton. After that his movements seem to have left no trace for some time. The council as usual were left to deal with routine matters in London, although after 14 July the magnates ceased to attend, and business was left to the officers and to knights such as Cheyne and Doreward. Sir Mathew Gournay was present on the 17th and on the 31st commissions were issued to collect shipping to take him to Aquitaine. The position was uneasy not only in Wales, for war with France remained likely. During the summer there were minor riots in Wiltshire, at Dartmouth and at Bristol. At Abergavenny on the Welsh march villeins attacked Sir William Lucy and set free three thieves whom he was about to execute.[1] Ships were needed in the Channel, troops in Aquitaine.

Within a few days of his appointment as treasurer on 31 May Lawrence Allerthorpe was writing not only to the King but also to some person of experience who was in the King's company, perhaps his own predecessor, John Norbury. The Bishop of Worcester, Tideman of Winchcombe, died on 13 June, and Allerthorpe immediately suggested that the temporalities of the see should be reserved for the expenses of the royal household. The necessary order was issued on the 27th.[2] In July he was writing to the King again. Henry had ordered him to make prompt payments to the Earl of Rutland, who had been appointed lieutenant in Aquitaine, and to Thomas, the King's second

[1] *Usk*, pp. 63, 228
[2] *Anglo-Norman Letters*, pp. 393–4, 401; *Cal. Pat.* (1399–1401), p. 504

on, who had a similar appointment in Ireland from 18 July. Rutland was to have £2,038 6s. 8d. and Thomas £1,000. Allerthorpe said that he could not manage it. He had recently paid ,000 marks for the expenses of the household, another 1,000 for the servants of Queen Isabel, £300 to the Prince of Wales, and various payments which he had to make 'by virtue of your letters and orders continuously sent me from day to day by divers persons.' The greater part of the money due from the parliamentary grant of fifteenths and tenths was already assigned before he took office. There was not even sufficient cash in the treasury to pay the messengers whom he had ordered to take summonses to a great council. Unless loans could be raised on the King's authority and with the aid of the council these payments could not be made.[1]

The one misfortune which neither Henry nor his council could have foreseen was the rapid decline in the volume of wool exports. Indeed it must have taken the exchequer officials with the very limited statistical information that was available to them several years to discover what was happening. It was most unfortunate for Henry that the end of the century and the beginning of his reign happened to coincide with a sudden drop, which reduced the customs revenues. Whereas the annual revenue from the custom and subsidy on wools had averaged £47,000 for the whole reign of Richard II, and £43,000 for the last three years, it fell to £39,000 in the first three years of the new reign, thus reducing the revenue which the exchequer might have expected to receive by at least £4,000 a year. Moreover in the fourth year, 1402–3, owing possibly to a series of exceptionally wet summers from 1399 onwards, which might have caused a fall in the number of sheep, it fell by another third to below £26,000. This collapse, despite a recovery to an average of £36,000 for the remainder of the reign, helps to explain the financial crisis of 1404 and the succeeding years.[2]

The summonses to the great council were dated 20 July. John Doreward was sent down by the council to see the King at Selborne, and came back with Henry's approval for the meeting of this council, which was to be even larger than a full

[1] *Anglo-Norman Letters*, pp. 396–7
[2] The figures are derived from Carus-Wilson and Coleman, pp. 51–6, 122–3. Meteorological information from Dr D. J. Schove

Parliament; all the lords spiritual and lay, and four to eight named knights from each shire, were to meet at Westminster on the morrow of the Assumption (16 August). The choice of date in the middle of harvest time emphasises the urgency with which the council viewed the situation. On the day after Doreward returned to London, the King sent Henry Bowet, now Bishop-elect of Bath and Wells, with a list of the names of persons who were to receive writs of privy seal summoning them to this gathering.

Meanwhile the council was working out the money which was needed, and reached a total of £130,000 apart from the day-to-day expenses of the royal household. The details are incomplete, but £13,000 was allowed for Calais, £5,000 for Ireland, £10,000 for Guyenne, £8,000 for sending Isabel to France, £16,000 for the wardrobe, £24,000 for annuities granted by the King, and £16,000 to repay the last loan. This leaves the very large sum of £38,000 for the Scottish marches, the war in Wales, and the defence of the sea. No doubt these were totals which the council and the officials of the Government would have liked to provide, but did not really expect to have available.

The full list of people summoned to the council included two archbishops, seventeen bishops, the treasurer and keeper of the privy seal, five abbots and one prior, the Prince of Wales, the Duke of York, nine earls, thirty-three lords and well over two hundred knights and squires, or about three hundred persons in all. Many of the same people would have been returned as knights of the shire had a Parliament been summoned, and many of them did in fact sit in Parliament during the reign. The borough members were omitted, and the meeting could not have the full authority of a Parliament. Nonetheless the fact of its being summoned at all especially at harvest time shows how much the King and council felt themselves to be in need of advice and support. Most of the ordinary councillors were summoned, as was Henry Percy, so that the meeting would be well-informed on all pressing matters, including the position in Wales. The question of making war on both France and Scotland is supposed to have been discussed. A month later a large embassy, including the Earls of Northumberland and Westmorland, Henry Percy, the Bishops of Bangor and Carlisle and five others were appointed to treat with the Scots, and there was also talk of further truces in Picardy, so evidently the decisions favoured peace rather than war.

In Wales Glendower was still at large, coming out of the mountains to slay and rob whenever he wished. Early in September Henry wrote from Kennington to the Prince to say that he had heard of a great assembly of Glendower's people, and would accordingly be setting out on the following Wednesday for Worcester where he hoped to be by 1 October.[1] On 7 September he was at Windsor and by the end of the month at Evesham. On the 18th orders were issued for proclamations to be made in the midland and south-western counties summoning all knights and squires, and all archers taking a yearly fee from the King to be with him at Worcester on 1 October, ready to resist the malice of Owen Glendower and other rebels of Wales.[2]

The treasurer, Allerthorpe, was still busy. Loans had been raised from leading London citizens, from civil servants, from Allerthorpe himself, and from his predecessor, John Norbury. The King's son, Thomas, and Rutland had at last received part of the money that was due to them, in assignments made on 2 September on the second part of the fifteenth and tenth, due to be collected on 2 November.[3] Besides issuing tallies of assignment Allerthorpe wrote to the Prior of Norwich, collector of the clerical tenth in that diocese, urging him to pay the 400 marks to Prince Thomas's attorneys, and take the tally in exchange, as soon as he possibly could.[4] In December the two lieutenants finally received the balance of the sums due to them, £333 6s. 8d. and £1,000, in cash payments. Meanwhile the treasurer reported to the King that on 20 September his ambassadors at Dordrecht had received the agreement for the marriage of his daughter, and also that the Countess of the March of Scotland had been paid £40 19s. 4d. from her husband's annuity, granted by Henry. All other of the King's commands he would be ready and happy to carry out to the best of his ability, and he prayed for the King's honourable victory.[5]

[1] *Anglo-Norman Letters*, pp. 299–300. K must be Kennington
[2] *Cal. Close* (1399–1402), pp. 421–2
[3] P.R.O., E 401/622
[4] *Anglo-Norman Letters*, p. 153
[5] ibid. pp. 394–5

Henry had perhaps need of his prayers. He was at Worcester on the day appointed, 1 October. On the 6th the Prince of Wales wrote him from Chester that he was sending two of his trusted counsellors to meet the King at Hereford and give him full reports on his activities.[1] Henry was at Hereford on the 10th and the 11th and it is possible that the Prince joined him there. According to Adam of Usk the English attacked the abbey of Strata Florida, and carried off from Wales a thousand children of both sexes.[2] Llewellyn ap Griffith Vaughan of Cayo was captured and beheaded at Llandovery in the presence of the King and the Prince. On the 14th the King wrote from there to Allerthorpe, acknowledging his letter dated from London on the 8th, thanking him for his diligence in the work of his office, but reproaching him for not having made any provision for the royal household, and finally commanding him to send 1,000 marks to the treasurer of the household at Hereford on the 28th. Allerthorpe sent his reply with John Ikelyngton, one of the chamberlains of the exchequer. He reminded Henry that the household had already had 1,000 marks since Michaelmas, and said that of the present 1,000, 700 should go to the treasurer of the household, and the remaining 300 'to your own coffers . . . for your private expenses and costs.'[3] It was at Dunstable however that Ikelyngton eventually found the royal household,[4] for Henry had soon tired of his campaign, and hampered by shortage of funds turned towards London once more. Before leaving Hereford he had seen to the punishment of a number of captured rebels, and the garrisoning of castles. The Earl of Worcester, who was to be made lieutenant of South Wales, was left as Captain of Cardigan, and a number of other appointments were made of surveyors of garrisons and constables of castles.[5] If the King could claim that he had put his strongholds in order and inflicted a minor defeat on the rebels, he had effectively done very little. Of Glendower himself, who was far too wise to come out into the open, he had seen nothing.

Owen now returned to North Wales, and attacked Welshpool,

[1] *Anglo-Norman Letters* pp. 312–14
[2] *Usk*, pp. 70, 237
[3] *Anglo-Norman Letters*, pp. 451, 392
[4] P.R.O., E 403/571
[5] *Anglo-Norman Letters*, pp. 302–3

here John, Lord Charlton of Powys died on 18 October. Hot-
pur being absent on the Scottish border, the Welsh secured con-
rol of the counties of Caernarvon and Merioneth.[1] Early in
November they attacked Caernarvon itself, but were driven off.
This advance southwards into central Wales meant that Glen-
ower's position was much stronger than in the previous year,
ven so he was still not committed to fighting to a finish. Indeed
vertures for peace seem to have been made about this time.
he Earl of Northumberland and his son, Hotspur, were not
nfriendly towards Owen, and the Earl reported to the Prince of
Vales that he had sent envoys to find out what conditions
Glendower wanted, but the latter said he was afraid to come to
England because he had heard that a number of lords had been
nurdered by the common people without trial and against the
King's will. The Earl had offered to plead his case with the King
f he surrendered, but nothing had come of that. At the same time
Northumberland was explaining that he could not accept the
King's invitation to visit him at Eltham at Christmas,[2] perhaps
n order to discuss these negotiations.

The Percies had nothing to lose in Wales, since all their estates
nd interests were in the north of England, and would probably
ave supported a settlement, whereby the King remedied some
of the grievances of Glendower and his followers, whilst they
on their part returned to their allegiance. Far different was the
position of the marcher lords, whose main estates were in Wales
or on the border. Any concessions to Glendower would be at
heir expense, and lords such as Grey of Ruthyn would certainly
ave opposed any settlement which did not ensure the complete
defeat of Glendower. In fact no serious attempt at a settlement
vas made, and King and council showed their determination
o hold the country by force. Henry's own sympathies are likely
o have lain with the marcher lords, for by his marriage to Mary
Bohun he was a marcher lord himself.

The Earl of Worcester had been left in Cardigan Castle with a
garrison of 50 men-at-arms and 120 archers, and with 30 men-at-
urms and 80 archers at Aberystwyth, then known as Lampadern.
At Builth was Sir John Oldcastle with 20 men-at-arms and 8
rchers, and four other castles had similar garrisons. The cost

Lloyd, *Glendower*, pp. 44–5
Anglo-Norman Letters, pp. 308–9, 304–5

of these troops was about £500 for a quarter of a year. The coun
proposed that Lord Burnell should be given charge of Welshpc
and the castles of the Earl of March, some of whose lands wou
help to pay the expenses of the Prince, who was to remain
Wales with Henry Percy. As a guardian for the Prince they su
gested either the Earl of Worcester, Lord Lovell, Sir Thom
Erpyngham or Lord Say. Glendower on his side was appeali
meanwhile for help from the Irish and the King of Scots
strengthen his position.[1]

The council also discussed the keeping of the Scottish marc
the sending of envoys to Picardy, and the reception of envo
from Bayonne. Finally they recommended that a great coun
should be held a fortnight after Hilary, that is at the end
January 1402, to discuss the summoning of a Parliament, and tl
raising of money for the passage of the Princess Blanche
Germany for her marriage. Without waiting for this howev
Henry, exercising his feudal privilege of levying an aid for tl
marriage of his eldest daughter, ordered the levy of an aid fc
Blanche on 1 December. He left London for Hertford, and the
made his way to Eltham for Christmas once more.

The second part of the fifteenth and tenth granted in tl
Parliament of 1401 was due to be collected at the beginning
November, but very little of it came into the exchequer in tl
form of cash, because it had already been assigned before it wa
due. In spite of the aid for Blanche the financial prospects we
still gloomy. The year 1402 in which no parliamentary gra
was due to be collected was to prove a difficult one for tl
exchequer.

In accordance with the advice of the council, the two Arcl
bishops, eleven bishops, the Prince of Wales, six earls and twent
four other lords were summoned to a great council on Monda
30 January. They were told to be in London by the previou
day, Sunday, in order to be ready. The King explained that he ha
intended calling a Parliament for that date, but had summone
them, a much smaller number, in order to cause less troubl
to the people. The writ of summons, which was issued on 1
January giving just a fortnight's notice of the meeting, did nc
specify the business to be discussed, but said that the membe
would be told of it when they assembled. The council was sti

[1] Lloyd, *Glendower*, pp. 46–7

itting on 4 February, and probably later.[1] The Prince and fifteen other lay lords, including all three Percies, were present, when a committee of four was set up to examine the assignments on the subsidies, customs, and fifteenths and tenths granted in the last Parliament. These four were the Bishops of Bath and Wells and Rochester (Henry Bowet and John Bottlesham), the Earl of Worcester and Lord Lovell. They were to meet early in the morning of Tuesday, 14 February in the chamber next to the exchequer.[2] The result of their examination is unknown, but as most of the money would already be spent it can have been of very little help in providing for the future. A fortnight later Lawrence Allerthorpe was replaced as treasurer by Bishop Bowet, one of the four examiners, but Allerthorpe was not punished except by dismissal, and was soon employed on the King's business in Ireland. There was no suggestion of misuse of the funds. It merely appears that the task of finding money for the King's needs had proved too much for him, as it did for all the other treasurers of the reign.

On the 19th of the same month of February Adam of Usk, the chronicler to whom we owe some of our knowledge of the early part of the reign of Henry IV, embarked at Billingsgate in London to sail to Bergen-op-Zoom. From there, as he tells us, he made his way across Germany, the St. Gotthard pass and northern Italy. Arriving in Rome on 5 April, he quickly established himself at the papal court. What he fails to tell is that he was forced to go into exile because he and two of his servants had been convicted of stealing a horse and 14 marks in Westminster in 1400. His sympathies with the rebels in Wales were perhaps also too great to enable him to remain as a loyal servant or subject of Henry IV. Certainly it was not until 1411, after many adventures, that he secured a pardon from the King and was able to return to England; so that his chronicle for the intervening

---

[1] P.R.O., E 28/11, printed by H. G. Richardson and G. O. Sayles, 'Parliamentary documents from formularies', *Bull. I.H.R.*, vol. xi, pp. 159–60. P.R.O., C 81/1540/31 refers to a great council of 4 Feb. Wylie, *H. IV.*, vol. i, p. 251, mentions a Parliament at Coventry immediately after this council, but this seems to be a misunderstanding.

[2] Nicolas, *P.C.*, vol. i, p. 180, from B. M. Cotton Cleopatra F III, f. 22b. My reading is that the Prince and fifteen other lords were present at the setting up of the committee, not members of it. The date given is 19 February, but this was a Sunday, and a misreading of 14 seems more likely.

years depended on the scanty news that he was able to pick up in exile, in Rome, the Low Countries, and perhaps with Glendower in Wales. Before he left however he was able to record the harrying of the lordship of Ruthyn by Owen and his men.

Glendower's rebellion was now approaching its most success-ful time. In mid-April Owen's great enemy, Lord Grey of Ruthyn, was ambushed and captured near his own castle of Ruthyn. A real prize for his captors he was carried off into the mountains. Two months later, on 22 June, an even more valuable prisoner, Edmund Mortimer, uncle of the boy Earl of March, was taken in battle at Pilleth, in Radnorshire, in the borderlands of the Mor-timers. Three knights and many other Englishmen were slain at the same time, a triumph for Owen and the Welsh archers.[1] Lord Grey, always a loyal supporter of Henry IV, was released within a year, on payment of a large ransom; but Edmund's capture was a more serious matter. Not only was he the uncle of the Earl of March, the rightful heir by the strict rules of here-dity to Richard's throne, but also related by marriage to the Percies, for his sister was Henry Hotspur's wife. When shortly after his capture he made peace with Glendower, and even married the rebel's daughter, Henry might well wonder what Edmund and the Percies would do next.

Hotspur had recently been away from Wales on the Scottish border, whilst the Prince was at Kennington from February to April 1402, but so far there were no obvious signs of any break between the Percies and the King. Hotspur, who had been justice of North Wales, Chester and Flint for life since 29 October 1399, was now on 31 March 1402 appointed the King's lieutenant in North Wales, by the advice of the council. The justice in South Wales had been William, Lord Beauchamp of Abergavenny, but after the King's last expedition Thomas Percy, Earl of Worcester, Hotspur's uncle, had been left in command there, and he was now confirmed as the King's lieutenant for the south.[2] These changes of title tacitly recognised the existence of a state of war in Wales. At the same time Worcester gave up his office of steward of the royal household to Lord Say, presumably in order to be able to devote his energies to the Welsh war.

[1] Lloyd, *Glendower*, pp. 48–52
[2] *Cal. Pat.* (1399–1401), pp. 33, 37; (1401–5) p. 53

The King had spent Christmas at Eltham, and stayed there during January, though he may have paid a short visit to the Archbishop who was at Canterbury, or at nearby Charing. In February they both came to London for the council, then Henry went back to Eltham and stayed over Easter, 26 March, whilst the Archbishop after visiting Winchester returned to Canterbury. He then stayed either at Canterbury, or at Ford between there and the sea until the later part of May, and was therefore absent from the important ceremony which took place at Eltham on 3 April.

This ceremony was no less than the King's marriage, albeit by proxy, to Joan, the widowed Duchess of Brittany. Joan was the daughter of Charles II, King of Navarre. She had married, as his third wife, the elderly Duke of Brittany in 1386, and on his death in November 1399 had become the regent of Brittany for her young son. The preliminary negotiations had evidently been conducted with some secrecy, and Henry's marriage came as a surprise to most of his people; but whether the secret had been kept from the Archbishop, his leading councillor, and the other members of the council, and what they thought of the marriage, can only be guessed. Nor is it easy for us to discover the significance of the marriage to Henry. If he hoped to gain political advantages in the control of, or alliance with, Brittany, he was speedily disappointed, and at home the cost of Joan's household and allowances added heavily to his difficulties. Almost a year was to elapse after the proxy wedding before they were able to meet. There is very little evidence as to their personal relations, but what there is suggests that the marriage was more than a mere political arrangement. Henry was now about thirty-five, and Joan perhaps five years younger. He can have seen her, if at all, only briefly, and that must have been before she was widowed, yet he would appear to have been early attracted by her, impatient to meet her when she landed in England, and thenceforward a faithful husband, always generous, and constantly careful to ensure that her needs and those of her household were fully satisfied. For the Duchess marriage with a King still in the prime of life, strong, handsome and renowned for his skill in arms, must have appeared a triumph, but it was not achieved without great sacrifices. She was forced to abandon her family, and their duchy, to come to Henry, and she was very soon deprived of the comfort of most of her familiar household servants by the Parliament's jealousy and hatred of foreigners. She remained on good terms with Henry during his life, and with all her stepsons until she was accused of witchcraft some years after his death. Her triumphant husband soon became a tired man struggling to maintain his position despite his own failing health, but perhaps they gave each other some happiness.

The problem as to how or when they first met still remains. It was long believed on the authority of Froissart that Henry had visited the Duke and Duchess of Brittany at Nantes and Vannes in 1399, but this story is very hard to reconcile with the known facts of Henry's movements. It is perhaps more likely that the Duke and Duchess visited Richard's court in England shortly before Henry's exile, and that he had met them there, but it cannot be proved that they had ever met at all. What is clear is that he was in constant correspondence with the duchy from the beginning of the reign, although the subject of the correspondence was kept secret.

As early as February 1400 Antony Ricz, Joan's envoy, who was eventually to act as her proxy at the wedding, was on his way back from a mission to Henry.[1] A few days later the Duchess wrote a letter to be delivered to Henry by a certain Joan de Bavalen, who was coming to see him in England.[2] Whether its terms are more effusive than common courtesy required is not easy to determine.

'Forasmuch as I am desirous to hear of your good estate,' she wrote, 'the which may our Lord will that it may at all times be as good as your noble heart knows best to desire, and in fact as I for my part could wish for you, I pray you, my most dear and most honoured lord and cousin, that it may very often please you to let me know the certainty, for the very good comfort and gladness of my heart; for whenever I am able to hear a good account of you it rejoices my heart most exceedingly. And if of your courtesy you would hear of the same from over here, my thanks to you, at the writing of these presents I and my children were altogether in good health of our persons . . .'

At least Henry might assume on the receipt of this that the Duchess was not ill-disposed towards him. No further letters

[1] *Cal. Close* (1399–1402), p. 43
[2] R. *Letters, H. IV*, vol. i, pp. 19–20

between them survive. Ricz and his fellow envoy, Nicholas Aldrewich, had with Joan, Lady Basset, been at Richmond in Yorkshire on 12 August 1399, acting as feoffees of the earldom of Richmond, which was anciently held by the Dukes of Brittany. On 20 October 1399 Henry granted the earldom and lordship of Richmond to Ralph, Earl of Westmorland, for life, the same three, Joan, widow of Ralph de Basset of Drayton, Ricz and Aldrewich, being said to have rights in the estate.[1] During their visit to England in February 1400 Antony Ricz and Nicholas Aldrewich, together with John Perian, entered into indentures of retainer with the Earl of Westmorland for life, taking grants in Lincolnshire. Ricz was to have £100 yearly from the manor of Crowhurst, a part of the lordship of Richmond.[2] Ricz and Aldrewich thus seem to have managed to be on good terms with both the new lord of Richmond, and the widow of the former one. Aldrewich was at the same time carrying letters from John Norbury, Henry's treasurer and confidant, to the Duchess.[3] The only subject mentioned in them was the piratical acts of English and Breton seamen in the Channel, but Norbury is described as the Duchess's 'very dear and good friend', and it may be that more important communications were entrusted to the messenger to deliver orally, or alternatively that there were separate and more personal letters, copies of which were not preserved. On 16 December 1401 Antony Ricz, this time accompanied by John Ruys (Ricz), perhaps a relative, was again about to cross from Southampton to Brittany.[4] After the marriage Ricz acted as the Queen's attorney in November 1403 and January 1404, and on 16 January 1405 the King granted him a ship called *La Grace de Dieu* with all its gear.[5] Aldrewich also entered the King's service, and on 31 May 1406 he and Perian entered into a bond for 100 marks on behalf of a Breton squire, who was a prisoner of Prince John, the King's third son.[6]

In March 1401 Joan secured a bull from Pope Benedict XIII at Avignon allowing her to marry anyone she pleased within the

[1] *Cal. Pat.* (1399–1401), pp. 24, 547,
[2] *Cal. Close* (1399–1402), pp. 104, 112–13, 115–16
[3] *Anglo-Norman Letters*, pp. 417–18, 430
[4] *Cal. Pat.* (1401–5), p. 67
[5] *Cal. Close* (1402–5), pp. 212, 237; *Cal. Pat.* (1401–5), pp. 347, 484
[6] *Cal Close* (1405–9), pp. 1, 138

fourth degree of consanguinity, thus surmounting the obstacle
provided by the fact that Henry and his subjects recognised the
rival Pope. About the same time, by letters under her signet
dated at Vannes, the Duchess empowered Antony Ricz and
John Ruys to act for her, and as already stated the proxy ceremony was accordingly performed at Eltham on 3 April. Henry
Bowet, recently rewarded for his long service to Henry by being
raised to the bishopric of Bath and Wells officiated at what must
have been a strictly private court ceremony. Also present were
the chamberlain, the Earl of Somerset, the constable, the Earl
of Northumberland and his son Henry Hotspur, the Earl of
Worcester, Thomas Langley, keeper of the privy seal, Richard
Kingston, now dean of the chapel of the King's household and
formerly his treasurer for the expeditions to Prussia and the Holy
Land, Nicholas Bubwith, the King's secretary, John Norbury and
Robert Pynart esquires.[1]

Meanwhile the exchequer was busy trying to raise money for
another marriage. Early in the previous year (1401) Rupert,
Duke of Bavaria and Count Palatine, who had just been crowned
King of the Romans at Cologne, sent envoys to England to
treat for the marriage of Henry's eldest daughter, Blanche, with
his son Louis, both of whom were about thirteen years of age.
The Bishops of Hereford and Rochester and the Earls of Northumberland and Westmorland represented Henry in the negotiations, and succeeded in reaching an agreement. Blanche was to
be sent to Cologne at Easter 1402, and to be married at Heidelberg. Her father was to give 40,000 nobles for her dower,
after which Louis was to provide for her. The final marriage
treaty was signed at Dordrecht in June 1401, Henry being
represented by Sir William Sturmy, John Kington and Robert
Waterton.[2]

In December Henry ordered the collection of an aid for the
marriage of his eldest daughter. The 'reasonable aid' for knighting
the King's eldest son, or marrying his eldest daughter, a truly
feudal conception, was fixed by the statute of Westminster of
1275 at 20*s.* on each knight's fee and on each £20 worth of land,
and confirmed by that of 1351, after Edward III had attempted
to collect double this amount for the knighting of the Black

[1] Lobineau, *Hist. de Bretagne*, vol. i, pp. 500–1; vol. ii, pp. 875–6
[2] Rymer, *Foedera*, vol. viii, pp. 179–80, 200–2

Prince in 1347. No aid seems to have been collected when Edward's daughter, Isabel, was married to Enguerrand de Coucy, a prisoner of war on 27 July 1365. This lack of any recent precedent did not worry Henry, who proceeded to levy the aid on the advice of his council and without consulting Parliament. It was to be paid into the exchequer by 16 February, but on 1 March letters were sent out requesting loans to help to pay for Blanche's clothes, dowry and escort, as well as for the Scottish and Welsh wars. The recipients are asked to send £40 each by Easter at the latest.[1]

These letters cannot have been very successful, for on the day after the King's marriage £2,500 was borrowed from John Hende, the wealthy London merchant, all the councillors present (the Bishops of Exeter, Bath, Hereford and Bangor, the Earl of Northumberland, Thomas Langley, Thomas Stanley, John Norbury, John Cheyne, John Curson and John Wodecock), pledging themselves for its repayment,[2] an indication that the King's credit did not stand very high. Another sum of 2,000 marks (£1,333 6s. 8d.) was borrowed from the City of London a week later, the customs of the port of London being pledged to repay it. Altogether more than £16,000 was raised in loans during the summer term, the highest total for any half year during the whole reign.

On 14 February letters under the privy seal were sent out asking the persons who were to escort the Princess Blanche to Cologne to be in London in mid-Lent, about 5 March,[3] but the usual delays ensued, due largely no doubt to the lack of funds, and it was not until 21 June, three months late, that the party finally left England. The escort was headed by the Earl of Somerset, the Bishop of Worcester and the Countess of Salisbury. Blanche duly met her future husband at Cologne, but the English were a little disappointed at the lack of pomp and fine clothes which they had expected to welcome their Princess. However she was married at Heidelberg on 6 July, and her marriage was apparently a happy one, though short-lived. Blanche died in May 1406, less than four years later. The question of her dowry was not so quickly settled, for it was nearly forty years before

---

[1] Rymer, *Foedera*, vol. viii, p. 245
[2] *Cal. Close* (1399–1402), p. 563
[3] Rymer, *Foedera*, vol. viii, p. 242

her husband's family was finally paid off by her nephew, Henry
VI, in 1444.[1]

Henry IV still had another daughter unmarried, and of course
his sons. By the edict of Calmar, 1397, the three Scandinavian
countries were united under one king, the fifteen-year-old Eric.
In 1402 envoys came over to England to treat for the marriage
of Eric with Henry's second daughter, Philippa, and also of
Eric's sister, Katherine, with the Prince of Wales. On 8 May at
the Tower in the presence of the King, the Bishops of Lincoln
and Bath, Edmund, Earl of Kent (the nineteen-year-old brother
of the Earl who was beheaded at Cirencester in 1400), Sir Thomas
Beaufort, Sir Hugh Waterton, Robert Mascall, the King's
confessor, Nicholas Bubwith, his secretary, John Norbury and
Robert Waterton esquires, the Prince appointed Sir William
Bourchier, Master Richard Derham and John Peraunt esquire
to treat for his marriage. A week later at Berkhamstead his sister,
Philippa, appointed the same three proctors, in the presence of
the King, her brothers, Henry, John and Humphrey, her uncle
the Bishop of Lincoln, the Earls of Arundel and Kent, Thomas
Mowbray (the young son and heir of Henry's opponent of
Coventry), Sir Thomas Erpyngham, the King's chamberlain,
Sir Robert Corbet, Nicholas Bubwith, and Robert Waterton,
squire of the chamber. In the following months the three com-
missaries were sent over to Denmark with the Bishop of Bangor
to negotiate for the marriages,[2] but no speedy settlement was
reached. A Scandinavian marriage for the Prince was not a very
brilliant prospect, and the provision of another dowry, for
Philippa, would be no easy matter. In the meanwhile Henry had
more pressing matters to engage his attention.

After the wedding ceremony at Eltham the King went to
Windsor, as he normally did in April for the feast of St. George.
Then he was at the Tower on 8 May and at Berkhamstead Castle
by the 14th, and there he stayed for some weeks. On 15 May
'greatly marvelling at the failure to provide' money for Blanche's
escort and wedding he sent his half-brother, Bishop Beaufort of
Lincoln, with a letter to the council, stopping other payments
meanwhile. At about the same time the council became worried

[1] Rymer, *Foedera*, vol. xi, p. 70; Wylie, *H. IV*, vol. i, pp. 255–6; *Bekynton
Corres.*, vol. i, pp. cxii–cxv
[2] Rymer, *Foedera*, vol. viii, pp. 257–60, 265–7

by rumours of plots against the King. A story was spread about that he was going to Brittany to marry the Duchess, and that in his absence, Richard, who was said to be still alive, would be restored. On 19 May the council ordered the arrest of Sir Roger Clarendon, said to be a bastard son of the Black Prince, and eight days later the prior of the friars preachers of Winchelsea, Stephen Lene, parson, and John Ayworth, Walter Walton, John Howeton and Henry Forster, all friars minor, were committed to the Tower.[1] All were shortly executed for treason, as was the Prior of the Austin canons of Launde in Leicestershire. The council was also informed by the Earls of Rutland and Northumberland that certain spies about the King's person were being paid for taking information to Cherbourg. John Norbury brought a draft writ from the council to the King and with his approval it was issued early in June. This ordered all the sheriffs to make proclamations forbidding the spreading of lying rumours, especially to the effect that Richard was still alive in Scotland, and would shortly invade the kingdom with an army of Scots. Persons spreading such tales were to be held prisoner until the King decided on their punishment.[2]

The friars were suspected of being the chief agents in spreading such treasonable rumours. Why they should have remained loyal to Richard is not at all clear, but travelling from place to place they were obviously in a position to convey discontent, which inevitably spread from the stories of war in the north and in Wales. It was also a very bad summer, with thunderstorms and floods, churches in Essex and Herefordshire being struck by lightning, incidents which could easily be made into portents of ill for the King and his Government. The council was not only worried about these things, but also, by asking that revenues should be paid in and out of the exchequer in the normal way, suggested that the King may have been trying to short-circuit the ordinary routine. Guyenne and Ireland were likewise claiming attention. Thomas, the King's second son, was sent to Ireland where many castles and fortresses were ill-kept and in a ruinous state. To Aquitaine it was proposed to send the Earl of Rutland, who became Duke of York on the death of his father on 1 August

[1] *Cal. Close* (1399–1402), pp. 527, 528, 568; *Cal. Pat.* (1402–5), p. 126
[2] *Cal. Close* (1399–1402), p. 570; Rymer, *Foedera*, vol. viii, p. 261; P.R.O., C 81/1540/25

1402, as lieutenant, and to give him the castle of Fronsac for his residence there, but he did not immediately set out to take up his command.

Glendower's successes had made Wales the most urgent problem. A rather full council meeting was held towards the middle of June, perhaps at the Prince's manor of Kennington, although there is no evidence that the Prince himself was present. A few days later the King wrote to the council from Berkhamstead. He had heard of the capture of Mortimer, and proposed to set out himself to wage war in Wales, starting from Lichfield on 7 July. He therefore asked the council to send out orders for the knights and squires of the midland counties to meet him in all haste mounted and arrayed for war, by that date at the latest. The northern counties were at the same time to prepare themselves to fight against the Scots, and the counties along the south coast to be arrayed to resist the King's enemies, presumably from France. Five days later on 30 June, still at Berkhamstead, he was able to write with news of victory in the north. The Scottish Earl of March with the garrison of Berwick had defeated a party of 400 Scots, and killed or captured 240 of them including Sir John Haliburton and three other knights. At the same time the Earl of Northumberland sent news of another Scottish raid near Carlisle, and further incursions were expected. Henry urged the council to ensure that his covenants with the Percies were observed lest ill befall the marches.

By 23 July the King had got as far as Lilleshall in Shropshire, where orders were issued for defending the towns of the English border against Wales. Since March the younger Henry Percy had been the King's lieutenant in North Wales, with his uncle Thomas, Earl of Worcester, lieutenant in the south; the Prince of Wales having an overall command, which was apparently far more than nominal. Hotspur was however spending more time on the Scottish than the Welsh border. Now the King created four new commands. Thomas, Earl of Arundel, was appointed lieutenant for the borders of North Wales from the castle of Holt in Denbigh to Wigmore in Herefordshire, and Edmund, Earl of Stafford, the same for South Wales from Wigmore to Chepstow in Monmouthshire. At the same time Richard, Lord Grey of Codnor was put in charge of the counties of Carmarthen, Cardigan and Pembroke, and Edward, Lord Charlton of Powys of the castle, town and lordship of Welshpool.[1] Henry wrote to tell his son, the Prince, that the Earls of Arundel and Stafford were under his command,[2] and then withdrew. He crossed England through Lichfield, Burton-on-Trent, and Tideswell to Ravendale in Lincolnshire, keeping himself either by accident or design equidistant from London, and the two borders with Scotland and Wales. At Burton, however, he stopped to issue instructions that victuals should be sent to towns on the Welsh border by 27 August, ready for another advance into the principality. At Ravendale he turned back and retraced his steps through Tideswell and Nottingham to Lichfield, where he was on 22 August.

By this time Glendower's men had attacked Abergavenny, Usk, Caerleon, Newport and Cardiff, their first incursion into South Wales. At the beginning of September the King's army did at last enter Wales, but once again the weather defeated him. On 7 September came one of the worst storms of a very bad summer, with rain, hail and even snow. The King's camp was almost washed away, his own tent blown down, and it was said that but for the fact that he was sleeping in his armour he would have been killed by its fall.[3] As always on such occasions it was claimed that such weather had never been known before. Naturally it was attributed to magic, worked by those black friars who were Richard's friends and the King's enemies. Repulsed yet again Henry turned towards London, without having met his enemies. His failure could be attributed to the difficulty of the country, to bad weather, or to the shortage of money, which prevented him from collecting and keeping an effective army in being; but it may be asked whether a more unified command, and a campaign carried through with more vigour, and less waiting to see what the Scots or the French might do, would not have met with more success.

On the very day of the disastrous storm in Wales, the Bishop of Bath and Wells, who had succeeded Allerthorpe as treasurer in February, was telling his colleagues of the council in London some of his difficulties in raising money. The chancellor was present, also the Bishop of Hereford, the keeper of the privy

[1] *Cal. Pat.* (1401–5), pp. 138–9
[2] *Anglo-Norman Letters*, pp. 286–7
[3] Capgrave, *Chron.*, p. 279

seal, John Scarle and John Prophet. The treasurer said that he
had tried every way to find money for the King. In order to raise
loans he had offered bonds under his own seal, as well as under
the King's, but the lenders insisted on having jewels as security
and furthermore authority by letters patent to sell the jewels
if the loans were not repaid by the date fixed. William of Wyke
ham, the aged Bishop of Winchester, had already on 1 July
received permission to sell some jewels which had been pawned
to him, if he was not repaid by Christmas. But on the general
question the council decided to consult the Archbishop of
Canterbury, so they went to Lambeth in the afternoon, where the
treasurer told his story over again. In view of the necessity for
the loans the Archbishop advised that the desired letters should
be given, and undertook to defend the councillors' action to
the King, provided that any surplus value of the jewels, above
the amount of the loans, should be paid over to the King.

Small forces of Scots had been defeated in June, but towards
the end of August a very much larger force, led by the Earl of
Douglas, with many Scottish nobles and knights, and some
thirty French knights, crossed the border. They advanced towards
Newcastle-upon-Tyne plundering and burning crops. The Earl
of Northumberland was content to await their return. He had
with him his son, Hotspur, the Scottish Earl of March, the Lord
of Greystoke, Sir Henry Fitzhugh and other knights. They took
up a position on Homildon Hill near Wooler, on the edge of the
Cheviots, and waited. The Scots returning home on 14 September
blundered into the English archers, and were defeated before
the knights had a chance to attack them. Defeated by the archers
they fled, pursued by Northumberland's knights and men-at-arms
right up to the border. Douglas himself was wounded and captured, along with the Earls of Fife, Moray, Angus and Orkney,
and a number of barons and knights including some of the Frenchmen. Sir Adam Gordon and several other knights were killed. A
squire called Merbury brought the news to the King at Daventry
on the 20th. He immediately wrote to the council to inform them
and also to tell them to give orders that no Scottish prisoners
were to be ransomed or freed without their authority. Orders
to this effect were issued by the council two days later. Henry
owed yet one more debt to the Percies, as both he and they were
no doubt aware, and neither he nor anyone else could avoid

comparing their success with his lack of it. Furthermore his order about the prisoners was an apparent interference with the just rights of the captors. Individual letters were sent to the leading captors, but the 'urgent reasons' prompting the King's action were not explained.

Chapter 11

The third Parliament and the revolt of the Percies,
September 1402–December 1403

B Y Tuesday 26 September 1402 Henry was back at his castle of
Berkhamstead. On the following Saturday the members of
his third Parliament assembled in Westminster Hall to answer
their names in the presence of the chancellor, the keeper of the
privy seal and other members of the council; and then adjourned
until Monday morning at nine o'clock. This time the chancellor
was a bishop, Edmund Stafford of Exeter, and it was he who
made the opening speech on 2 October. He was able to point out
that Henry, as 'the most powerful king in the world', had been
asked by the King of the Romans to do his best to help to heal the
schism in the church. He also reported the recent victory of the
Percies over the Scots but apart from this the outlook was not
bright. There was the usual, or rather worse than usual, shortage of
money, and the continuing troubles in Wales and Ireland, about
which the King wished for the advice of the Parliament. Finally
before sending the Commons away to choose their Speaker, who
was to be presented to the King the next morning, the chancellor
said that in the past a number of both Lords and Commons had on
coming to Parliament paid more attention to their private business
than to the common profit of the kingdom. Now the King
expected them to attend daily and devote themselves to the
business of Parliament.

Amongst the shire representatives were twenty-eight who are
not known to have sat before, a little less than the average
number, and eleven including Sir Arnold Savage who had sat in
the last Parliament. But Savage was not elected Speaker this time.
Instead the Commons presented Sir Henry Retford, a comparatively obscure knight, who, although this was only his
second Parliament, was not without valuable experience in other
fields. He had been on diplomatic missions both to Avignon
and to Rome, and had recently led troops to Shrewsbury to take

part in the Welsh campaign.[1] He might well therefore have some contribution to make to discussions both of the schism in the church and of the rebellion in Wales. Unlike the other Speakers of the reign he was never a member of the royal council. On being presented as Speaker he made the usual protest, after which the King told him that he would send certain lords, his officers, to the Commons on the following day, to explain to them the reasons for the summoning of Parliament.

A week later the chancellor reported that the Commons had asked to be allowed to 'commune' with the Lords on the matters before Parliament, as had sometimes been done in the last reign, and that the King had granted this as a special grace, which was not to be taken as a right or custom. To emphasise the special nature of the favour the King instructed the clerk of the Parliament to note the fact on the Parliament Roll, and also sent William Heron, Lord Say, the steward of his household, and Master John Prophet, his secretary, to tell the Commons that it was not to be taken as a precedent. Twelve peers were thereupon named to consult with them, the Archbishop of Canterbury, the Bishops of London, Lincoln and St. David's, four earls, Somerset, Northumberland, Westmorland and Worcester, and four barons, Roos, Berkeley, Abergavenny and Lovell. All twelve were at some time members of the council, and therefore aware of the King's problems if not always in sympathy with his policy, but the constant attacks of the Commons made Henry jealous of his prerogatives, and no king could be expected to welcome the presentation of a united front by Lords and Commons. However, at this moment the Commons did take the unusual step of expressing their gratitude to the King and his family. They thanked Henry for his great labours against the Scots and the Welsh, the Prince for his service in Wales, and Prince Thomas for his work in Ireland. In addition they asked Henry to thank the Earl of Northumberland for his victory at Homildon Hill, and to allow the Lords Roos and Willoughby to raise a loan of 10,000 marks to ransom the Lord Grey of Ruthyn.

Four days later on 20 October Northumberland came before the King and Parliament in the White Hall at Westminster, bringing some of his prisoners – Mordake, Earl of Fife, son of the Regent Albany, three other Scots, Lord Montgomery, Sir

[1] Roskell, *Speakers*, pp. 141–2

William Graham and Sir Adam Forster, and three Frenchmer
Sir John de Heley, Sir Piers Hazars and John Dormy – in
triumphant parade. The prisoners knelt firstly at the entrance t
the hall, secondly in the middle of the hall, and finally in front c
Henry on his throne, after which they were treated it was sai
with the courtesy of chivalry. Most conspicuously absent fror
this ceremony was the Earl of Douglas, prisoner of the younge
Henry Percy. Hotspur refused to obey the King's order to han
over his prisoner, and his refusal was probably followed by
stormy interview between Percy and the King, but no one coul
yet guess that this withholding of prisoners was the first ste]
towards rebellion. Another Scot who was present was Georg
Dunbar, Earl of March, who had fought on the English sid
against his compatriots at Homildon Hill, and now asked tha
his services should be rewarded, but all that he received wa
a promise that he should have possession of his own estates in th
unlikely event of being captured by the English.

The most important business of the Parliament was as always
at least to the King, the grant of money. The Commons suggeste
that all alien priories except the conventual ones, which were ver
few, should be taken into the King's hands, and that Henry
should make no more grants of lands, revenues or annuities
The Commons were evidently aware that Henry had already mad
an exceptionally large number of grants, rewarding his owr
friends, as well as appeasing those of Richard, by confirmin
their grants; and this despite the fact that the first Parliamen
had asked that grants of lands escheating to the Crown and nev
grants of lands and annuities should only be made with the advic
of the council. But a king could hardly bind himself not to rewar
his own friends and supporters, and Henry's reply – that he
would only make grants to deserving cases as agreed by himsel
and his council – was effectively meaningless, involving no
real restriction on his freedom. There was still a suspicion tha
the King had a hoard of money either of his own collecting o
else taken over from Richard II's hidden treasure. The truth tha
he had nothing at all was difficult to prove and impossible fo
the Commons to believe. However, on 24 November they di
grant him the custom and subsidy on wools and woolfells at
the rate of 5os. per sack exported by natives, and 6os. by aliens, fo
a period of three years, and also tunnage and poundage for two

nd a half years from the following 3 April. One fifteenth and
enth was also to be levied from the laity, half to be paid on 2
February 1403 and the other half on 24 June; and the clergy in
onvocation, following the lead of the laity, granted a correspon-
ling clerical tenth. Thus the King had got his money, and got it
vithout the prolonged discussion and nagging criticism which
nost of his Parliaments produced.

Regulations were made about youthful recruits to the orders of
nendicant friars, whose disloyalty had recently been marked,
.nd about the sanctuary of St. Martin-le-Grand. The Commons
>roposed that the Earl of Somerset should resume the title of
narquess, which he had given up in the first Parliament, but
his he declined as being an alien rather than an English title.
Finally on 25 November the Commons asked the King to help
leal the schism in the church, provided always that no charge fell
>n the common people of the realm. This notably unenthusiastic
juggestion regarding the greatest problem of the day brought a
:omparatively quiet session to an end, and displayed the extreme
nsularity of the English Parliament. In the absence of the steward
>f the King's household, the Earl of Northumberland conveyed
he King's invitation to both Lords and Commons to feast with
iim on the next day, Sunday, 26 November, and on that day the
expenditure of the royal household rose from its usual figure
>f about £40 to £182.[1] So it would appear that the members were
well dined. Indeed it was not until Christmas Day that the departments of the royal kitchen again spent so much in a single day.

Henry had passed the time of the Parliament between Westminster and Eltham. He was now beginning preparations to send
for his new wife to be brought from Brittany. In December he
went to St. Albans and Berkhamstead and then to Windsor for
Christmas. By then his two half-brothers, the Bishop of Lincoln
and the Earl of Somerset, who with the Earl of Worcester had
been entrusted with the task of fetching the Duchess, were on
their way to Brittany. They all sailed together from Southampton,
but were forced by wind and weather to put into Plymouth, and
from there they wrote on 9 December asking the council for
more money and further instructions. If eventually they did get
across to Brittany, which is very doubtful, they did not wait
for the Duchess, because they were all three present in the council

[1] P.R.O., E 101/404/21

in London on 20 January, whilst she left Nantes on 26 December, embarked at Camaret on the evening of 13 January and landed at Falmouth, instead of Southampton as had been intended, on 19 January 1403, after five storm-tossed days.[1]

Once the Christmas festivities were over the royal household left Windsor and passed through Easthampstead to Berkshire to spend ten days at Reading and a week at Farnham in Surrey. On 28 January it was at Clarendon in Wiltshire.[2] So far it may be supposed that the King was as usual with his household, but for the next few days the evidence for his movements is somewhat conflicting. The household stayed at Clarendon until 3 February and then moved to Winchester perhaps without its head, for it seems likely that in his eagerness to meet his bride the King had himself by this time left the main body of his household behind. If this were so, he must have set out with a small party, which included his brother-in-law, Sir John Cornewaille, and the ever-faithful John Norbury, immediately on hearing of the Duchess's arrival in Devon, and ridden the ninety miles or so to Exeter. He would then have met her in or near that city towards the end of the month. According to the municipal records of Exeter the King and Queen were royally entertained there by the citizens, who also provided a carriage and horses to take them to Bridport. By this time the Queen, who was accompanied by Nicholas Aldrewich, her daughters, retainers and servants, had probably been joined by Bishop Beaufort and the two earls of her escort.[3] On 3 February the Bishop, the two earls and John Norbury were with her at Dorchester and borrowing money to take her on to Winchester,[4] which suggests that if Henry had joined her at Exeter he had now returned ahead to be ready to welcome her when she arrived at Winchester, thoughtlessly leaving her and her escort without funds meanwhile. What is certain is that by the 5th they were all feasting at Winchester, and that on the 7th Henry Beaufort, the Bishop of Lincoln, who had been entrusted with the duty of escorting his half-brother's bride, completed his

[1] Lobineau, *Hist. de Bretagne*, vol. 1, pp. 502–3
[2] P.R.O., E 101/404/21
[3] Exeter City Receiver's Account Roll, 4–5 Henry IV; Cecily Radford, 'An unrecorded royal visit to Exeter', *Trans. Devon Assoc.* (1931), vol. 63, pp. 255–63
[4] P.R.O., S.C. 1/51/22

task by conducting the marriage ceremony in Winchester Cathedral. 'The expenses of the marriage day at Winchester were put down at £433 6s. 8d. Besides this the Prior of Winchester obligingly lent 200 marks, which had afterwards to be paid from the exchequer. The young Princes, John and Humphrey, had handsomely ordered a pair of tablets from a London goldsmith at a cost of £79, as a present for their new mother. The King's marriage-gift was a collar purchased from a London jeweller for 500 marks (£333 6s. 8d.).[1] Lavish feasting and gifts were a normal part of any wedding and more especially a royal one; extravagance would be expected even of a moneyless king. After the wedding the King and Queen journeyed in state to London, being met at Blackheath by the citizens, and passing by way of Cheapside to Westminster. There the Queen was crowned and given a coronation banquet. Jousts were also held to celebrate the occasion, the Queen's own champion being Richard, Earl of Warwick, who had succeeded his father in 1401, and was now just twenty-one.

On 8 March Queen Joan was granted an income of 10,000 marks a year dating from the day after her marriage. This was to be paid by the exchequer until such time as the King could grant her lands to that value. This he soon began to do, but even so this princely gift was a burden which the royal finances could ill afford, and it remained a burden not only during the rest of the reign, but for most of that of Henry V as well, until in fact her stepson's council charged her with witchcraft, imprisoned her and seized her revenues in 1419. Now, although the first part of the grant of the last Parliament was beginning to come in there were many pressing needs apart from the Queen's dower.

Henry Bowet, Bishop of Bath and Wells, had been replaced as treasurer by Guy Mone, Bishop of St. David's, on 28 October during the session of Parliament. Mone was an experienced administrator who had been keeper of the privy seal to Richard II, but was to prove no more successful as treasurer than his predecessors. All through January and February he was kept busy with the other members of the council examining the status of the alien priories to decide which of them were conventual, and how the King might best profit from the revenues of the others. On 28 February shortly after celebrating the royal marri-

[1] Wylie, *H. IV*, vol. i, p. 310

age, Henry Beaufort, Bishop of Winchester, became chancellor. The first two chancellors of the reign had not been men of out-standing personality or rank, and the council had relied a good deal on the Archbishop of Canterbury, who had not attended the meetings very frequently but was always at hand, and often consulted on the more important matters. But the appointment of Beaufort was bound to make a difference to the Archbishop's position. Beaufort was now about thirty years of age, and had been Bishop of Lincoln for five, a man of royal birth and outstanding ability, although this was not yet so evident as it was later to become. Henceforth he would preside over all the routine meetings of the council, and was not so likely as his more lowly predecessors to rely on referring matters to the Archbishop. A fullish council meeting on 20 January had been attended by the Archbishop, the Bishops of Lincoln, Exeter, still chancellor, St. David's the treasurer, and Rochester, with the Earls of Somerset, Northumberland, Westmorland and Worcester, the keeper of the privy seal, John Scarle, the ex-chancellor, Sir Thomas Erpyngham and Sir John Cheyne. After that most of the meetings were attended only by the chancellor, the treasurer and Scarle, until 5 March when another full meeting is recorded. Then the Bishops of Exeter (no longer chancellor) and Rochester had dropped out, and John Norbury was added. Otherwise the same persons were present as in January.

King and Parliament had been united in their desire to secure the release of Lord Grey, and released he was, although at a cost which impoverished him for the rest of his life. It was other-wise with Mortimer, a great-grandson of Edward III, who might be held to have a better claim to the throne than Henry himself. No efforts were made by the King to secure his release, although the Earl of Northumberland did have the King's permission to communicate with him as a possible intermediary between Glen-dower and the English Government.[1] But nothing came of this. Mortimer shortly married Owen's daughter, and made the Welsh cause his own, whilst Hotspur, whose wife was Mortimer's sister, cherished one more grievance against the King.

On 8 March 1403, a few days before his uncle became chan-cellor, the Prince was made lieutenant in Wales, an appointment which presumably superseded that of the two Percies made on

[1] Lloyd, *Glendower*, pp. 57–8; Nicolas, *P.C.*, vol. ii, pp. 59–60

1 March in the previous year. Within two months he was able
to report some successes. He had led raids into Wales, had captured Glendower's ancestral lands, and taken some notable
prisoners. He had nevertheless to write to the council on 30
May, asking for payment for his men, and pointing out the
urgent need for relieving and provisioning the garrisons of
Aberystwyth and Harlech, which the Welsh had long been
besieging. But King and council, although directing that £1,000
should be sent to pay the Prince's troops, were not prepared for
any immediate action. In the early part of July Glendower was
moving freely about Wales with a large force, and his movements
were reported in a series of surviving letters.[1] On the 3rd he was
at Llandilo and on the 6th the castle and town of Carmarthen
surrendered to him after a short siege.

Richard Kingston, Henry's former treasurer on his foreign
travels, and now Archdeacon of Hereford, had already written
to the King about the perils of the moment in Wales, when the
news of this last disaster drove him to write the following postscript in English:

And for Godes love, my lyge Lord, thinkith on zour' self and zour'
astat, or bemy trowthe all is lost elles; but ze come zoure selfe with
haste all other wolle folwin aftir. And ol on Fryday last Kermerdyn
town is taken and brent and the castell yolden be Richard Wygomor,
and the castell Emelyn is hi zoldin; and slayn of the toune of Kermerdyn mo thanne l. persones. Writen in ryght gret haste on
Sunday; and y crye zow mercy and putte me in zoure hye grace
that y write so schortly; for be my trowthe that y owe to zow, it
is needfull.[2]

Three days later the English position was slightly improved
by Thomas, Lord of Carew in Pembrokeshire, who defeated a
party of Glendower's men in that county. Henry does not seem
to have been worried by the state of affairs in Wales, nor to have
had any suspicion that the Percies were shortly to come out in
open rebellion. The reasons for their discontent remain as much
of a mystery to us as they probably were to the King. No doubt

[1] Lloyd, *Glendower*, pp. 61–70; Ellis, *Orig. Lett.*, vol ii, pp. 14–23; *R. Lett.
H. IV*, pp. 138–51
[2] Ellis, *Orig. Letters* 2nd ser., vol. ii, pp. 17–19, from B.M., Cotton Cleopatra
F III, f. 121b

there was some disagreement with the royal policy in Wales, the Percies both felt that they had received but a very small proportion of the money that was their due, and Hotspur regarded the prisoners of Homildon as his own property to be ransomed and when he chose without royal interference, but above all it seems to have been personal ambition which led the younger Percy to rebel. Too much pride was their fault according to Adam of Usk.[1]

But in the spring things were quiet. After the coronation of the Queen the court went to Eltham, then on a tour of Kent, returning to Eltham for Easter. May and June were spent at Windsor, Easthampstead and Henley-on-the-Heath. Thence they went to London by way of Sutton and Kennington. On 30 May Northumberland wrote to the council from Newcastle-upon-Tyne. He and his son had to be at Ormiston in Roxburghshire on 1 August to receive the surrender of the castle there. He mentioned the labour and expenses which they had both undertaken, and asked that they might be paid what was due to them. Nearly a month later on 26 June he wrote to the King himself from Healaugh in Yorkshire. The King had told him that some money would be sent to him, but had not specified the sum. He asked to be told how much it would be and that it should be sent quickly so that he would not disgrace the chivalry of the realm when he met the Scots, and also dishonour himself and his son. It was not true, as he believed the King had been told, that he and his son had been paid £60,000 since the coronation, and they were certainly owed £20,000. He asked that they should be paid. It was a strong letter, but in no way disrespectful or disloyal to the King. Styling himself 'Your Mathathias' the Earl signed the letter with his own hand. This was not likely to alarm Henry, for he was accustomed by now to the constant demands for money, which he could not satisfy. Its tone does not suggest that the writer is on the verge of rebellion, nor on the other hand does it look like an elaborate deception reassuring the King of the Percies' loyalty. Probably Northumberland had no thoughts of rebellion and would have gone on as before, but for his impatient and impetuous son.

Certainly Henry had no suspicions. He set out northwards from Kennington at the beginning of July, apparently on a normal

[1] *Usk*, pp. 85, 256

summer itinerary, by way of Waltham Abbey, Hertford, Hitchin and Newnham Priory in Bedfordshire to Higham Ferrers on the 10th. From there he wrote to the council. He was glad to be able to report some success of the Prince of Wales, and asked them to send the Prince £1,000. He himself was going to Scotland to assist Northumberland and his son. Thereafter he would hasten to Wales to put an end to the rebellion there. He sent two squires, John Wodehouse to report on the Prince's activities, and Elmyng Leget to report on his own. He then continued on his way to Leicester on the 11th and Nottingham on the 12th. From Nottingham his usual route to the north was through Pontefract, but instead of going there he turned aside, was at Derby on the 13th and 14th, and at Burton-on-Trent on the 15th. This move suggests that by the 12th he had heard rumours of Hotspur's revolt and turned westwards ready to meet it. Three days later at Burton-on-Trent he knew for certain that he was in for trouble.

His letter to the council on the 17th was therefore on a far more urgent note than the leisurely one of a week earlier. Now he had heard that Henry Percy was in revolt in Cheshire, issuing proclamations calling the King 'Henry of Lancaster', and asserting that Richard was still alive. The Earl of Northumberland was also said to be in revolt, and Thomas Percy, Earl of Worcester, the third member of the family, had deserted the Prince at Shrewsbury, and taken part of the Prince's army to join his nephew. The King therefore wanted all members of the council to hasten to join him, except for the treasurer who was to stay behind and try to raise loans. On the letter is a note to the effect that a member of the council, unnamed, had met the messenger hastening south with it on the Wednesday, the day after it was sent. He had opened it, read it, and then despatched it on its way. On the same day Henry ordered the sheriffs of all the midland counties to go with him against Sir Henry Percy, who had, as he said, joined with the Welsh rebels and some of his Scottish enemies. Two courses were now open to the King, to withdraw and wait until he had collected an adequate army to crush the rebels, or to advance quickly in the hope of defeating them before they had time to unite and organise themselves. The more cautious procedure would have left the Prince, now deserted by Worcester, isolated with a small force at Shrewsbury. For Henry the natural policy was the bold one, and this according to the chroniclers was also urged on him by the Scottish Earl of March. Passing through Lichfield he reached Shrewsbury in three days, the speed of his movements surprising Hotspur, who had hoped to secure the town in order to provision his army, and helping to ensure his victory.

According to John Hardyng, Hotspur's own squire (and here this generally untrustworthy writer is not without confirmation from other sources), the Percy candidate for the throne was now the young Edmund, Earl of March, and not Richard, whose death was acknowledged. Hotspur now said that he had been wrong in supporting Henry's claim to the throne, because Henry had sworn at Doncaster that he came only to claim his own inheritance, whilst Richard remained king, with the real authority vested in his council. Henry had not only broken this oath, he had also broken his promises not to exact taxes except in case of dire necessity, he had ordered the sheriffs to return to Parliament only members known to be favourable to himself, and he had refused to ransom the elder Edmund Mortimer, and kept the younger, the rightful king, a prisoner.[1] This is the first time that the famous oath at Doncaster was brought out as a charge against Henry, and its exact nature as well as its very existence remain in doubt, because those chroniclers who do mention it disagree as to its terms, and it was not mentioned at all by chroniclers favourable to the King. According to these last the rebels merely asked for better governance, the employment of wise councillors, and the proper expenditure of the money raised by taxation, which was being spent neither to the worship of God nor the profit of the land.[2] Such demands were no more than those habitually made in Parliament, and hardly constituted grounds for armed rebellion; but the Percies had certainly challenged Henry's title to the crown – whether in support of Richard or the Earl of March made no difference – and the outcome could only be decided by force of arms.

The battle was fought about two miles north-east of Shrewsbury on 21 July. Once again, George Dunbar the Scottish Earl of March urged Henry to attack quickly. A speedy victory was essential because Hotspur was expecting help both from Glendower in Wales, and from his father in the north. For the

[1] Hardyng, *Chron.* pp. 351, 361; Bean, 'H. IV and the Percies', pp. 221–2
[2] Capgrave, *Chron.*, p. 282; *Annales R. II et H. IV*, pp. 362–3

moment his chief supporters were his uncle, and his prisoner, the Earl of Douglas, who was now ready to fight by his side. His own personal following was reinforced by his uncle's men, and by such Cheshire archers and others as he had been able to enlist on his way south. Before attacking, however, Henry had formally to ask the rebels what they were about. He sent the Abbot of Shrewsbury and a clerk of the privy seal office with offers to discuss their grievances, suggesting that Hotspur should come to a personal interview. It was however his uncle, Worcester, whom he sent with the reply, and it has been suggested that Worcester, instead of acting as a mediator, attempted to exacerbate the differences between the two sides, and even failed to convey the King's messages honestly. Certainly nothing came of the negotiations except the determination on both sides to fight the quarrel out.

Hotspur, who had been told by a soothsayer that he would die at Berwick and had naturally thought of Berwick-on-Tweed, was somewhat disconcerted to find that Berwick was the name of the nearest hamlet to his army. However, after the somewhat heated altercation between the King and his uncle he had no alternative but to fight, and as soon as the King gave his men the signal to advance the fire of the Cheshire archers was directed upon them. The Earl of Stafford, to whom Henry had given the command of the vanguard, was killed, and some of his men fled from the field. Sir Walter Blount was one of eight or nine knights, two of them dressed to resemble the King, who were also killed, whilst the Prince was wounded in the face by an arrow. Some of the rebels sensing that victory was within their reach raised the cry of 'Henry Percy, King', a cry which may accidentally have revealed the true object of the revolt, hitherto disguised by the use of the name either of Richard or of the Earl of March, but more probably rose spontaneously from the heat of the moment. In any case it was immediately rendered meaningless by the arrow which killed the leader himself, and the shouts turned to 'Henry Percy, slain.' Without him all was over for the rebel army. Glendower had failed to come to their aid in time. The Earls of Worcester and Douglas were captured with many others, and the remainder fled from the field. On the next day, Sunday, Worcester wept over the body of his nephew, and on the Monday he was executed as a traitor taken in arms against the King, along

with Sir Richard Vernon and Sir Richard Venables. Thank
largely to an unknown archer Henry had won his only full-scal
battle.

On this same day that the second Percy perished, the third
the Earl of Northumberland, was met on his way south by hi
cousin, the Earl of Westmorland and Robert Waterton. There
upon he withdrew to Newcastle-upon-Tyne. The citizens how
ever would admit only the Earl and his household, and no
his armed followers. After staying one night he retired to his
castle of Warkworth. Westmorland then sent Lord Say to the
King, urging him to come north as soon as he could leave Wales, a
far for example as Pontefract, for some people were busy spread
ing rumours and others were riding about the countryside ir
armed bands. He also wanted the King to send siege engines to
enable him to capture the Earl of Northumberland's castles
As to the calling of a Parliament, he said that was a matter for
the King to decide. For Westmorland this was not only ar
opportunity for showing his loyalty, it was also a chance to
destroy, perhaps permanently, the power of his only rival in the
north.

The King did in fact turn northwards almost at once, and was at
Pontefract in the early days of August. Proclamations were
ordered warning everyone that the suppression of rebellion
should not be used as a cover for robbery. The customs collectors
were ordered not to make any more payments to the Percies,
who held many assignments on them, and on 9 August to bring
all their documents before the council. The cancellation of the
debt to the Percies would at least provide some relief to the royal
finances. The King reached York, where the Earl of Northumberland surrendered to him on 11 August.[1] The Earl had to give
up both his castles and the office of Constable of England, which
was given to the King's third son, John, now aged fourteen.
The surrender of Northumberland, who was set at liberty and
restored to his estates some six months later, meant the end of
the rebellion in the north, even though some of his castles still
held out. The King stayed in Yorkshire for about a fortnight
and then decided that it was time to turn once more against
his long-standing enemy in Wales. Levies of all the counties
were ordered to join him at Worcester on 3 September to be

[1] Capgrave, *Chron.*, p. 283

ready to go into Wales. He made his way south through the midlands by Leicester, Lutterworth and Daventry to Woodstock, where he stayed until 2 September, and then went on to meet his army at Worcester.

On the same 3 September Richard Kingston was again writing from Hereford 'in very great haste, at three of the clocke after noon.' This time he signed himself Dean of Windsor, an office to which the King had appointed him in July 1402, although he remained Archdeacon of Hereford until 1404:

War' fore, for Goddesake, thinketh on zour' beste Frende, God, and thanky Hym as Hee hath deservyd to zowe; and leveth nought that ze ne come for no man that may counsaille zoew the contrarie; for, by the trouthe that I schalle to zowe zet, this day the Walshmen supposen and trusten that ze schulle nought come ther', and there fore, for Goddeslove, make hem fals men. And that hit plese zowe of zour hegh Lordeship for to have me excused of my comyng' to zowe, for, yn good fey, I have nought ylafte with me over two men, that they beon sende out with Sherref and other gentils of oure Schire, for to with stande the malice of the Rebelles this day . . . For in god fey, I hope to Al Mighty God that, zef ze come zoure owne persone, ze schulle have the victorie of alle zoure enemys. And for salvacion of zoure Schire and Marches al aboute, treste ze nought to no Leutenant.[1]

Whilst this letter was on its way to Henry he was holding a council at Worcester. There according to the Parliament Roll of the following year the lords renewed their oaths of loyalty to the King, perhaps because the rebellion had cast doubts on the loyalty of some who were not openly concerned in it. Evidently, despite his proclamations, the King was still short of men, and during the week that he spent at Worcester he called on the sheriffs for further proclamations for men to meet him at Hereford, and for others to provide him with victuals. The captains of the Welsh castles were enjoined to guard them safely. At Worcester he had neither money nor supplies enough for an expedition into Wales. The Archbishop and some of the bishops who were at the council pleaded that they could not afford to provide him with money, whereupon some of the knights and squires,

[1] R. *Letters, H. IV.*, vol. i, pp. 158-9; from B.M., Cotton Cleopatra F III, f. 79

whose Lollard sympathies were apparent, suggested that they should take the prelates' horses and their money and send them home on foot. To which Arundel is said to have retorted that any knight who tried to despoil one of his brethren should have as good a knock as ever Englishman had.[1] The King moderated and the Archbishop went off promising to see what he could do. He summoned a convocation of the Canterbury province to St. Paul's and there secured a grant of one and a half tenths, and some loans meanwhile to cover the period until the tenths came in.

On 9 September William, Lord Roos of Hamelake was appointed treasurer, the fifth treasurer to hold office within the four years of Henry's reign. The office clearly presented a thankless and well-nigh hopeless task, but there was always a hope that a new man might have new sources for borrowing, untapped by his predecessors, for the exchequer depended partly on the treasurer's credit, as well as the King's. From Worcester Henry went to Hereford, and after a few days there, he did at last enter Wales once more. He got as far as Carmarthen, but as always Glendower's men kept out of his way, and leaving a garrison there he returned to Hereford. On 8 October the Earl of Somerset, the Bishop of Bath, Thomas Beaufort and Richard Grey wrote from Carmarthen that the King had left them there for a month, and they would like the council to appoint a suitable captain with a force of men-at-arms and archers to come and relieve them. The King went from Hereford to Gloucester and then to Bristol, still hoping to make head against the Welsh despite the lateness of the season. The mayor and citizens of London had advanced £2,000 on the strength of the grant from the clergy, and Henry was still hoping to raise more troops. On 14 October he ordered the Earl of Arundel, Hugh Burnell and Edward Charlton to array an army at Shrewsbury. But none of his plans were successful. On 23 October he wrote from Bristol to the council asking them to issue letters of protection for certain people who were to serve under the Earl of Warwick in the defence of Brecknock, and to the signet letter he added an explanation written in his own hand, and signed 'H.R.', incidentally showing not only that he could write French as well as English, but even excused himself with a Latin tag:

[1] Capgrave, *Chron.*, p. 284

Nessescitas non habet legem. Et pour tant volons que noz lettres de protection soient fais selonc la contenue de cestes noz lettres, considerantz qa cause de guerre move contre nous dedeins nostre reaume nous pourrons fere toutez noz courtez cesser, en sauvacion de noz et nostre reaume.[1]

vidently he did not like placing anyone beyond the reach of ne law, and knew that the council would also be reluctant, ut could see no alternative.

In the interim the Bretons had burnt Plymouth on 10 August 403 and the men of Plymouth had attacked Breton ships off enmarch and Brest. Whatever else it had done the King's narriage had signally failed to improve relations with Brittany. Next year the French also raided Dartmouth and the Isle of Vight. A Parliament was originally summoned to meet at Coventry on 30 November, but there was neither sufficient ood nor lodging there for the members. It was postponed to he New Year and the place was altered back to Westminster. o November saw the King returning to London after his fourth nsuccessful expedition into Wales. It was true that this year te had survived a great danger, suppressed a revolt and pacified he north. But the position was as difficult as ever. The French vere still threatening the south coasts, the rebellion of Owen Glendower still prospered, and the financial position was still lesperate. Lollard doctrines were being widely preached and liscussed.[2] The Archbishop of Canterbury was now attending he council more regularly, perhaps aware of the need to defend he interests of the church, or fearing that Bishop Beaufort peing chancellor, he would not be consulted unless he were ictually present.

On 30 November a great council was held at Westminster, vhen once again the lords renewed their oaths of allegiance, his time in the presence of the heralds of France.[3] If this second enewal of oaths had been rendered necessary by the uncertain-

---

P.R.O. *Catalogue of the Museum* (1948), p. 34. 'Necessity knows no law; nd therefore we wish that our letters of protection be made out in accord-nce with the contents of this letter, seeing that war having been made igainst us in our kingdom we can suspend all our courts, for the safety of ourselves and our realm.'
Capgrave, *Chron.*, p. 280; Walsingham, *Hist. Angl.*, vol. ii, pp. 252–3
Rot. Parl., vol. iii, p. 525

ties following the rebellion of the Percies, it must also have been
painful reminder of some of the events of the last reign. Th
year the King and Queen spent Christmas at Abingdon Abbe
instead of at one of his own manors or castles. It is possib
that the abbey was at least equally comfortable, and there a pa
of the cost would fall on the monks rather than on the roy
finances. On 26 December Henry summoned the Archbisho
the chancellor, the Bishops of Bath and Rochester, Hugh Wate
ton, Sir Arnold Savage and John Norbury to join him at Sutto
in Chiswick, which was a favourite halting-place on the journe
from Windsor to Westminster.

Chapter 12

The year of two Parliaments, 1404

THE councillors summoned by the King to Sutton duly met him there on 11 January 1404. Amongst them was Sir Arnold Savage, the protesting Speaker of the 1401 Parliament. On Monday 14 January the new Parliament met at Westminster, fourteen months after the dissolution of the last one. Of the Commons twenty-three had sat in Parliament during Richard II's reign, thirty-six in the first three Parliaments of the present reign, and thirty-three were, so far as is known, new to Parliament. Bishop Beaufort of Lincoln began his first opening speech as chancellor with the customary introduction. It was the King's will that not only the church, but also the lords, spiritual and temporal, and the cities and boroughs, should continue to enjoy their accustomed liberties. He went on to explain the reason for summoning Parliament, comparing the realm to the human body, and saying that the King needed the advice, counsel and assent of its members. There was first of all the rebellion in Wales, then the threat of attacks by the Duke of Orleans and the Count of St. Pol, the latter having recently raided the Isle of Wight, the dangers to Calais and Guyenne, the wars in Scotland and Ireland, and the recent rebellion of the Percies. All these things considered how was the King to maintain the peace of the realm? The answer of course would be by raising more money, but this was not mentioned. The chancellor ended by enjoining the Commons to be in their places every morning at eight o'clock, and to present their Speaker on the next day before nine.

On Tuesday morning accordingly the Commons presented Sir Arnold Savage, who asked to be excused for several reasons, which were not stated, but the King insisted on his taking office. Whether this had all been carefully rehearsed at the council a few days before, or represented the genuine difficulties of an over-conscientious man cannot be discovered from the record. Savage was earnest and well-meaning and spoke a great deal too much in trying to justify himself, and it may be that he found the

dual role of Speaker and royal councillor too onerous. Certainly
he must have been aware of the growing unpopularity of the
King, especially since his marriage. Forced apparently to accept
office, Savage now begged forgiveness for any offence that his
words might give through ignorance or negligence, asking
that the Commons might criticise the King's government, and
that the King would not take amiss any malignant information
from anyone, to all of which Henry agreed. Finally Savage asked
the chancellor to repeat the King's order to the Commons to
be in attendance in their house, the refectory of Westminster
Abbey, by eight o'clock at the latest each morning. The chancellor
did so, and also charged the Lords to attend likewise.

The chronicler who said that this Parliament lasted for twelve
weeks, and that much was said, but little achieved in it for the
common good, was guilty of only slight exaggeration.[1] It lasted
in fact for 67 days against the 51, 50 and 57 for the first three
Parliaments of the reign, and the opposition to the King was
stronger and more open than before. The first record of the Parliament after the opening business of the session is dated 25 January,
the end of the second week. On that day the Commons referred
to matters discussed at a great council shortly before the previous
Christmas, and then adjourned for the Parliament to consider.
These included the keeping of the seas and the suppression of the
rebellion in Wales. Now the Commons had also examined the
revenues from the customs and other sources, which had, so
they said, suddenly dwindled, and the grants of annuities made
by the King. He had sent the chancellor and the treasurer to the
Commons in the refectory of the abbey to explain the financial
difficulties to them, and especially the costs of defending the
realm and the seas, and maintaining the royal household. Some
questions were answered verbally by the chancellor, and the
treasurer dwelt on the heavy cost of the administration, but other
questions, notably those about Wales, remained unanswered.
The Commons now asked that certain of their members, led by
Savage, should be allowed to consult with the Lords to advise on
these matters, and this was granted.

The Commons urged that the statute against liveries should be
enforced, exceptions being made only for the retinues of the King
himself and of the Prince. Savage called on his colleagues to

[1] *Annales R. II et H. IV.*, p. 378

Letter of Henry IV to his council concerning the Battle of Homildon Hill, 20 September 1402

witness that he was giving the view of the Commons, and not simply his own, as he had been accused of doing in the past. He then complained that the King's manors and castles were in a ruinous state, especially Windsor Castle, that a large number of grants were made neither rightly nor discreetly, and that the cost of the royal household was excessive. The Commons urged that the Lords should be fearless in giving their advice, without dissimulation or adulation, and the King himself with his own voice commanded them likewise. The Commons were ordered to give honest counsel.

So far nothing had been achieved by the voicing of grievances, and the next business dealt with could hardly be very pleasing to the King. This was the consideration of the petition of the Earl of Northumberland. He had already asked the King's pardon at York, for his connivance in the rebellion of his brother and his son. He was now pardoned at the request of the Commons, and took an oath of loyalty to the King. The Commons then persuaded his rival the Earl of Westmorland to make his peace with Northumberland and embrace him. A week later they secured a similar peacemaking between Northumberland and the Scottish Earl of March. Furthermore Archbishop Arundel asked that he, the Duke of York, and others who had been accused of sympathy with the rebels should be declared loyal, and this was done. The rebel Percies and their adherents, unless specifically pardoned by the King, were declared guilty of treason. This was the least that could be expected, and a king who had been obliged to defend his crown in battle might perhaps have hoped for a little more support for himself and a little less enthusiasm for the father of the leading rebel than his Parliament showed.

But loyal support for the King was conspicuously lacking. On the next day, Saturday, 9 February, his household was attacked. The Commons thanked Henry for pardoning the Earl of Northumberland, thanked the Lords for their judgment in his case, and thanked the King also for certain articles to which he had agreed. Oaths of loyalty which had been taken by certain lords and others at great councils in the previous year were then renewed both to the King and to the Prince as heir apparent. The Commons then asked that four persons should be removed from the royal household. One of the four, the Abbot of Dore, was not present, but the other three, the King's confessor, Master Richard

Derham, Warden of King's Hall, Cambridge, and 'Crosseby of the Chamber', came before Parliament. Although as he said he knew of no reason why they should be dismissed, Henry nevertheless agreed to dismiss them from his household. Thereupon the Commons asked for an ordinance of the household to be made, laying down that it should comprise only persons whose loyalty and honesty were known.

The presence of a foreign queen with foreign courtiers had always been unpopular, and had aroused considerable opposition during the two preceding centuries, but it was also true that the fourth year of the reign, 1402–3, had proved an unusually expensive one for the household. The wardrobe of the household, the department which accounted day by day for the cost of food, wine and other provisions for the King and his court, received £25,000 from the exchequer during that year against an average for the reign of about £19,000. The presence of the Queen and her court put up the daily expenses, and in addition £522 had to be found for the wedding feast, and £631 for the Queen's coronation feast. In the ensuing years some reduction in the daily expenditure was achieved, either as a result of the complaints of the Commons, or enforced by actual shortage of cash. Economies were perhaps more obvious in the other two spending departments of the household, the great wardrobe, which was mainly responsible for clothing and liveries of cloth for the King, his court, the judges, and the officers of chancery and exchequer; and the chamber, the funds of which were at the King's personal disposal. The great wardrobe, as in the later years of Richard II, received an average of nearly £10,000 a year from the exchequer during the first four years of the reign, but in some of the later years it had to make do with less than £2,000. The chamber's income of about £5,000 in each of the early years of the reign was very much reduced in the fifth and sixth years, 1403–5, but rose again thereafter.[1]

Foreign affairs were not altogether neglected by this Parliament. On 14 February a letter addressed to the lords spiritual and temporal and the whole community of the realm of France from their opposite numbers in England, about the truce between the two countries, was prepared, and sealed by the two Archbishops, the Bishop of Lincoln, the Abbot of Westminster, the Prince of

[1] P.R.O., E 361/5, 6, 7; E 101/404/13, 20, 21; E 101/405/6: E 403/564–611

Wales, the Duke of York, the Earl of Northumberland, Lord Roos and Arnold Savage, the Speaker,[1] but there is no evidence that it was ever sent, and it is clear that domestic affairs were considered much more important. A dispute between the Prince of Wales and his aunt, Elizabeth, and her husband, Sir John Cornewaille, was settled; and the Prince asked to be allowed the same rights in the duchy of Cornwall, as had been enjoyed by his great-uncle, the Black Prince. The Commons objected to certain provisions in recent commissions of array, and having secured a promise of amendment there returned to their attack on the royal household. A new steward of the household was appointed in the person of Sir Thomas Erpyngham, one of the King's oldest and most loyal comrades. At the same time on 21 February at the instigation of Parliament Henry appointed the Archbishop of Canterbury, Bishop Beaufort the chancellor, the Bishop of Rochester, the Earl of Somerset, chamberlain, the Earl of Westmorland, marshal, Lord Roos the treasurer, and Lord Willoughby, that is all the leading members of his council, to see that all aliens were expelled from the kingdom. The three household officers, Erpyngham, the new steward, Thomas More the treasurer, and Roger Leche the controller, were required to ensure that no livery was made to any aliens in the household. But for the sake of the Queen and her daughters, certain exceptions were made. She was allowed a severely limited foreign establishment, comprising Marie Sante, Nicholas Aldrewich and John Perian, the wives of these last two, Charles de Navarre Montferant, Guillem Arnaud, 'Demoiselle Peronelle', two valets and one maid, and for her daughters, two squires, one nurse and one valet, or fifteen persons in all. Also Antony Ricz was to be allowed to go backwards and forwards between England and Brittany, but not to stay permanently.

Having given way to all the demands of the Commons for controlling his household, the King might perhaps have hoped to receive some financial concessions in return. But the Commons were still on the aggressive. They pointed out that the King had all the revenues of the Crown, and of the duchy of Lancaster, the profits of some forfeited lands and of wardships, as well as the revenues from the customs and subsidies, which had greatly

[1] H. G. Richardson and G. O. Sayles, 'Parliamentary documents from formularies', *Bull. I.H.R.* vol. xi, (1933–4), pp. 160–2

increased during Richard II's reign. He could hardly expect them to grant him direct taxes as well. Henry replied that he still needed a grant for defence, and could not agree with the Speaker that such a grant would enable the customs to be reduced. Finally on Saturday, 1 March, Archbishop Arundel, on the King's instructions, put proposals first before the Lords and afterwards before the Commons. These proposals probably embodied the compromise which was the Archbishop's own suggestion. the common law was to be maintained without any exceptions being granted to individuals under the signet or the privy seal, or in any other way. The royal household was to be well regulated, and it was to be provided with the rather modest sum of £12,100 out of certain revenues specially assigned for the purpose.

The grant of taxation was then made in an original form. Twenty shillings to be levied from each knight's fee, and one shilling from each pound's worth of land, goods and other sources of income. Half was to be paid at Whitsun and the other half at All Saints (1 November). The Commons insisted that no record should be kept of this tax, lest it should be used as a precedent, and not only were the records destroyed, but no mention of the tax was even made on the Parliament Roll. The last experiment in taxation, the poll-taxes, had ended disastrously in 1381, and this appears to have been another attempt to escape from the full rigour of the fifteenths and tenths, which proved much too efficient a tax from the point of view of the payers as represented in Parliament. The Commons made it clear that they trusted neither the exchequer nor the royal household. The proceeds of this novel tax were therefore to be paid to four treasurers of war, who were also to receive that part of the wool subsidy not allocated to the royal household or the payment of debts. These treasurers, who were to ensure that the money was spent on the objects for which it was intended and were to be accountable for it, were appointed on 25 March, a few days after the end of the Parliament. Two of them were exchequer officials, Master John Oudeby and John Haddeley, clerk, and the other two London citizens, Thomas Knolles and Richard Merlawe.

Meanwhile the Parliament concluded with other important business. Alien priors of conventual priories were ordered to give sureties for their loyalty, and other French-born priors were to be expelled from the country. As he had perhaps done in 1401 the King gave Parliament the names of his continual council, and for the first time these were recorded on the Roll of the Parliament. Thus the membership of the council was for the first time formally defined, although the King was clearly not bound in any way by his statement. He could still vary the membership whenever he chose. The Commons no doubt hoped that by fixing responsibility they were ensuring better government. The members now named were in fact mainly those who had been councillors from the beginning of the reign: the Archbishop of Canterbury, the Bishops of Lincoln (chancellor), Rochester, Worcester, Bath and Bangor, the Duke of York, the Earls of Somerset and Westmorland, Lord Roos, the treasurer, the keeper of the privy seal, the Lords Berkeley, Willoughby, Furnival and Lovell, and Peter Courtenay, Hugh Waterton, John Cheyne, Arnold Savage, knights, John Norbury, John Doreward and John Curson, twenty-two in all. The succession to the crown was declared to belong to the Prince of Wales and his heirs, followed by his brothers and their heirs in turn. The behaviour and privileges of alien merchants in England were regulated by statute, and two cases arose in which the Commons were able to assert their own privileges. The sheriff of Rutland was committed to the Fleet prison, after his case had been examined in Parliament, for failing to return Thomas Thorp, elected in full county court, as one of the knights for that county; and penalties were ordained for assaulting the servants of members during the time of Parliament as a result of the injuries suffered by Richard Chedder, an esquire of Thomas Brook, one of the members for Somerset. Of the many private petitions that were granted the most important was that of the Queen, who asked that she should have £4,963 11s. 2d. still outstanding from her grant of 10,000 marks. After all this business Parliament at last came to an end on 21 March.

The end of such a humiliating session must have been very welcome to the King. Instead of being received in triumph as the victor of Shrewsbury, he was upbraided for the misdoings of his Government, and had repeatedly to submit to the will of the Commons. His enemy, Northumberland, was quickly forgiven. His household, and especially his wife's entourage, were attacked, and he gave way. He had to name the members of his council, and the strange and very limited grant which the Commons did make was entrusted to special war treasurers, for fear that the King might get hold of it for his own expenses. Moreover the Commons further insisted that no record of the grant should be kept, lest they be asked to repeat it. That this grant, so absurdly veiled in secrecy, was quite inadequate is evident from the fact that within seven months Henry was meeting another Parliament, for after such a session it is impossible to believe that anything but sheer necessity would have persuaded the King to meet Parliament again within the year.

When Parliament ended the Michaelmas term at the exchequer was already over, and the Easter term was quite exceptionally inactive. None of the usual payments of annuities or grants was made. Issues from the exchequer totalled only about £8,000 of which £2,000 went to the royal household, and the remainder for the payment of debts, and the salaries of judges, the officers of chancery and exchequer and other employees of the Crown. Apart from this the four war treasurers were responsible for spending £6,500.[1] These figures may be compared with the £40,000 to £50,000 which was the normal total of issues for the Easter term, and in fact it was almost Christmas before payments out of the exchequer began to return to their usual frequency.

As soon as the Parliament was over Henry withdrew to Eltham for a week or more, spending Easter, 30 March, there. He then returned to London, and spent some days at the Tower, which still served as an occasional residence. Convocation met at St. Paul's and proved less obstructive than Parliament, granting a tenth, which was to be collected at Martinmas (11 November) and the feast of St. John the Baptist (24 June), on condition that the King promised to defend the privileges of the church. He then left London for Windsor, and went on by way of Woburn, Leicester, Nottingham and Doncaster to the Lancastrian stronghold of Pontefract, where he spent three weeks or more from 17 June onwards. There on 24 June after several summonses the Earl of Northumberland came to the King bringing his three grandsons. Another visitor to the court was Sir William Clifford who brought with him Serle, the alleged murderer of the Duke of

[1] P.R.O., E 403/579

Gloucester, the King's youngest uncle. William Serle, who had been devoting himself to Richard's cause in Scotland, and had surrendered to Clifford at Berwick-on-Tweed, was now condemned as a traitor, to be drawn by horses through various cities and towns, before final execution at Tyburn.[1]

Meanwhile a French force invading the Isle of Wight demanded tribute for the expenses of Queen Isabel. Harry Pay, a notorious Devonshire pirate, had some successes against the French, but they nevertheless landed at Dartmouth, from where they were driven off with considerable losses, peasants and even women joining in attacking them. The Lord of Castellis was killed. Towards the end of May the Earl of Somerset, who was Captain of Calais, captured some Spanish ships in the straits. On 23 April the council authorised payments by the treasurers of war to certain persons for the defence of the realm, including Sir Thomas Beaufort, the admiral for the northern parts, and citizens of Bristol for arming ships, and preparing them for victualling castles in Wales. At the same time messengers had been sent out to raise loans and to arrange for the collection of the subsidy granted in Parliament. Two days later the council discussed the answer to be given to the ambassadors of Denmark about the marriage of the King's daughter Philippa, which they wished to postpone for the moment, probably because there were no funds to pay for it. They also discussed a number of other matters for all of which money was needed, the possibility of sending the help for which Bordeaux was asking, the embassy from Prussia, the keeping of the sea, and the governance of Wales.

The Prince had now been entrusted with the subjugation of Wales, having as his lieutenants, the Duke of York in South Wales, and the Earl of Arundel in the north. Glendower, however, was still prospering. He captured the two towns of Harlech and Aberystwyth after long sieges, thus securing strong points in which to store his supplies, and was even able to hold a 'Parliament' of his own in this year, at which representatives from Scotland, France and Castile were present. On 10 June the sheriff and gentry of Herefordshire wrote to the council to report a Welsh raid and ask for help in defending the county. On the 26th the Prince of Wales wrote to his father from Wor-

[1] *Cal. Close* (1402–5), p. 354

cester confirming the news of this Welsh raid, reporting on the strength of the Welsh, whom he would do his best to defeat, but asking for assistance and money. He wrote to the council in the same terms on the same day, and again five days later to say that without aid he could not continue the struggle. To Archbishop Arundel he wrote separately, asking him to inter- vene with the King, who had sent him to Worcester. The Prince said he was paying all his expenses himself and had been obliged to pawn his plate. In July he was writing again to say that he was supporting all the men who were defending Herefordshire, and was still in urgent need of money. The Duke of York, who had given good service, had gone to the King at Leicester, to explain their needs.[1]

At the same time envoys of Glendower were negotiating for help from France; and the mother of Richard's favourite, Robert de Vere, Maud Countess of Oxford, was believed to be trying to persuade the Duke of Orleans and the Count of St. Pol to land a force in Essex to support the cause of Richard and Isabel, his queen. There was much plotting, especially amongst the dis- contented religious, but nothing came of it, and Isabel mean- while was so sure of Richard's death that she became engaged to Charles of Angoulême, son of the Duke of Orleans. The Countess of Oxford was sent to the Tower, but eventually pardoned, as were the three Abbots of Byleigh, Colchester and St. Osyth, and a number of other religious and laymen, all of whom were tried for, or at least charged with, treason at Colchester.

When the Duke of York went to Leicester to report to the King on the situation in Wales, Henry was on his way back from Pontefract, where he and his council had been negotiating with the Earl of Northumberland. The Earl finally agreed on 9 July to hand over his castle of Berwick on certain conditions. Most of the royal councillors were present to witness the agreement. In addition to the royal seals, those of the Archbishop of York, the Bishop of Lincoln the chancellor, Lord Roos the treasurer, the keeper of the privy seal, Lord Grey the chamberlain, Lord Willoughby, Sir Thomas Erpyngham the steward, the Abbot of Leicester, the King's confessor, Roger Leche controller of the household, John Norbury and John Curson, were also affixed to

[1] Nicolas, *P.C.*, vol. i, pp. 223–5; *Anglo-Norman Letters*, pp. 359–60, 355–6

the agreement, which was confirmed at Lichfield on 27 August. After a long stay at Pontefract Henry had made his way to Leicester by the end of July, then curved southwards through the midlands, and come to Lichfield in the second half of August. At Lichfield he met his council again to discuss the financial position. Orders were sent to the sheriffs and other royal officers to stop paying annuities until further instructed by the council, the exchequer, as already said, having stopped making any such payments since Easter. This was an admission of bankruptcy. The grant made by the last Parliament and a number of loans raised by the exchequer during the summer had not saved the situation, and now it was decided to summon another Parliament to meet at Coventry in October.

Repayment of the loans from the wool subsidy and the clerical tenth was promised by the council which also suggested that £2,000 due from the county of Chester should be allotted to the Prince for his expenses, that the county of Salop should be allowed to make a truce with the Welsh until the end of November, that the Prince should remain in Herefordshire to defend it with the same forces that he already had, and that at the beginning of October he should be ready to ride into Wales with a force of 500 men-at-arms and 2,000 archers, and stay there for twenty-one days to chastise the rebels. Certain castles were to be garrisoned.

The council was also informed that sixty ships had been assembled at Harfleur laden with men-at-arms and supplies ready to go to the help of Owen Glendower in Wales, and therefore decided that letters should be sent to certain people on the south coast, Lord Berkeley, the admiral, Sir Philip and Sir Peter Courtenay, John Hawley, John Bolt and Henry Pay, urging them to intercept the French, or oppose them as best they could. Signet letters to this effect were despatched on 29 August. There were not sufficient forces available to accompany the King into Wales, and he was therefore advised to stay at Tutbury or thereabouts until the meeting of Parliament in October. The Bishop of Coventry was asked to lend a hundred marks, and the customers of Bristol to send provisions to the town and castle of Carmarthen, to enable them to be held against the rebels. Henry accordingly spent the month of September at Tutbury Castle, or at least not very far from it, and arrived at Coventry on 5 October in time for the Parliament which had been summoned for the following day.

The writs had laid down that no lawyers should be returned to this Parliament, because, it was alleged, lawyers were apt to devote their time to their own or their clients' business, rather than to the King's. Hence it was known as the Unlearned Parliament, but in fact it is difficult to discover any way in which its members differed from those of other Parliaments. The session was opened at Coventry on Monday, 6 October 1404. Bishop Beaufort as chancellor began with the same words as in the last Parliament concerning the maintenance of the liberties of the church, and of the lords, the cities and the boroughs. The King, he went on, needed counsel to deal with the Welsh rebels, and with his enemies of France, Brittany and elsewhere. Contrary to normal usage he immediately mentioned money, saying that the grant made in the last Parliament was not, as had been supposed at the time, sufficient. But for this the Lords and Commons might be surprised to find themselves recalled so soon, but the King was receiving news day to day of the attacks of his enemies. He had just heard of a new attack in Guyenne, and matters were urgent. On the next day the Commons presented as their Speaker Sir William Sturmy, an experienced member, who was now representing Devonshire. He had been for some time a royal councillor, and served the King on a number of diplomatic missions. He made the usual protestation, and the King accepted him and promised to excuse his mistakes. Then the chancellor urged the Commons to get on with the consideration of grants of supply, fixing their times of meeting at one hour earlier than usual, the Commons to be in their places at seven and the Lords at eight o'clock in the morning.

The knights of the shire were however in no great hurry to give their own money to the King. First they seem to have discussed confiscating the wealth of the clergy. Lollard feeling was strong, and we are told that many people, including some of the King's own household, failed to reverence the Host in the streets of Coventry. If this Parliament earned the title of 'Unlearned' it was in the eyes of the clergy not so much because of the exclusion of lawyers, as for their attacks on the Church. The chroniclers' story of the altercations between the Speaker and the Archbishop is somewhat muddled by the fact that the Speaker is called

Sir John Cheyne, and this well-known Lollard knight was certainly not Speaker, and is not known to have sat in Parliament after 1399. The Archbishop is said to have spent his nights in prayers and tears. He summoned his colleague of York and other bishops and lords to his aid. Certainly anti-clericalism was rife, and the Commons suggested that the temporalities should be taken for one year. The Archbishop lectured them, and Richard Young, the newly-elected Bishop of Rochester threatened excommunication. Finally the Commons gave way, and some of them sought absolution for their attack on the Church.[1] On 12 November, after just over a month of debate, a grant was made to the King, and when at last it came it was a generous one, two whole fifteenths and tenths. The first was to be payable at Christmas, and the two halves of the second on 24 June and 11 November in the next year, 1405. The Commons also granted 43s. 4d. on each sack of wools or 240 woolfells exported by native merchants, and 53s. 4d. on similar exports by aliens, with 106s. 8d. on each last of leather, for two years from the coming Michaelmas, and likewise tunnage and poundage for the same period. All these grants were to be paid to two new war treasurers, Lord Furnival and Sir John Pelham, who were named to replace the four previously appointed. On no account were tallies for anything except the purposes of war to be levied against these grants. Then the lords for themselves and their ladies and other temporal persons with more than 500 marks annual revenue from land, granted 20s. on each £20 of land to be levied at Christmas and 24 June in the next year. This small tax which did not bring in very much revenue looks like an effort by the magnates to appease the Commons, who no doubt felt that too large a share of the taxes was paid by them. As before it was emphatically stated that the grants were not to be taken as a precedent, and the two new war treasurers then swore before the King and Lords in Parliament to execute their office in accordance with the conditions laid down in Parliament.

Certain lords then lent money for the rescue of Sir Alexander Berkrolles, the Lord of Coity, who was besieged in his castle by the Welsh. The money was to be paid to John Curson, and the lenders who were spiritual lords were to have it allowed out of the next tenth granted by the clergy, whilst those who were lay

[1] Walsingham, *Hist. Angl.*, vol. ii, pp. 264–7; Capgrave, *Chron.*, pp. 287–8

lords were to be allowed it out of the 20s. on each £20 of revenu
from land, which they had just granted. On 26 October th
Commons had requested the King to honour his sons, th
Prince and Thomas, making them dukes, or duke and earl
and to give more possessions to John and Humphrey, but th
King was reluctant to grant any new honours. Doubtless h
remembered Richard's lavish distributions, which had brough
both the King and the 'little Dukes' into contempt. The Common
also asked him to reward the Duke of York for his great labour
in Guyenne, and not to forget the Earl of Somerset, and hi
brother Thomas Beaufort.

To the more vital petitions about financial regulations Henr
took the unusual step of replying in English, perhaps considerin
this more appropriate than the normal French for an 'unlearned
Parliament. In order that he might the better be able to live of hi
own, the ideal of all medieval Parliaments, they wanted al
grants made since the fortieth year of Edward III to be resumed
The King and his advisers were no doubt aware of the numbe
of complications to which this would give rise, and all he pro
mised was an enquiry to find out what these lands were, an
what would be involved. He did however agree that all annuitie
should be suspended for one year from Easter last until Easte
next, a step which had already been taken by the exchequer
and commanded of sheriffs and other royal officers. The salarie
of the officers of chancery and exchequer, the judges and othe
public servants were exempted. The Queen and the King'
sons were likewise exempt. The Prince of Wales who had been
granted 1,000 marks for Wales at the council at Lichfield in
August asked that the second half of this sum should be paid.
He was promised both this and sufficient funds to pay his forces
in the future. The Parliament ended on 14 November, and al
were no doubt glad to hurry away from Coventry, where an
outbreak of dysentery had resulted from the overcrowding of the
little town.

On 25 November the convocation of the Canterbury province,
following the lead of Parliament, granted the King one and a
half tenths from the clergy. A stormy autumn brought great
floods to the estates of the Archbishop and the cathedral of
Canterbury, and also at Calais. More ominous for the King was
the desertion of John Trevor, Bishop of St. Asaph, who after

supporting him almost from his landing now went over to the rebel Owen Glendower. Henry returned slowly to London, and then went to Eltham to spend one more Christmas. A special council was summoned to London to discuss the difficulties in Guyenne.

Chapter 13

The Hanse, Northumberland, Scrope and Glendower, 1405

ONE of the less controversial decisions of the Parliament of
Coventry was to send an embassy consisting of Sir William
Sturmy, the Speaker, Master John Kington, a senior chancery
clerk, and William Brampton, fishmonger and alderman of
London, on an embassy to Prussia and the Baltic towns of the
Hanse. The Baltic trade was vital both to England and to Prussia
and the Hanseatic towns, but its conduct led to constant friction.
In exchange for English wool, or cloth made from it, the northern
states sent to England fish, principally herring and dried cod,
large quantities of furs, timber for shipbuilding and bowstaves,
pitch, tar and even grain. Some of the wine from Guyenne also
found its way to the north. By the end of the fourteenth century
the league of German and north European cities, known as the
Hanse, had emerged as a political power, though handicapped by
the great number of its members and the lack of any central
authority. Its main object was to secure and preserve for its
members a monopoly of the trade of the Baltic and North Sea.
In England they enjoyed considerable privileges from the time
of Edward I. Their colony of the Steelyard – on the site which
is now occupied by Cannon Street station – in London was
largely self-governing, and other settlements were established at
King's Lynn, Boston and Hull. The other power in north
Europe, to which some of the Hanse cities were subject, was
the Order of Teutonic Knights, which, originally a crusading
order, had become the ruler of large tracts of Prussia and the
Baltic lands, under its High Master, who was elected for life by
the knights.

On his accession Henry confirmed the privileges of the German
merchants in England, but added three conditions: that English
merchants should be allowed to traffic with equal freedom in
Germany, that the Master of Prussia and the Hanse towns
should send envoys to the English council before midsummer
1400 to make restitution for injuries done to English merchants,

and lastly that the Hanse should not introduce strangers to England without authentic letters under the seal of the towns. Both sides had long lists of ships detained and goods seized in almost every year back to 1393, but settlement was put off and trade went on. Two envoys of the Grand Master arrived in England in the summer of 1403, with a claim for over £6,000 for damages suffered by the Prussians at the hands of the English,[1] and on 29 September concluded an agreement with the chancellor and treasurer of England. All ships taken from the Prussians with their cargoes, if still intact, were to be returned forthwith, and all goods which could not be so restored to be paid for. Compensation for 'persons thrown overboard or slain in the sea' was to be settled between the King and the Grand Master. Trade was to continue normally until the following Easter, to allow time for negotiation. In June 1404 Henry sent a letter by a merchant of King's Lynn, John Brown, promising to send ambassadors to treat with the Grand Master, but asking that normal trade should continue meanwhile.[2] The Germans however were getting impatient; in January and again in June 1404 the Hanse towns meeting at Bruges complained of the seizure of their ships, and of the losses inflicted on them by the English, and on 5 June the Senate of Hamburg had a similar complaint. Correspondence went on between Henry and the various German authorities.[3] On 16 October Konrad von Jungingen, the Grand Master, decided to expel the English from Danzig, and to limit their trade in the future. This was the moment at which the Coventry Parliament decided to send an embassy to the Baltic, but it was not until 2 April 1405 that Henry summoned the three chosen ambassadors to meet him at St. Albans to receive instructions for their journey.

Sturmy and Kington had already been on several embassies for Henry. In 1401 they went first with Robert Waterton to the Duke of Guelders, and afterwards into Germany. In 1402 they were sent to arrange for the payment of the dowry of the King's daughter, Blanche, and for her journey to Germany for

---

[1] Hist. MSS. Comm., *Fifth Report (D & C. of Canterbury)*, p. 443, nos. M 303, M 201, K 8, X 9; Hakluyt, *English Voyages*, vol. i, pp. 128, 150–7; Kunze, *Hanseakten*, pp. 223–5, 265

[2] Hakluyt, *English Voyages*, vol. i, pp. 133–8

[3] R. *Letters, H. IV*, vol. i, pp. 208–9, 238–9, 242–4, 251–408

her marriage. Early in 1404 Sturmy was in Rotterdam negotiating
with Flemish merchants, whilst Kington was taking part in
discussions with the ambassadors of Prussia.[1] The third member
of the party, William Brampton, was perhaps the most prominent
of the merchants of London experienced in trade with the northern seas. They left London at the end of May and after nine
weeks arrived in Marienburg to begin two months of hard
bargaining. Finally they secured freedom for English merchants
to trade in Prussia, and most of the claims and counterclaims for
damages were postponed for consideration at Dordrecht in the
following year. Brampton then set off for home, and was apparently shipwrecked on the way, losing all his papers, whilst
the other two visited the chief cities of the Hanse, Griefswald
Stralsund, Lübeck, Hamburg, Bremen and Dordrecht, negotiating
agreements in each place. They got back to London on 17
February 1406, and Brampton did not arrive until a month
later.[2]

The ambassadors returned just in time to report their success to
the next Parliament, where it was no doubt the more welcome
for coming after another year of very limited achievement. At
the beginning of the year 1405 the outlook for Henry was as
gloomy as ever. In Wales the Prince and the other English
commanders seemed barely able to hold their own against
the rebels. The duchy of Guyenne was in imminent danger from
the French, the Channel was still at the mercy of Breton and French
pirates, and in the north of England the Earl of Northumberland,
father and brother of rebels, was able to treat with the King
almost on equal terms. To strengthen his position the King
needed men, and for men money; but the Coventry Parliament
had spread its grants over the year 1405 so that there could hardly
be an occasion for asking for more, and the grants themselves
were already allocated before collection, through special treasurers, appointed with the avowed purpose of preventing the King
from laying his hands on them.

[1] J. S. Roskell, 'Sir William Sturmy', *Trans. Devon. Assoc.* vol. 89 (1957),
p. 82; P.R.O., E 364/36 m. A; Rymer, *Foedera*, vol. viii, pp. 253-4; R. *Letters*,
H. IV, vol. i, pp. 99-101; *Lit. Cant.*, vol. iii, pp. 78-9; Nicolas, *P.C.*, vol. i,
p. 223
[2] P.R.O., E 364/39 m.E; Hakluyt, *English Voyages*, vol. i, pp. 130, 139-50;
Kunze, *Hanseakten*, pp. 216, 217; *Hanserecesse*, vol. v, pp. 189, 194, 374

Great Seal of Henry IV
(Majesty side)

Effigies of Henry IV and Joan of Navarre on the tomb in Canterbury Cathe

In January 1405 the council was discussing the problem of Guyenne, whither it was proposed to send the Earl of Somerset with 2,000 men-at-arms and 3,000 archers, and the victualling of the Welsh castles.[1] The Prince wrote to his father from Hereford. He had heard that the rebels were assembling at Builth to attack Herefordshire, and asked for help to repel them. A few days later the Earl of Arundel wrote from Oswestry where he was stationed with 30 men-at-arms and 150 archers, saying that unless he received some reinforcements he would soon have to withdraw from the castle there. In March the news from Wales was a little better. The Prince again writing to Henry from Hereford was able to report that a small force which he had despatched under Lord Talbot, Sir William Newport and Sir John Greyndour, had defeated a larger force of Welshmen who had been ravaging Monmouthshire. The King received the news at Berkhamstead and passed it on to the council in London. Soon afterwards Griffith, the eldest son of Glendower, was captured by Lord Grey of Codnor, whilst attacking Usk. He was sent to the Tower and died there six years later. Owen's brother was killed in the same skirmish, making it a disastrous day for the rebel leader.

The four Bishops of Hereford, Rochester, London and Winchester had died during the year 1404. At London the death of Robert Braybrooke, who had been bishop for more than twenty years, enabled a place to be found for Roger Walden. Walden had been given the see of Canterbury by Richard II in place of the exiled Arundel, and driven out of it on the accession of Henry IV, but evidently neither Arundel nor the King wished to keep him out of the episcopate, and he was allowed to spend the last year of his life as Bishop of London. He died early in 1406 to be succeeded by Nicholas Bubwith, then keeper of the privy seal. Most important of the vacancies however was that at Winchester caused by the death of the aged servant of Edward III, William of Wykeham, on 27 September 1404. To this, probably the richest of all the episcopal sees, the King's half-brother, the chancellor, Henry Beaufort, was translated from Lincoln. He was destined to occupy it for forty-two years, even longer than the thirty-seven years of his predecessor, and to play a leading part in English politics for almost the whole of that

[1] Nicolas, *P.C.*, vol. i, pp. 244-5

time. The first result however was his resignation of the chancellorship, in which he was succeeded by Thomas Langley,
keeper of the privy seal and Dean of York, on 28 February 1405.
Eighteen months later Langley also secured a fat bishopric, the
see of Durham. His elevation left the privy seal office free for
Nicholas Bubwith, who had been King's secretary in 1402, and
since then keeper of the rolls of chancery, but he only retained
the privy seal for eighteen months until he became Bishop of
London.

Another prelate who was now approaching his end was Henry
Despenser, Bishop of Norwich since 1370, and now in his sixties.
From his zeal in suppressing the revolt of 1381 and crusading in
Flanders he had come to be known as the fighting Bishop, but
he never seems to have reconciled himself to Henry's occupation
of the throne. In the first years of the reign he was repeatedly
summoned to the King's presence, and constantly excused himself, but never openly rebelled. Instead he devoted himself to a
dispute with the townsmen of Lynn, where his officers failed to
repair a staithe and distrained goods in the market. Commissions
were appointed to enquire into the rights of the affair, and the
King had to intervene to protect the town. Although he enjoyed
the friendship of the King's sister, Philippa, the old Bishop was
evidently a nuisance to Henry, and his death in August 1406
cannot have been unwelcome.[1] Nor did the election of the prior
Alexander Tottington in his place please the King, who had the
Bishop-Elect imprisoned in Windsor Castle for a year, before
Arundel persuaded him to recognise the election.

In the middle of February 1405 a son was born to the King's
other sister and Sir John Cornewaille, and baptised by the Abbot
of St. Albans, Henry acting as godfather, but other events were
not so pleasing to the King. The young Edmund, Earl of March,
and Roger his brother, the great-grandsons of Lionel, Duke of
Clarence, whose claim to be the heirs of Edward III and Richard
II was too obvious to be comfortable to Henry, were being kept
at Windsor during the winter in the charge of Constance, Lady
Despenser, sister of the Duke of York. In the middle of February
they were taken from Windsor, Constance and her son going

[1] Nicolas, *P.C.*, vol. i, pp. 165–8; *Anglo-Norman Letters*, pp. 45–7, 53, 372;
Cal. Close (1399–1402), pp. 166, 272; (1402–5) pp. 358, 384; *Cal. Pat.* (1401–5),
p. 274

with them, and the party made for South Wales, the lands of the Despensers and the Mortimers. Henry himself set off in pursuit, but they were captured near Cheltenham and brought back to him. On the 17th Lady Despenser was brought before the council in London, whereupon she not only accused her brother, the Duke of York, of planning the escape of the boys, but also of having plotted to kill the King at Eltham during the previous Christmas festivities. The story seems to be an echo of the plot of 1400; the times were full of treason. York was arrested and sent to the Tower, but released after a few months, and restored to his dignities in the Parliament of the following year. Thomas Mowbray, known as Earl Marshal, the nineteen-year-old son of the late Duke of Norfolk, confessed that he knew of the plot, but he was pardoned, and even Archbishop Arundel asked to be cleared of the suspicion of complicity.

Henceforth the two Mortimer boys were well guarded, but harmony was not immediately restored. In councils held at London and St. Albans the lords continued to dispute with each other, and with the King, to whom they declined to make any grant of money.[1] There was a great deal for Henry and his council to discuss, though the subjects were not new. The war against the Welsh, the garrisoning of the castles there, and arrangements for the defence and administration of Bordeaux and Guyenne were evidently considered in great detail. Letters had to be sent to Prince John and the Earl of Westmorland, who since the rebellion of the Percies had shared the command on the Scottish border. Finally there was the mission of the Bishop of Bangor, Richard Aston, Nicholas de Ryssheton and Thomas Pickworth, who had gone as ambassadors to treat with the Flemings. On 5 April Robert Thorley, the treasurer of Calais, one of the most important financial officers of the Crown, was suddenly relieved of his post, a symptom perhaps of the general uneasiness and mistrust prevailing in the administration. The treasurer of England, Lord Furnival, was temporarily empowered to act in his place, and the customs collectors were forbidden to hand over any money to Thorley.[2]

If there was nothing that Henry could do about his baronage, a number of whom seemed to be discontented if not disloyal,

---

[1] Walsingham, *Hist. Angl.*, vol. ii, p. 268
[2] *Cal. Close* (1402–5), p. 439

he could at least attack his open enemies in Wales. He left St
Albans towards the middle of April to spend Easter and the feas
of St. George at Windsor. Once that was over he marched rapidl
westwards. Commissions of array had been issued to all th
sheriffs on the 3rd calling on all knights, squires and fencibl
men to prepare themselves to march against the King's enemies.
Henry was at Wycombe on 24 April, Oxford on the 26th, Wood
stock on the 27th and 28th, Chipping Norton on the 29th
Evesham on the 30th, and Worcester on 1 May. From almost ever
place he wrote to the council in London. At Worcester he stayec
for about a fortnight, preparing yet once again for an invasion o
Wales. Meanwhile his son, Thomas, as admiral, was writing
from Sandwich to the council asking for the payment of his men
However, there were some successes to report. On the night o
12 May the Count of St. Pol attacked the fortress of Marck ir
the pale of Calais. The Calais garrison counter-attacked. Some
French ships were driven off, and the coast of Normandy ravaged,
but these were minor matters, the real crisis was to come.

On 9 and 15 May the council found it necessary to write to the
sheriffs of all the counties of England, telling them to make proclamations against the circulation of lying rumours, and ordering
the arrest of rumour-mongers, which shows that a general state
of uncertainty prevailed. On the 10th the council discussed the
raising of loans. About the 14th the King moved to Hereford,
ready to strike into the heart of Wales, but he had not been there
very long when he received a lengthy letter from the council.
They acknowledged the receipt of his letter dated at Worcester
on the 8th. They were glad to hear of the King's good health, and
assured him that they also were well. As he had said that it lay
near his heart to have full knowledge of how the affairs of their
government had progressed since his departure they were pleased
to tell him. They had raised a loan for Prince Thomas, who should
be in his ship with his retinue by the following Thursday, and
also one for Calais, from the command of which the Earl of
Somerset, the King's half-brother, had been forced by ill-health
to return to England. They were still trying to raise a loan for
Guyenne, and hoped to do so before Sir Thomas Swynbourne,
who was preparing an expedition, sailed for Bordeaux. As for
his own troops for the expedition to Wales they had payment for a

[1] *Cal. Close* (1402–5), p. 503

quarter year, by assignment of £1,000 to the treasurer of his household. The Prince of Wales had agreed to take an assignment on the half fifteenth payable at the coming feast of St. John the Baptist (24 June), and they suggested that the King should ask the commanders in South Wales, the Lords Abergavenny and Grey and Sir Thomas Beaufort, to be satisfied with similar assignments. They were hoping that Sir Thomas Pickworth would undertake the governance of Jersey, and Sir John Lisle of Suffolk that of Guernsey. They also forwarded letters of Sir John Pelham about the need for repairs to the castle of Pevensey.

After all that came the ominous part of the letter. The council had learnt from members of the council of Prince John and other reliable sources in the north that Thomas, Lord Bardolf had quietly made off towards the north, which surprised them since, as they thought, he had been ordered to join the King ready to go into Wales. Bardolf, who had always been a close ally of Northumberland, had strongly opposed the granting of any money to the King in the recent councils at London and St. Albans. As a precaution to avoid trouble if any should arise the council had therefore in the King's name ordered Lord Roos and Sir William Gascoigne, the chief justice, to go north and see what was afoot. Finally, since they knew that the King was very short of money for his own person, they had borrowed 1,000 marks on the revenues of the kingdom and were sending them for him to spend as he pleased.

Henry very soon had worse news from the north, whether from Roos and Gascoigne, or some other source is not known, but on 23 May he suddenly left Hereford, abandoned the Welsh expedition, returned to Worcester and set off for the north. Once again he was at the head of his army, pressing forward to save his throne. On 28 May he was at Derby and wrote to the council from there. He supposed that the council would have heard that the Earl of Northumberland, the Earl Marshal, Lord Bardolf and others had risen and taken the field against him. He himself was hurrying from day to day towards those parts, and wished to have their advice. He therefore commanded them to meet him at Pontefract as soon as possible. Two days later he was at Nottingham, by 3 June at Pontefract and on the 6th at the Archbishop's palace of Bishopsthorpe outside York. By then the rebellion was over.

The castles of Berwick and Jedburgh had been restored to Northumberland by the King in the previous November, and he was now busy provisioning and strengthening them and his other strongholds. He was certainly in touch with Glendower, and was said to have signed a partition treaty with him and Mortimer at Bangor in North Wales at the end of February. By this Glendower would have had a principality enlarged beyond the traditional borders of Wales, Northumberland the north of England and Mortimer the south. The old Earl may also have been aware of the plot to release Edmund, Earl of March and his brother. Mowbray, the Earl Marshal, certainly was so. Now they were apparently plotting with Lord Bardolf and Sir William Clifford Bardolf's son-in-law, and another loyal retainer of the Percies.

The initiative on this occasion seems however to have been taken by the Archbishop of York. Richard Lescrope, a younger son of Lord Scrope of Masham, and Archbishop since 1398, had hitherto given little indication of either support for, or opposition to, Henry. Now he may have drafted and certainly approved the manifestoes against Henry which were being circulated and posted on the doors of churches in York. The accusations against Henry were very similar to those made by Hotspur. He was said to be a usurper, who had broken his oath, and falsely dethroned Richard. He had promised to abolish levies of fifteenths and tenths and the subsidies and customs on wool and wine, but had broken that promise also. King Richard, the rebel earls and Henry Percy had been wrongfully put to death without trial. Statutes had been made against the Pope and the universities, and misery brought on the country. They asked for help to put the right heir, carefully unnamed, on the throne; to make peace with the Welsh and the Irish; and to free the realm from all exactions, extortions and unjust payments for ever.[1] In support of this programme Archbishop Scrope collected an army mainly composed of the citizens of York outside the city. With him were the Earl Marshal and three knights. Their intention was to go to the north and join forces with Northumberland and Bardolf, but the Earl of Westmorland acted too promptly.

Ralph Neville always remained loyal to Henry, perhaps because the rival house of Percy was consistently disloyal. In company with Prince John he advanced towards York, and came

[1] *Annales R. II et H. IV.*, pp. 403–5; *Historians of York*, vol. ii, pp. 292–304

up with the Archbishop at Shipton Moor, six miles from the city. He sent to ask Scrope what he wanted, and Scrope replied 'peace not war'. A parley was therefore arranged between the two armies, at which the Archbishop and the Earl Marshal were promised redress of their grievances. Agreement having been apparently reached the Earl suggested that the Archbishop should disband his army. The citizens were quite ready to return to their homes, and once they were gone Westmorland arrested both Scrope and the Earl Marshal as traitors. They were brought as prisoners to Henry when he arrived at Pontefract, and he took them back to York.

Archbishop Arundel on his way north learnt of the taking of his brother archbishop, and also that the latter was in immediate danger of suffering a traitor's death. Although it was Whit Sunday he rode all day and through the night to arrive at the King's court at Bishopsthorpe early on Monday morning to intercede for the life of Archbishop Scrope. To execute an archbishop would be an unheard-of crime. When his own brother was executed as a traitor to Richard II he himself had only been sent into exile and deprived of his see. But this time Henry felt that he had been lenient too often. He must make it clear that no rank could save a traitor. He urged the Archbishop to rest after his long and tiring journey, and to discuss the fate of his colleague later. Meanwhile a hastily created court which included the Earl of Arundel, Sir Thomas Beaufort and a judge, Sir William Fulthorpe, condemned Scrope, the Earl Marshal and Sir William Plumpton as traitors. They were immediately beheaded outside the city of York. Henry had his revenge, and also made one of the big mistakes of his life. Sir William Gascoigne, the chief justice, was said to have refused to take part in the trial of an archbishop, but most members of Henry's court had no such scruples.

The King had killed an archbishop. Miracles were soon reported at his tomb in York, and the King's illness which began soon afterwards was naturally regarded as God's punishment. He had also deceived and acted against the advice of Archbishop Arundel, who although accused more than once of treason, had worked harder than anyone else to keep Henry on the throne. However, once the deed was done he did not waste time on regrets. The unpopularity which he incurred could not be measured. The terrified citizens of York humbly sought his pardon, which, having been given, he left the next day for Ripon. After a week there he continued his journey northwards by way of Thirsk, Northallerton, Darlington and Durham to Newcastle-upon-Tyne, and by the beginning of July he was at Warkworth, whence he wrote to the council on the 2nd. He was able to announce that he had captured Prudhoe, that Warkworth itself after some resistance had surrendered on the day before, and that he now held all the Earl of Northumberland's castles except Alnwick. By the 6th he was at Berwick-on-Tweed and stayed there a week. Northumberland and Bardolf had not been able to meet him in battle, but had taken refuge in Scotland. Apart from the escape of his foes Henry's victory was complete; he had shown that he was King in the north as well as the south.

Once more he could turn his attention to Wales. On 18 July he left Newcastle to retrace his steps to Worcester. The urgency was over, and the return journey took more than a month. He was back on 23 August, just three months after being called to the north. The French had been promising aid to Owen Glendower for over a year, and a small force had at last arrived at Milford Haven in August 1405. Although their ships had been attacked by Lord Berkeley, Sir Thomas Swynbourne and Harry Pay, they had with Glendower's men taken Carmarthen, and by the time Henry arrived at Worcester they were within ten miles of the town. However, they were short of provisions, and not strong enough to attack. Henry for his part had no forces with which to pursue them. After ten days at Worcester he spent a week at Hereford, from which town he wrote to Archbishop Arundel. He had heard that the French were both assisting his enemies in Wales and attacking fortresses in Guyenne, and he proposed to set off into Wales on the next day. The remainder of a lengthy letter was concerned with his financial difficulties, the expenses that he had borne, his present lack of money, and the measures he proposed to alleviate this. He had written to all the counties asking them to raise a loan on the security of the half fifteenth granted by the Parliament of Coventry and due to be collected in November. This loan they were to pay to the war treasurers by 26 September at Worcester. He asked the Archbishop to make similar arrangements for an advance on the clerical tenth. As the Archbishop had to write to each archdeaconry, get the loans raised and the money delivered to Worcester by the 26th of a month which had already begun, the King cannot be said to have allowed overmuch time.[1]

The expedition into Wales was fated to meet with Henry's usual ill-fortune on these incursions. A storm swelled the rivers of Glamorgan into torrents, part of the royal baggage train was captured, and the King's men failed to make contact with the rebels. Once more the King had to return by way of Hereford to Worcester with nothing achieved. There a number of magnates are said to have gathered for a meeting of the council, at which the knights revived the cry they had raised both at Worcester in 1403 and in the Parliament of Coventry. Let the King take the revenues of the bishops to pay for any army to go against the Welsh. Once again the Archbishop had to fight hard for his money and that of his clergy. After his unsuccessful ride to York, he had got back to Lambeth on 28 June, attended council meetings and visited Canterbury, before setting off again at the end of September to come to the King at Worcester. Now he promised to negotiate once more with the clergy for funds for the King.[2]

With that the King and his knightly counsellors had to be content for the moment. This story is so similar to that of the proceedings at Worcester in 1403 and Coventry in 1404 that one is bound to ask whether the chroniclers were muddling their dates, but it may well be that some Lollard-minded knights did raise this same proposal at every possible opportunity during these years. Almost anything was better than that they should pay taxes to relieve the King's difficulties.

The Archbishop returned to London, and the King went to Kenilworth to rest after a very active summer. He stayed there almost a month, an unusually long stay in one place, and returned to London early in December to stay partly at Westminster but mainly at the Tower until 8 December.

Wales continued to engage most of the attention both of the King and of his council. Lord Grey of Codnor, who had been left in charge of the royal forces in South Wales, was demanding more men and more money as a condition of retaining the command. A remarkable story came to light in December when John Cokayn visited Huntingdon with other justices on a

---

[1] *Anglo-Norman Letters*, pp. 343-5
[2] *Annales R. II et H. IV*, pp. 414-15; Walsingham, *Hist. Angl.*, vol. ii, p. 272

commission of gaol delivery. Two thieves John Oke and John Veysey claimed that they had been employed in collecting money for Owen Glendower, and delivering it to Sir John Scudamore, who was, they said, Owen's treasurer. They named a number of persons mainly religious whom they said had sent gold to Glendower. These included the Abbots of Bury St. Edmunds, Warden, Woburn and Lavendon, and the Priors of Huntingdon, Newnham, Thetford and Ixworth, with other religious and a few laymen including three former members of Parliament. Oke said that he had collected nearly £7,000. If not complete fabrications their stories were probably greatly exaggerated, and all the accused were acquitted; but it is not impossible that there was some foundation of fact, and the mere fact that they could be told at all is proof of the strong anti-clericalism, and general feeling of alarm and suspicion which prevailed.[1]

Meanwhile the council had agreed on 7 December to the restoration to the Duke of York of all his estates. He had been arrested in February after the escape of the Earl of March and his sister's plot. How long he had been in captivity is not known, but now he was evidently forgiven and restored. The escheators who had seized his lands were ordered to pay him all the revenues collected in the interim. On 12 December the Duke was named as a witness to a royal charter, which he had not been on the last charter dated the 2nd, and from the 19th he took his place once more in council. So with all in apparent harmony once more the court went to Eltham again for Christmas. This was the fourth out of his seven Christmases as King that Henry had spent at this manor, so conveniently near to his capital.

---

[1] R. Griffiths, 'Some secret supporters of Owain Glyn Dŵr?', *Bull. I.H.R.*, vol. xxxvii (1964), pp. 77–100

Chapter 14

The Long Parliament of 1406

THE restoration of the Duke of York might seem to imply the end of dissension in England, but the French attack on Guyenne was being intensified, the revolt in Wales was apparently no nearer to an end, and as ever the shortage of money continued. The last part of the fifteenths and tenths granted at Coventry in November 1404 had now been collected and spent, and a whole year having elapsed it might not be thought unreasonable to ask another Parliament for a new subsidy. Accordingly on 21 December 1405 a new Parliament was summoned to meet at Coventry on 15 February 1406, but on 1 January the place of meeting was changed to Gloucester in the march of Wales, because, it was said, the Prince was shortly to begin a campaign against the rebels and finally conquer them, and it would be convenient for King and council, Lords and Commons, to be near at hand. This however was not to be. On 9 February only six days before the Parliament was due to meet, when members from the most distant shires should already have been setting out, and carpenters were preparing the buildings at Gloucester, the place of meeting was changed to Westminster and the opening put off to 1 March.

The writs ordering these changes explained why the King and council thought them necessary.[1] The merchants of the realm had called on the King to come to their aid, because a large force of French ships laden with men-at-arms was lying off the Thames, preventing Gascon and other ships from coming in, and English ships from putting out. It was felt that the Prince with his retinue and the loyal forces of the adjacent counties were strong enough to subdue the Welsh rebels, and it seemed better for the King himself and his lords to be nearer to the new danger, especially as he intended to embark and sail against the enemy himself. Moreover victuals and other supplies needed by members of the

[1] *Cal. Close* (1405–9), pp. 93–5

Parliament were most plentiful at Westminster, which was th
fittest place for meeting.

A Parliament of King, Lords and Commons, with all the re
tainers and servants who habitually accompanied them, mus
always have added up to over a thousand persons, perhaps neare
to two thousand. No small town could conveniently house s
many visitors for any lengthy stay. Westminster and Londo
were therefore no doubt normally preferred by most of the mem
bers, the more so as they would usually have the moral support o
the London merchants, and the noisier support of the mobs
unless overawed by a strong force of archers as in 1397 and 1399
in any opposition to the King. The King on the other hand wa
likely to prefer a provincial town, where the Commons bein
uncomfortably housed would want to complete their busines
quickly and go home, especially if they were surrounded by th
tenants of the King's own estates. Parliaments held away fron
London tended to be both readier to comply with the King'
demands, and shorter in duration. In this case the change to
London led to a very long meeting, and thereby frustrated any
plans which Henry might have had to campaign himself, whethe
in Wales, on the sea, or in Guyenne. It is likely however that ill
health would in any case have kept him from such activities.

When it did meet, the Parliament of 1406 was destined to
prove one of the longest of the Middle Ages. The Lords and
Commons assembled on 1 March in the painted chamber at
Westminster to hear a new chancellor but not a new speech
Thomas Langley, shortly to become Bishop of Durham, made
the usual statement about the safeguarding of the liberties of the
Church, of the Lords and of the Commons, explained how zealous
the King was for the welfare of his people, and mentioned the
troubles caused by the Welsh rebels, and the enemies in Guyenne,
Calais, Ireland and the Scottish march. The King therefore needed
the advice and counsel of the estates. On the following day the
Commons presented Sir John Tiptoft as their Speaker. Although
he had been in Henry's service in 1397-8, and had sat in both
Parliaments of 1404, Tiptoft was probably still only in his
twenties, so that the plea of youth and inexperience which he
advanced as his reasons for the customary request to be excused,
was perhaps justified. He was nevertheless accepted by the King.
The Commons as usual were told to attend in their house each

morning at eight and the Lords at nine. Receivers and triers of petitions were appointed to deal with the mass of petitions which every Parliament received from Guyenne as well as from England.

On 3 March the chancellor announced the result of the negotiations with Prussia and the Hanse, from which the ambassadors appointed in the last Parliament had just returned. After that the Commons began to get down to their grievances, and Tiptoft was able to show that he could speak as forcibly as his predecessors, Savage and Sturmy, even if he was not quite so long-winded as Savage, or so experienced as Sturmy. The complaints of the Commons lost nothing from being more shortly and openly expressed. After three weeks Tiptoft asked for the same liberties as his predecessors, and requested that if anything was put in writing by the Commons, they should be permitted to have the writing back during the Parliament in order to amend it. To these things the King agreed. Referring to the chancellor's opening speech the Speaker then requested that urgent steps should be taken for the keeping of the seas, the defence of Guyenne and the defeat of the Welsh rebels.

On the Saturday before Palm Sunday, April 3, Tiptoft asked if he could speak again under his protestation, which protestation he wanted safeguarded and entered as a record on the Parliament Roll. As usual the King agreed. Then the Speaker returned to matters of substance. First he asked that the Prince should remain continuously in Wales to wage war there, that no castles, lordships or lands recovered from the rebels in Wales should be granted to anyone for at least three months, that new controllers should be appointed to take musters there, that the powers granted to the Prince should be set out and enrolled in chancery, and that he be thanked by letters under the privy seal for his good and continual services. Secondly he went on to demand that all aliens, Breton and French, should be sent out of the kingdom, which despite repeated demands had not yet been done. The King now promised that it would be done as soon as possible. Tiptoft said that some members of the Commons were said to have spoken disrespectfully of the King's person, and asked to be excused on declaring themselves loyal. Only one important item of business had been concluded, or almost concluded, and that was an agreement between the council and the merchants as to the keeping of the seas. As time was getting short and Easter approaching the Commons suggested that they should appoint a committee to assist with the final details. This committee consisted of John Tiptoft the Speaker, Sir Hugh Luttrell, Sir Roger Leche, Sir Thomas Skelton, Sir John Dalyngrigg and Lawrence Drue, all knights of the shire. On the same day Parliament was adjourned for Easter, five weeks had been spent in discussion, but the King was evidently no nearer to getting a grant of money.

The agreement with the merchants and seamen was concluded by the council on the King's behalf and enrolled on the Parliament Roll. As his admirals had failed to safeguard the seas, these merchants, mainly from London, would try to defend them against all the privateers and pirates who were providing hazards for merchantmen. A royal fleet from France, or any other country, would still require the King's intervention, but this was not a likely contingency. The merchants were to police the seas from 1 May until Michaelmas in the next year, 1407. From 1 May to 1 November they would provide for two thousand fighting men, and in the winter months (November to April) one thousand. In return they were to receive the revenue from tunnage and poundage and one quarter of the wool subsidy from 1 April 1406 to Michaelmas 1407, and also an equivalent for the period from 2 February to 1 April 1406, to be taken out of the remaining three-quarters of the wool subsidy. The King would name one collector of customs in each port, and the merchants would name the other, and account for their receipts. They were to have letters under both the great and privy seals authorising them to collect the monies. Also they were to have all the profits of war except the ransoms of high-ranking prisoners, which were reserved for the King, but they would be given a fair reward for them. They also asked for a further £4,000, but were firmly told that no more money was available. If in spite of all their efforts the enemy should still triumph, the King remained under an obligation to send a fleet to sea and give them protection. If on the other hand peace should be made they were to have a sufficient reward for their efforts, and if the subsidy proved insufficient, they were to have further assignments. Finally they were to appoint admirals for the north and for the south parts, who would be given the King's commission. Nicholas Blackburn, one of the customs collectors for Hull, and Richard Clitheroe, a Kentish squire and member of Parliament, were accordingly named for the north and south respectively.

After Northumberland's victory at Homildon Hill in September 1402 the northern counties were less troubled by the Scots, although the Duke of Albany was always ready to shelter any enemies of Henry. Now during the parliamentary recess Henry gained an unexpected advantage. James, the young King of Scotland, was brought to him as a prisoner. After the death of the Duke of Rothesay his younger brother, James, had become heir to his father Robert III. Early in 1406 Robert decided to send James to France to be educated there, or possibly to put him out of reach of the Regent Albany. The ship in which he was sailing was captured off Flamborough Head, despite the current truce, at the end of March 1406. On 4 April Robert III died, so that when the young Prince was brought as a prisoner to Henry's court he was already the nominal King of Scotland. So long as James remained in captivity the Duke of Albany's position was likely to go unchallenged, and thus the boy became a valuable hostage for Henry, who could always threaten to release him if his northern neighbours became too troublesome. The illegality of the capture does not seem to have worried anyone in England, and certainly not the King, who is said to have remarked that he could educate the Prince as well as the court of France. Since James was destined to remain for twenty years in England, a 'guest' not only at Henry's own court, but also at those of both his son and grandson, he was to have ample opportunity to complete his education.

On the adjournment of Parliament the King and his court went to Eltham for Easter. From Eltham Henry went to Greenwich, and from Greenwich he was probably rowed up the river to Windsor for the feast of St. George. This was a bad moment for Henry. Several times since 1399 Henry had ridden at the head of his household and his army, dashing across England to save his throne. Now it appears that he was unable to ride even from Eltham to Windsor. Since his expedition to Wales in the previous autumn, some said since he had caused the execution of Archbishop Scrope at York, Henry had been afflicted by the mysterious sickness, which in more or less acute form was to remain with him for the rest of his life. The nature of the illness was not understood at the time, and contemporary reports of it have not enabled later generations of doctors to diagnose it, but it certainly disabled him from time to time, and eventually restricted his movements to a very small area. However, on this occasion he was able to reach Windsor and take part in the celebrations of the feast of St. George. Parliament was due to resume on Monday 26 April.

Two days after that, on 28 April, Henry wrote to the council from his manor house in Windsor Park. He had hoped, he said, to have been at Westminster the day before, but a malady had suddenly come to his leg and prevented him from getting there. His doctors advised that he could not travel without great danger, especially on horseback. His squire William Philip, who was bringing the letter, would tell them about it, as would his dear and loyal cousin, the Duke of York. He now hoped to reach Staines that night, and London from there by water in two or three days. Later in the same day he wrote again. So bad was the disease that he could not even hope to carry out the programme mentioned in the first letter. He asked them meanwhile to get the Parliament to discuss the present needs of the realm, and such matters as the Duke of York would tell them of. He wished them to make provision for the defence of Guyenne, and for sending his daughter Philippa to Denmark, whither it had been promised that she should go at the beginning of May.

Owing to the non-arrival of the King and other lords from Windsor the opening of the new session was put off from Monday to Tuesday, and so from day to day until Friday, 30 April. Then, the Archbishop of Canterbury, the Duke of York, and a number of bishops having arrived, discussions were able to begin. No more is heard of the King's illness at this time, and he was evidently sufficiently recovered to reach London by 4 May. On the 8th he was able to agree with the Lords that the demand of the Commons for the expulsion of all aliens should be conceded, for that rather than the safety of the realm was the subject which had engaged their attention in the meantime. A list was given to the steward of the household, of some forty persons who were to be expelled by 24 May. The people concerned were mainly cooks, valets and grooms, hardly of sufficient importance to warrant the exertions of the Commons, who were however relentless in the pursuit, either from a genuine fear that aliens might be agents of the King's enemies, or simply as a means of attacking the King himself. The money thus saved to the royal household could make but a very small contribution to solving the problems of the kingdom's finances. By 18 May it had been found possible by raising a large number of loans to pay over some £3,500 to the Prince for his expenses in Wales, most of it being delivered to him or his officers at his castle of Tutbury, in Staffordshire,[1] but the exchequer remained empty.

On Saturday, 15 May after repeating the usual protestation the Speaker asked that Richard Clitheroe, one of the admirals, should be released from his parliamentary duties so that he could go to sea, that the King should not listen to any slander of him in his absence, and that Robert Clifford, the other knight of the shire for Kent, should be allowed to speak for him. A week later Tiptoft reminded the King that they had been promised good governance, and that the Archbishop had said that the King would be advised by the wisest councillors, who would oversee the whole government of the realm. Such reminders or requests were becoming almost routine entries on the Parliament Roll, but this apparently flat statement undoubtedly glossed over one of the greatest crises of this Parliament if not of the whole reign. Henry desperately in need of money from an unyielding Parliament was forced to make concessions.

Speaking himself, Henry agreed that what the Speaker had said was indeed his own wish. A bill was then read, which, it was rather overmuch emphasised, had been drawn up by the King of his own free will, giving the names of his councillors and some proposed rules for the conduct of the administration. The councillors so named were Archbishop Arundel, Bishop Beaufort of Winchester, and Stafford of Exeter, the Duke of York, the Earl of Somerset, Lords Roos, Lovell, and Willoughby, the chancellor, treasurer and keeper of the privy seal, the steward and chamberlain, and three knights, Hugh Waterton, John Cheyne and Arnold Savage. This was very much the same council as had been serving since the beginning of the reign, except that the squires dropped out, leaving the knights as the lowest in status. Thus the King was not appeasing the Commons by changing his council, except in so far as he was leaving out the most humble members, whom perhaps they distrusted as being too much under his personal influence. It was more per-

[1] P.R.O., E 403/587

haps the councillors themselves whom he was trying to please with his bill. Amongst other provisions, whose significance is not very clear, the bill laid down that certain instructions to the chancellor, treasurer and keeper of the privy seal should only be effective if endorsed or made by the advice of the council. This was obviously intended to prevent the King from granting away lands and revenues without the council's agreement. The Commons had long been protesting against the lavishness of his grants, which reduced his own revenues, and so in their view led to increased demands for taxation, which they both resented and resisted. How far this measure did restrict Henry's freedom of action and transfer authority to the council is very difficult to discover or to assess.

That the councillors themselves were not very happy about their position is clear. First of all the chancellor declared that Lord Lovell, who was included, had several times asked to be excused because he had a number of pleas waiting to be heard in the courts of law, and the King agreed that his name should be removed from the list. But then all the other councillors also asked to be excused. Whereupon the King had to ask them again to serve. This they agreed to do 'seeing that the bill was of the King's own will, and not of their seeking', and provided that it was entered on the Parliament Roll as a record, and that if it was found that it could be advantageously amended during the session of Parliament, this should be done and recorded. This might appear to have settled matters, but on Monday morning Tiptoft, the Speaker, was still not satisfied. He summarised Saturday's proceedings and then asked whether or not the Lords named by the King would now undertake to serve as councillors. Arundel replied for himself and the other members of the council, if sufficient funds could be provided to enable good governance to be maintained, they would serve as the council, and do their best for King and kingdom, but otherwise not. Thus he neatly threw back to the Commons the demand for a grant of taxation.[1]

They, however, preferred to talk first of many other matters. The Speaker next referred to the danger to Calais, to recent destruction in Guyenne, in Ireland and in the north on the Scottish march, to the rebellion in Wales, to the expenses of dwellers

[1] This is fully discussed by A. L. Brown, 'The Commons and the Council in the reign of Henry IV', *E.H.R.*, vol. lxxix (1964), pp. 1-30

by the coast in safeguarding the seas, and to the great poverty of everyone. For all these things the Commons asked for remedies, and the King promised that what could be done would be. The Earl of Somerset for example was intending to go to Calais, and this prompted Tiptoft to ask that all captains of garrisons should go to their posts. Finally he asked once more to be forgiven if he had given offence, and once more Henry promised forgiveness.

On the next day Lord Lovell brought before the Lords his dispute with William Doyle, and witnesses were directed to appear at the beginning of July. On 4 June it was agreed that the clergy should be exempt from commissions of array, and a commission comprising the Bishops of Exeter and Bath, the Prior of St. John of Jerusalem, Lord Burnell and two judges, William Rickhill and William Hankford, was appointed to enquire into the grievances of the Prussians and the Hanse merchants, whose ships had been seized by English pirates and privateers. On Monday, 7 June after a fortnight's lull the Speaker returned to the attack. He asked that he might speak as any former Speaker had done. Once more the King assented. Tiptoft praised the Prince of Wales, and then recalled how at the council held at Worcester, and then at Westminster and in the Parliament of 1404, the Lords had sworn to obey the King, and after him the Prince, as was set out in a Commons petition, the succession to be in the Prince and his heirs male, and each of his brothers in turn. Exemplification of all this was now requested and granted, Archbishop Arundel, eleven bishops, three abbots, the Duke of York, five earls, nineteen barons and Speaker Tiptoft putting their names to it as witnesses. Tiptoft went on to ask that the Prince should be sent to Wales to fight the rebels. He complained that money for Calais had been misappropriated by the collectors of customs, and that in musters held there boys and foreigners had been counted as men-at-arms so that pay could wrongfully be drawn for them. He further complained that too much was spent on Ireland and on the King's household, and that many members of the latter were not fit to be there.

The Commons wanted the accounts of the treasurers of war appointed at Coventry, Lord Furnival and Sir John Pelham, to be audited. According to one chronicler[1] the King at first refused

[1] *Eulogium*, vol. iii, p. 409

on the ground that kings do not render accounts, and the Commons thereupon refused to make any grant of money. This is evidently a gross oversimplification. According to the Parliament Roll the two treasurers had repeatedly asked for a final discharge from their office, and now at the request of the Commons the King had granted this. At the same time Lord Roos and the chief baron of the exchequer were appointed to audit their account, and the Commons understood that they had to name further auditors to assist them. Accordingly six members of the Commons, Hugh Luttrell, Richard Redman, Lawrence Drue, Thomas Chelrey, David Holbache and William Staundon, were appointed. On the same day (19 June) after the usual protest Tiptoft once more asked that the council might give good governance, and also suggested that they should be reasonably rewarded for their work. After which he said that the Queen's endowment should be fully made up to the promised 10,000 marks, and that the King should consider rewarding his sons, and certain persons who had done good service against the Welsh rebels. These included Richard, Lord Grey of Codnor, Sir John Greyndour, Lord Charlton of Powys and the whole counties of Chester and Salop. Sir Thomas Erpyngham's many services to the King and kingdom were also mentioned, and the Commons wanted Richard, the Duke of York's brother, to have reparation and payment for certain jewels of his which had been in the care of the late King.

Then at last the Commons did agree to some financial concessions. They granted tunnage and poundage for one year from 24 June; and also agreed that the King should have one noble, that is 6s. 8d., on each sack, from the wool subsidy granted at Coventry, and that the three quarters of it left after satisfying the merchants for their sea-keeping, should be spent on defence and good governance at the discretion of the council. If however the council were to be discharged before the subsidy expired then the arrangements made at Coventry should stand. All aliens were to quit the realm. All grants made since the first day of the Parliament, apart from those to members of the council, the Queen and the Princes, should be annulled and the money applied to the royal household. The household was to be reformed as quickly as possible to cut down expenses. A further enquiry was to be made into the administration of alien priories in order to raise more money, and the King must not make any gifts until his household debts were settled.

On 19 June, considering their great labours, the needs of the harvest and the great heat, as well as the enemies by land and sea, the Parliament was adjourned until 15 October. The Commons had shown their great mistrust of the King, and they had talked for four months about the need for good governance and defence, but they had shown no willingness at all to pay for it. Much as he disliked the Speaker's endless complaints Henry could not finally discharge the Parliament until they had granted him a real subsidy.

Some financial relief was however provided by the clergy. The convocation of Canterbury met in St. Paul's on 10 May, granted a tenth from their clergy and broke up on 16 June. The convocation of the province of York met in that city on 12 July and made a similar grant on 18 August. Messengers were hastily sent out to the bishops and the keepers of the temporalities of the vacant sees asking for the speedy appointment of collectors to get the money in. At the same time the collectors and controllers of customs in all the ports were summoned to attend a great council at Westminster on 8 July, and commissioners were appointed to enquire into the accounts of sheriffs, escheators and all other officials who collected revenues for the exchequer. A great effort was being made to get every possible penny in with the utmost speed, and to ensure that none of the revenues of the Crown were being misappropriated. The council also attempted to raise such loans as it could.

Despite the 'great heat' the King stayed in London for another month after the adjournment, a most unusual procedure for him. He may not have been feeling fit for much travel, but more probably he was watching the financial activities of the council, anxious to know how much money was to be at their and his disposal. This was the more important to him as one of the main objects for which the money was needed was the sending of Philippa, his second daughter, to Denmark. Thomas Langley, the chancellor, was in the process of being elevated to the bishopric of Durham, and for most of the time up to the middle of July Henry stayed at the Bishop of Durham's house in the City, where he would be in the closest touch with the work of the council.

As early as 1402 envoys of Eric, the youthful King of Denmark, had been negotiating for the hand of Henry's younger daughter. After four years of intermittent discussion Henry had finally agreed to the marriage. A proxy ceremony was celebrated at Westminster on 26 November 1405, Philippa being then eleven, and Eric nearly twenty. It was then agreed that she should be sent across to her husband early in May 1406, but the King's illness, the proceedings in Parliament and the shortage of money, forced him to put off the date of her departure. On 22 June orders were issued for the second time for chartering ships for the Princess, and several appeals for loans were made in order to pay for her clothing and the necessary ships and equipment. For although the King of Denmark had agreed to take her without a dowry these charges for herself and her escort amounted to more than £4,000. This escort was to be led by Bishop Bowet of Bath and Wells, Richard, brother to the Duke of York, Henry, Lord Scrope of Masham, Sir Henry Fitzhugh and Master Richard Courtenay. It also included six knights, of whom one, Sir Walter Hungerford, acted as her chamberlain, and another, Sir Peter Bukton, as steward of her household, three ladies, eight damsels, three squires, eight clerks, an usher, eight minstrels, fifteen pages, and eighty grooms or yeomen.

Leaving London on 18 July Henry went to Hertford, and then set out accompanied by the Queen and three of his sons, Henry, Thomas and Humphrey, to take Philippa to Lynn. They went by Babraham, near Cambridge, Newmarket, Bury St. Edmunds, Walsingham and Castle Rising, and by 7 August all were at King's Lynn, where they spent nine days.[1] Among others who were with the court were three Scottish prisoners, the Earls of Fife, Douglas and Orkney. Philippa and her escort sailed in mid-August and the marriage was celebrated at Lund in October, after which most of the escort returned to England. Philippa, who lived until 1430, never saw England or her family again.

The King was evidently better for the moment. From Lynn he went on to Spalding in Lincolnshire, and thence to Horncastle by 20 August. The next evening he arrived at Bardney Abbey, and then followed the one day in the whole reign on which, thanks to an eyewitness account by an unknown monk of Bardney, we can see how the King spent his time, enjoying as it

[1] Capgrave, *Chron.*, p. 292

happened a leisurely day of rest.[1] As the King and his party approached the abbey, the Abbot, John Woxbrigg, and his monks filed out to meet him at the lower gate. Seeing them Henry dismounted, dropped to his knees, and kissed their crucifix. He was then sprinkled with holy water and led into the church and so up to the high altar. After a short service, which included a hymn and an address by the Abbot, he kissed the sacred relics and went through the cloister to the Abbot's lodging, where he spent the night. The next morning being Sunday he came down into the cloister at about six, and so into the church and St. Mary's chapel, which was richly decorated with scarlet hangings and other ornaments, and there he heard two masses. He followed the procession round the cloister to the choir, remained in the chapel whilst the major mass was said, and then went up to the Abbot's room for breakfast with his two sons, Thomas and Humphrey. On the other side of the room sat the three Scottish earls, who were still accompanying the court. The Abbot himself presided at the high table in hall with Thomas Peverel, Bishop of Llandaff, and a number of lords and knights. These included Lord Grey of Codnor, the King's chamberlain, Richard Kingston, treasurer of the household, John, Lord Harington, who was twenty-two and had succeeded his father but three months before, Sir John Strange, the King's steward, Sir Henry Rochefort, Sir William Frank, Sir Richard Goldsburgh, Sir John Lyttlebury, and Robert Waterton esquire. All the Waterton family were amongst Henry's most devoted followers, and Robert, like Goldsburgh, had been with him on the first Prussian expedition sixteen years before.

Two other old friends called to see Henry during the day. Philip Repingdon, his former confessor, now Bishop of Lincoln, rode over with a party which needed twenty-four horses, and was received by the Abbot and eight or ten monks. Later came William, Lord Willoughby, another companion both in Prussia and on the ride from Ravenspur in 1399. After they had gone Henry came down into the cloister and to the church to see the monastic library, and there he read from several books, so long as he wished. Then he went up to dinner and so to bed. Apparently there were no ladies with the court on this occasion. What happened to the Queen and her ladies after they left Lynn is

[1] Leland, *Collectanea*, vol. vi, p. 300; Dugdale, *Mon. Angl.*, vol. i, p. 625

not known. The Prince of Wales had also left the court, no doubt to return to his post in Wales.

Henry went on to Lincoln, Leicester and Northampton, and so back to St. Albans and London by mid-September. There on the 15th his brother-in-law Sir John Cornewaille once more distinguished himself in the lists, this time against a number of Scottish knights. Just before Parliament was due to reassemble the King went to Merton in Surrey, but was back in time for the start of the third session on 15 October. In fact owing to late arrivals the opening had to be postponed from day to day until the 18th. Even then it was a whole month before any business considered worthy of record was done. Henry had meanwhile been down to Hertford for the feast of All Saints, waiting for the Commons to get round to making a grant of money, and needing all the patience that he possessed.

It was not until 18 November that the Speaker made his usual request to be allowed to speak under his protestation, and even then he had apparently no matters of great moment to bring forward. He asked the King to charge the Lords to declare what they thought was wrong with the government of the realm. It was pointed out that at the opening of Parliament both Lords and Commons had been charged to tell the King what they thought best for the kingdom. However Henry assented to the Speaker's request, and agreed also that the absent lords should be told of it. Tiptoft next said that the castle of Mauléon, at the foot of the Pyrenees, was in the hands of Charles of Navarre and garrisoned by aliens. He asked that an English captain and loyal men should be appointed to it. He further requested that treasurers and controllers should be appointed for Wales, so that monies intended for Wales should be seen to be spent there. He asked that certain castles should be put 'in hostage' for the Earl Douglas, and that the other Scots prisoners should not be allowed too much freedom, seeing that the flower of Scottish chivalry was in the King's hands, for which, as he said, God be praised.

The days went by and the King kept the members in London. It was not until 22 December, too late for most of them to get home for Christmas, that the Commons agreed to make a grant of taxation so that they could be released and get away to their homes. Even then it was only on conditions which imposed very severe restrictions on the King. But some other matters were dealt with first. Tiptoft asked that the Commons might commune with the Lords, after which the Archbishop spoke for both Lords and Commons. He said that the settlement of the Crown made on 7 June should be exemplified, with an amendment from the heirs male to the heirs general of each prince in turn. This was then done with a much longer list of witnesses than in June, comprising the Archbishop himself, fifteen bishops, and the keepers of the spiritualities of the vacant sees of York, Norwich and Rochester, twenty-four abbots and priors, the Duke of York, eight earls, thirty-three barons and the Speaker of the Commons. Henry had been negotiating once more for the marriage of the Prince to a daughter of Charles VI of France, and it was probably to satisfy the French King that an arrangement which would have cut out any daughters of the Prince in favour of his brothers and their sons was changed.

A petition for the punishment of Lollards and contrivers of novelties was accepted, the auditors appointed in Parliament were given full powers to discharge the war treasurers, Lord Furnival and Sir John Pelham, after hearing their accounts, and it was conceded that no one should be punished for any actions taken in suppressing riots or rebellions. The Commons then appointed a commission consisting of Tiptoft, Sir Thomas Skelton, Sir John Pelham, Sir John Dalyngrigg, Lawrence Drue, David Holbache, Richard Baynard, John Wilycotes, Esmond Brudenell, William Staundon, Henry Somer and Nicholas Wotton, any six or more of whom were to be present at the enactment and engrossment of the Parliament Roll. The appointment was a clear statement that the Commons did not even trust the King and his officials to compile the Roll honestly.

Then once more the names of the council were given to Parliament, and thirty-one articles were sent out which they were to be sworn to observe. When the list of the council was given to Parliament on 22 May the squires had been left out, now, exactly seven months later, the knights were left out as well. The council was reduced to thirteen, apart from the Prince of Wales who now joined it for the first time, namely Archbishop Arundel, the Bishops of London, Winchester and Durham (the chancellor), the Earl of Somerset, Lords Furnival (the treasurer), Burnell, Roos and Grey of Codnor (the King's chamberlain), the keeper of the privy seal, the steward and treasurer of the household. The councillors said that they would only undertake their charge and swear to observe the thirty-one articles, if the King made it clear that it was his wish that they should so do. Accordingly the King of his own free will commanded them to take the oath, and also agreed that Lord Roos, who was the only absentee, should be sworn later, as well as all the judges.

These articles laid down that some of the councillors were always to be about the King's person until the next Parliament, to report the King's wishes to the other members. The King was to hear petitions on two days in each week, Wednesdays and Fridays, when some of the councillors would be present. They were to be paid as members of the council, to guide the King, and control the details of the administration, including the running of the royal household, for which certain revenues were allotted. No grants of lands or revenues were to be made from the 17 December, that was five days earlier, until the ending of the next Parliament. In return for all these concessions a grant was made of one fifteenth and tenth payable in the first week of Lent, 1407, together with the usual subsidies on wool and tunnage and poundage for one year from the following Michaelmas. All was to be expended by the advice of the council, except for £6,000 which was placed at the King's disposal. There were no more war treasurers and the control of receipts and issues reverted to the normal exchequer procedure. As a final act of the session the merchants were discharged at their own request from their task of keeping the seas. The experiment had evidently not proved a success and was quietly terminated a year before it was due to end. The Long Parliament was then at last dissolved. It had had so many sittings that the expenses of the seventy county members alone amounted to £2,500.

If the terms which the Parliament had exacted in return for their grant were literally observed very little initiative was now left to the King. The thirteen members of his new council were endowed with full powers to administer the kingdom until the meeting of the next Parliament. On 8 December the council had recommended that the King and his household should spend a normal Christmas, but that afterwards he should withdraw to some place where the expenses of the household could be kept down. In fact they went immediately to Eltham for the holiday, and then probably returned to London before going down to Merton in Surrey for a time. On the same 8 December John Tiptoft, the Speaker, was made treasurer of the royal household. There and in his next office of treasurer of England, which he was to hold from July 1408 to January 1410, he would learn some of the difficulties of the Government, which he had been so freely criticising. How far Henry welcomed the spokesman of his critics as the administrator of his own household there is no means of telling. Tiptoft was also granted all the lands of Rhys ap Griffith in the counties of Carmarthen and Cardigan, and the office of keeper of the forest of Waybridge and Sapley in Huntingdonshire,[1] presumably as a reward for his work as Speaker through the long weeks of the Parliament.

[1] *Cal. Pat.* (1405–8), p. 318

Chapter 15

Archbishop Arundel, chancellor, January 1407–December 1409

HAMPERED both by ill-health and the lack of an hereditary title to the throne, Henry fought a losing battle with his Parliament throughout 1406. Council, Lords and Commons all seem to have been united against him. For the remaining six years of his life a great deal of the work of government was taken out of his hands, and although he attempted at times to assert his authority and remained King in fact as well as in name, he was often compelled by illness, if not by Parliament, to leave decisions to his council. The dominant figures henceforth were Archbishop Arundel and the Prince of Wales, working at first in harmony, but later in bitter opposition to each other. Arundel had been the King's most prominent supporter, taking the leading place in council from the beginning of the reign. Then in 1405 Henry, in executing his colleague of York, not only went against his very sound advice, but even is said to have tricked him by causing the execution to take place whilst he slept after an exhausting journey. Such behaviour must have been hard for so serious-minded a prelate to forgive, especially as, although more than once accused of treasonable actions, he had remained a loyal and strong supporter of Henry. In fact he had little choice but to be loyal, for the King's enemies were his enemies too, and a change of king might well have put his own position at Canterbury in jeopardy. According to his recent biographer Arundel was 'a man of independent views . . . a mediator and conciliator . . . some thought him wise, and many respected him.'[1] During 1406 his attendance in council had become more regular, and in the Parliament he had acted as spokesman for the councillors, but what his attitude to the King then was the records do not reveal. Little more than a month after the Parliament ended, on 30 January 1407, he became chancellor in place of Bishop Langley. It was in the chapel of St. Stephen's, West-

[1] Aston, *Thomas Arundel*, p. 377

ninster, that Langley surrendered the great seal to the King, who thereupon handed it to Arundel. The Archbishop took the oath of office as chancellor in the presence of the Prince, the Earl of Somerset, Bishop Beaufort of Winchester and others. Doubtless he could have held office earlier in the reign had he wished, and now, according to one chronicler,[1] only accepted it against his own will, in response to requests from many people.

The Prince of Wales, unlike Arundel, was now coming to the fore for the first time. At nineteen he had already taken part in six years of campaigning against the Welsh, and for the last three years since the defeat and death of Hotspur had been virtually in charge of the war. The many letters exchanged between 'his revered lord and father' the King, and himself, 'the very dear and entirely beloved son',[2] suggest that they were on terms of mutual trust, respect and affection, at least in these early years. Moreover Parliament had several times expressed its confidence in the Prince, and he had already proved himself as a commander. The year 1406, the first in which his father had not come to the border to take charge, was also the first in which some real progress had been made against Glendower. On St. George's Day, 23 April, the Prince had won a victory in which one of Glendower's sons had been killed, later some of the French who had been sent to help Glendower were captured, and the English continued to hold their own. On 25 November 1406 the Prince's name first appeared as a witness to one of his father's charters. On 8 December he made his first known attendance in council, and thenceforth continued to attend frequently as a full member, although exempted from taking the oath with the other councillors on account of his high rank.

Supported in the council by twelve of the most experienced administrators in the country, Archbishop and Prince formed a very strong combination, for Arundel was an expert in the arts of administration and politics, whilst the Prince was proving his ability as a commander in the field. One of their first acts however seems to have been deliberately provocative, for in February the King, who could for the moment hardly act but by the advice of his council, confirmed the act legitimating his three half-brothers, the Beauforts, and in so doing added the

[1] Galbraith, *St. Albans Chron.*, p. 10
[2] *Anglo-Norman Letters*, *passim*

words '*excepta dignitate regali*' which did not occur in the document
laid before Parliament in 1397. Since the King had four sons, all
of whom might be expected to have heirs, the possibility of the
Beauforts succeeding to the royal dignity must have appeared
remote. The words were nonetheless added between the lines
on the patent roll, and seemed to constitute a quite unnecessary
insult to two members of the ruling council and their brother,
Thomas. It was said that the Beauforts never forgave Arundel
for this, and thenceforward supported the Prince against him.

The measures of December 1406 having deprived letters and
warrants under the King's signet of much of their authority,
these ceased to be written, or at least preserved, in any numbers;
and as they normally provide one of the the surest guides to the
King's own whereabouts, it is much more difficult to trace his movements in the early part of 1407. Indeed all we know is that he paid
a short visit to Merton in January, and that he was at Hertford,
at, or shortly after, Easter, and then went on to Windsor for
the feast of St. George. Although restricted in domestic affairs
Henry remained in charge of foreign relations, and on 23 March
Arundel wrote him a long letter from Canterbury about relations
with Scotland. Both countries were anxious to prolong the truce
which was due to expire at Easter, and Arundel suggested that
Henry should take advantage of Albany's desire for an extension
to get some concessions especially the handing over of 'that fool
who was calling himself Richard II'. Arundel hoped to be in
London on the Tuesday week when he would see the full texts
of previous truces and agreements, which were there in the hands
of the Bishop of Durham and other members of the council.[1]
The truce continued in fact to be renewed from year to year, and
some Scottish prisoners were ransomed, but King James,
whose return was feared rather than desired by the Regent
Albany, now calling himself Governor of Scotland, remained
in England.

In France, or at least Guyenne, the position was slightly
improved with no help from Henry or his council. Through
1405 and into 1406 the French had continued their advance
towards Bordeaux, capturing one stronghold after another
with monotonous regularity. In April 1406 the Archbishop of
Bordeaux began a series of letters to the King in England plead-

[1] *Archaeologia*, vol. xxiii (1831), pp. 297–8

ing for reasonable help for Bordeaux, which was, he said, in danger of being completely lost. On 30 June he wrote even more urgently. He had cried for help until his voice was hoarse, he declared, and now the people despaired of ever receiving help from the King. And well they might for Henry was far too much involved in his argument with the Long Parliament to concern himself with Guyenne. By 22 July the French were threatening the very outposts of Bordeaux, Fronsac, Libourne and St. Emilion in the heart of the vineyards. Under its English mayor, Sir Thomas Swynbourne, Bordeaux itself was put into a state of defence ready to withstand a siege, whilst some help was sent to the outlying fortress towns. As well as to the King, appeals were sent to the council, and to the merchants who had the defence of the seas, but mostly in vain for the Commons would not vote any money. A fleet under the Earls of Arundel and Warwick did appear off the coast, and Harry Pay with his Cornish pirates brought some solace to the Gascons, who thought they might be a royal fleet coming to their rescue. But in the end the people of Bordeaux had to rely on their own exertions.

Once more the Duke of Orleans came south to take part in the final triumphant capture of Bordeaux. He joined the constable at Barbezieux, forty-five miles north of the city, in October, and sent an ultimatum to Libourne and St. Emilion demanding their immediate submission to Charles VI. The French army numbered nearly 10,000 men, with whom it was hoped to cut off Bordeaux from England by capturing both sides of the Gironde. On 31 October the French laid siege to Bourg, which was the last stronghold before Bordeaux on the Gironde. The people of Bordeaux counter-attacked, and defeated the French in a river battle on 23 December, the day after Henry's Long Parliament was at last dissolved. As a result the French withdrew from before Bourg in January, and much territory round Bordeaux was recovered from them. But in the spring of 1407 the safety of Bordeaux was by no means assured. No one knew that the Duke of Orleans would withdraw to Paris in the autumn and be assassinated there.

At Calais on the other side of France the problem was rather different. By the beginning of March 1407 some £25,000 out of the subsidy granted in Parliament had reached the exchequer, which also borrowed £900 from the Earl of Westmorland, and

£200 from Thomas Knolles, a London merchant, but the garrison of Calais were willing to wait no longer for their pay. Their wages had been grossly in arrears for several years, and they now seized the wool which was awaiting sale in the merchants' warehouses in Calais. The council thereupon replaced the treasurer of Calais, Robert Thorley, by Richard Merlawe, a London merchant, on 9 March. On the next day the exchequer closed for the Easter vacation, and four days after that, 14 March, Lord Furnival, the treasurer of England, died. It is not perhaps surprising therefore to learn that the council which met after Easter sat for nine weeks, and that it was much concerned with the raising of loans.[1]

The cost of Calais to the English exchequer was about £17,000 a year, and payments had inevitably fallen into arrears during the years of financial stringency. Now by seizing the merchants' wool the garrison had brought the matter to a head, and also strengthened the hands of King and council in dealing with the merchants. The council was able to insist on the merchants making a loan as a condition of their wool being released. First of all a new treasurer, Nicholas Bubwith, was appointed to succeed Furnival. For Bubwith this was the culmination of a long official career as King's clerk which had brought him through the offices of King's secretary, master of the rolls and keeper of the privy seal. As a reward for these services he had been made Bishop of London in the previous year, and was shortly to be translated to Salisbury on his way to Bath and Wells. Within a fortnight he and his colleagues on the council had reached agreements by which Richard Whittington and other merchants of the staple had lent £4,000 to be repaid them out of the wool subsidies. Whittington was at this time mayor both of London and of the Calais staple, and in addition to the corporate loan he lent £1,000 on his own account. Probably the only wealthier London merchant at this time was John Hende, who lent another £2,500 himself, for which he was promised the keeping of the cocket seal in the port of London, thus securing control of the collection of the wool subsidy there. Two other London merchants made small loans, and the Albertini of Florence £1,000 on condition that they were allowed to export free of subsidy until the money was recovered. Thus the revenues from the

[1] Galbraith, *St. Albans Chron.*, p. 11

subsidy on wools were pledged in advance for some time to come.

All these loans enabled £7,000 to be issued for the current expenses of Calais, but did not suffice to pay off the accumulated arrears of debt. A further loan of £2,000 was made by John Norbury, £500 by the Earl of Westmorland, £400 by a number of members of the council, and 500 marks by the clerks of the chancery. The raising of these loans was facilitated by the fact that bonds guaranteeing their repayment were signed by all the members of the council. Apart from Lord Furnival who had died these were the councillors nominated in Parliament in the previous December, evidently still acting efficiently together as the Government of the kingdom. An expedition to Guyenne had been planned to sail under the King's own command. Several postponements had brought the date for its departure into April, but by then it became clear that the French were withdrawing and agreeing to local truces, and there being no money to pay for it the proposal was allowed quietly to lapse.

The nine weeks for which the council was said to have sat would have ended on 29 May. Henry if not attending its meetings had stayed near enough to be in close touch, and was then at Rotherhithe. Three weeks later he left the London area and set off for the midlands, going more slowly than in earlier years by way of Leicester, Nottingham, Rothwell Haigh near Leeds, to York, Beverley and Bridlington. This was a more leisurely progress than that of the warlike expeditions of the past, the itinerary suggesting that it may have been of the nature of a pilgrimage, an attempt to atone for the murder of the Archbishop. Perhaps Henry hoped that he might thus be cured of his recurring illness. From Bridlington he went to the Archbishop's palace at Bishopsthorpe. The see was still unfilled as he could not agree with the Pope on a successor to Lescrope, and it was not until October of this year that his lifelong servant, Henry Bowet, was translated from Bath and Wells. By then the King was at Gloucester, having completed his summer in the north with visits to his castle at Pontefract, to Nottingham and Evesham. At Nottingham on 12 August he was present at a trial by battle between John Bulmer, a Bordeaux seamster, and Bertrand Usana, a merchant of the same city, whom Bulmer had accused of inciting him to treason. Eventually after they had belaboured each other, the King stopped the fight and declared both to be loyal. Encounters between professional fighting men in the lists afforded an entertaining spectacle, but such meetings as this bordered on the ridiculous.

The summer brought a visitation of the plague and talk of an invasion by the Scots, but for the rest it passed quietly, enabling the leading members of the council to leave London. Arundel was at Canterbury and Saltwood Castle near Hythe presiding over the trial of William Thorpe, a Lollard and disciple of Wycliff, who had been arrested and charged with heresy whilst preaching at Shrewsbury in April. The Prince was in Wales. The castles of Harlech and Aberystwyth were still held by the followers of Glendower, and they must be recaptured if he were to be defeated. Siege was accordingly laid to Aberystwyth, where some of the Prince's followers deserted him. However, by the mediation of Richard Courtenay, Chancellor of Oxford University, he was able to arrange a truce on 12 September. Under the terms of this the castle was to be surrendered if not relieved by Glendower before 1 November. However, to the surprise of both sides Glendower did collect a new army and relieve it in time. With the Prince this summer were the Duke of York, Richard, Earl of Warwick, the new Lord Furnival, and a number of lords and knights including Roger Leche, John Oldcastle, John Greyndour and Humphrey Stafford.[1] Glendower was not yet beaten, but as the next few months were to deprive him of a number of potential allies, it soon became merely a question of how much longer he could hold out.

From Leicester on 22 June Henry had written to Arundel acknowledging a letter written in the Archbishop's own hand. The Minister General of the Franciscan friars wished to visit England with a party of about thirty followers to restore harmony to the English province of his Order, and was seeking the King's permission to do so. Henry agreed that Arundel, as chancellor, might grant permission, and not to be outdone by the Archbishop he added a postscript in his own hand; 'I thonk the wryter of youre lettre, and byd God gyve hym good lyff and Long, Vostre, H.R.'[2] Another letter of Henry to Arundel, of uncertain date, suggests that he could sometimes see the lighter side of the job of being king. He asked the chancellor to issue a

---

[1] Lloyd, *Glendower*, pp. 130–3; Galbraith, *St. Albans Chron.*, pp 22–7
[2] R. *Letters, H. IV.*, vol. ii, pp. 179–80

protection for a certain woman called D. 'We have', he wrote 'at the importunate suit of the aforesaid D. and in order to get rid of her out of our company, promised her our said letters, if in your judgment this seems feasible, requesting that as you think best, you will let this same D. have our said letters for a certain time under our great seal in due form, and we believe that you will be as weary of her company and boring persistence as we became before she would see reason.'[1]

Towards the end of the summer Arundel or the council had evidently decided that another Parliament was needed, but did not want another long session in London. Accordingly on 26 August one was summoned to meet at Gloucester on 20 October. Henry himself was in Gloucester by the appointed date, but as many of the members had failed to appear, the opening was put off for four days. Being away from London this Parliament, like the Coventry one, had a very short session, thirty-nine days. In several of the earlier Parliaments Arundel had played a leading part especially as a mediator between King and Commons, but on this occasion he seems to have dominated the whole proceedings. As chancellor he preached the opening sermon taking as his text the words 'honour the King', something which previous Parliaments had conspicuously failed to do. He said that the King had maintained the liberties of the church and of all his subjects, he had ensured that all statutes and good laws, especially the Great Charter and the Charter of the Forest, were enforced, he had defended his subjects, and treated them with mercy and justice, and therefore they should honour him. Just as the parts of the body honoured the head, so they should honour the King who was their head, and assist him in time of need. He asked them to consider the rebellion in Wales, the safe-keeping of the sea, and of Guyenne, Calais, Ireland and the march towards Scotland, and to come to the aid of the King on this occasion. His address was differently worded from the orations of his predecessors, and for the King refreshingly flattering, but the meaning was the same, and the Commons very soon showed signs of resuming their usual critical course.

First they elected as their Speaker an Oxfordshire squire, who, although this was his fourth Parliament, had not so far been very much to the fore. This was Thomas Chaucer, whose father

[1] *Anglo-Norman Letters*, p. 435

was Geoffrey the poet, and whose mother was the sister of Katherine Swynford. He was therefore the first cousin of the three Beaufort brothers, and very well connected for a squire. Like all Speakers he asked to be excused from taking the office, and this being refused, asked to speak under the protestation that if he said anything displeasing to the King, this should be forgiven him, to which the King assented. A fortnight later on Wednesday 9 November he came back with his protestation, and reminded the King of the grants made in the last Parliament on condition that certain lords should be of the council and should ensure good governance. Arundel did not receive him with the patience which the King had shown to previous Speakers. He said shortly that he had already dealt with these matters, firstly in a speech, and secondly in a written schedule which had been given to the Commons in the frater of Gloucester Abbey which was serving as their meeting place. The councillors had honestly carried out their duties without receiving much in the way of thanks, and now asked to be released from the oaths which they had sworn in the previous Parliament, and for any blame for what they had done in the meanwhile. The King agreed to this, but in fact no change was made in the council for more than another year.

The Speaker then turned to another grievance and complained about purveyance for the royal household, whereupon the steward and treasurer of the household replied that if specific charges were brought against particular purveyors these would be investigated, and the purveyors, if found guilty, punished. Eventually William Wydcombe was brought up to answer the charges of Sir Thomas Brook. His case was twice postponed and finally referred to the council to be dealt with in London in the following January. Five days later the Commons complained of the losses in men and merchandise which had resulted from the failure to keep the seas, and once again urged that lords with possessions in the marches of Wales should stay there to guard them. It was agreed that Richard Clitheroe should have £2,668 for expenses incurred when he was acting as one of the admirals for the merchants, and that the council should negotiate with the other admiral, Nicholas Blackburn, about his expenses. Then Henry gave permission for the Commons to commune with the leading members of the council, the Archbishop, the Bishops of Winchester and Durham, the Duke of York, the Earl of Somerset and the Lords Roos and Burnell.

On Monday, 21 November the Lords were asked what grant was needed for the defence of the kingdom, and they replied that it should be one and a half fifteenths and tenths. Twelve members of the Commons were summoned to be told of this and eventually on 2 December it was granted together with the usual subsidy on wool and tunnage and poundage for two years. The Commons however protested at the Lords being consulted as to the amount of the grant. This was a breach of their right of granting subsidies, for if the Lords were to tell them how much was needed their initiative in money matters would be lost. They were promised that this procedure would not be used again. Nothing would be reported to the King until Lords and Commons had agreed, and then the report would be made by the Speaker of the Commons. Once more the Speaker reiterated the Commons' demand for the safe-keeping of the seas and for resistance to the King's enemies and rebels. As usual they also wanted to give thanks for his good service to the Prince, who had arrived from the siege of Aberystwyth by way of Hereford on 30 October and was now staying at the nearby priory of Llantony. He for his part went down on his knees before his father to declare the loyalty, and describe the faithful service, of the Duke of York, who was continually being accused of treasonable acts. The Commons' suggestion that the King's other three sons, Thomas, John and Humphrey, should be honoured with titles and lands, was, as in the past, ignored. A statute of the last Parliament had laid down that in the payment of annuities priority should be given to those who held the oldest grants from the Crown; but Henry now announced that preference would be given to those serving him from day to day, and that others should only be paid so far as was possible. A king could not afford to fail his own immediate servants. Finally he undertook that for two years from the Annunciation next to come, 25 March 1408, he would not ask for another parliamentary grant; and strangely enough this promise was almost kept, for it was not until January 1410 that the next Parliament met, after by far the longest interval between Parliaments of the whole reign.

On 23 November whilst Parliament was still sitting, Louis,

Duke of Orleans was murdered in a Paris street at the instigation of his rival, the Duke of Burgundy. Orleans had been Henry's worst enemy at the French court, responsible for directing all the attacks on Guyenne. His violent death and the consequent deepening of the divisions at the court of Charles VI, on whom madness was descending with increasing frequency, could not fail to be of advantage to the English King. On 27 September a safe-conduct had been issued to four French ambassadors allowing them to come to England with a following of not more than a hundred persons in all and to stay until Christmas in order to negotiate a truce. They had no doubt arrived at Gloucester during the Parliament, for on the day before it was dissolved, 1 December, Henry appointed the Bishop of Durham, Sir Thomas Erpyngham, Hugh Mortimer esquire and Master John Catryk to treat with them. Since neither Henry nor Charles VI recognised the other's title as 'King of France' a permanent peace was not possible, and perhaps not very much desired by either party, but a continuing truce was convenient for both. On this occasion agreement was reached on the 7th that a truce should endure for three months from the 15 January following, and this was renewed from time to time for short periods up to 1 May 1410.

After the execution of Archbishop Scrope in 1405, the Earl of Northumberland and Lord Bardolf fled to Scotland. Their possessions were confiscated, and Henry summoned them to York to answer charges of treason, but they no doubt valued their lives too highly to answer such a summons. On receiving a hint that the Regent Albany, who was constantly negotiating with Henry, might be willing to hand them over in exchange for some Scottish prisoners, they hastily made their way to Wales to join the prince of rebels, Owen Glendower. Their presence in Wales may well have provided the occasion for the sealing of the famous 'indentures tripartite' between Glendower, Northumberland and Sir Edmund Mortimer, under the terms of which Glendower was to have as an independent principality a much enlarged Wales, whilst Mortimer took England south of the Trent, and Northumberland 'the remnant northward lying off from Trent'. If Northumberland was present when the indentures were drawn up it must have been in February 1406, but some authorities believe that it was done in an earlier year, the parties to it not being present in person. All that is certain is that it did not, as in Shakespeare, take place before Shrewsbury.[1]

Glendower's own problems were however too great for him to be able to give anything but promises to the English rebels, who soon took themselves off to Paris, and then to Flanders, vainly hoping to enlist help against the Lancastrian usurper. Before the end of 1407 they were back in Scotland, corresponding with anyone in England who was sufficiently discontented to listen to them. Then in January 1408 they crossed the Tweed. No one expected an invasion in the depth of winter, and this proved to be one of the worst which Europe had known for many years with snows from December to March. Many of the Percy tenants in Northumberland would still turn out for their Earl, who soon had with him, besides Lord Bardolf, Lewis Bifort, Glendower's Bishop of Bangor, the Abbot of Halesowen, the Prior of Hexham, monks from both Hexham and Fountains, and a collection of disaffected people mainly from the lower classes. They were therefore able to advance unopposed through Durham to Darlington, Northallerton and Thirsk, which they reached on 16 February. The sheriff of Yorkshire, Sir Thomas Rokeby, had raised a small force and was then at Knaresborough. Northumberland is believed to have had hopes that Rokeby, with whom he had corresponded, might join him, but when they met at Bramham Moor on the 19th the sheriff's forces attacked. The old Earl was killed in the battle, Bardolf was captured and died of his wounds the same night, whilst the Bishop, the Abbot and the Prior were all made prisoners by the sheriff's men. Thus Henry's most persistent enemy, apart from Glendower, perished in a miniature battle on the Yorkshire moors, and for the rest of his reign Henry had peace at least in England.

After Parliament ended on 2 December the King stayed at Gloucester for some time, but whether he spent Christmas there is uncertain. By early January he was back at Eltham, and remained in or near London until the end of February. Then, when he must have heard the news of Bramham Moor, he set off for the north once more by way of Leicester and Nottingham to Wheel Hall, the Bishop of Durham's palace near Selby in Yorkshire. The Abbot of Halesowen was hanged, but the other rebels were pardoned after short periods of imprisonment, and Rokeby,

[1] Shakespeare, *Henry IV*, Part 1, Act 3, sc. i; Lloyd, *Glendower*, p. 93

the sheriff, was rewarded with a grant from the lands of the Earl of Northumberland. Easter and the remainder of April were spent by the King at his castle of Pontefract, without the usual visits to Eltham and Windsor, and then the court moved slowly back to London by the end of May; the rest of the year being spent at Mortlake, Hertford, Canterbury, Windsor, Langley and Lambeth, with Christmas once more at Eltham with the Queen.

The council met frequently in January, February and March 1408, both the Archbishop and the Prince being present. Arrangements were made to assign the revenues from alien priories, from the temporalities of vacant sees and abbeys, and from wardships and marriages, to pay some of the expenses of the royal household. In March a long petition was received from the merchants of the staple of Calais, whose loans had served to appease the mutinous garrison in the previous year. Now they were anxious to make sure of recovering their money from the wool subsidies. In June the council received a long letter from the ambassadors, who were at Calais negotiating a treaty with Flanders, and in July they were arranging a complicated indenture for paying Thomas, the King's second son, for the government of Ireland. Money had also been found during the summer to equip a fleet under the young Earl of Kent, who had been appointed admiral in the previous year, after a brief hard-hitting career in both battle and the lists. In September he was killed whilst besieging Bréhat in Brittany. At the end of the exchequer term Bishop Bubwith gave up the treasurership after fourteen months to be succeeded by Sir John Tiptoft, who had been treasurer of the household since the end of 1406. His place was taken by Sir Thomas Brounflete, a former controller of the household, who remained in the office until the end of the reign.

Meanwhile the Prince went off to devote himself to the Welsh war once again, and Arundel to ecclesiastical business. The siege of the castles of Aberystwyth and Harlech was vigorously resumed with the result that the former was captured in the autumn, and Harlech in the winter, probably in January 1409. This last was a severe blow to Glendower. His son-in-law, Mortimer, died during the siege, and Owen's wife, two daughters and three granddaughters (Mortimer's children) were all captured and sent to London. Glendower was left without any stronghold for use as his headquarters, and for the storage of his treasure.

Apart from the business of the Government the Archbishop of Canterbury was very much occupied with efforts to heal the great schism in the Church, and at home to suppress the Lollards. In the summer he held a convocation of the province of Canterbury in St. Paul's, to which doctors from Oxford and Cambridge were invited, to discuss the withdrawal of allegiance from Pope Gregory XII and the sending of a delegation to the general council which was shortly to be held at Pisa. Another convocation met at St. Paul's in January 1409 for further discussion of the schism and the council, and also promulgated a series of constitutions against heretics, which Arundel had drawn up. These attempted to prevent religious disputation, and forbade the translation of the Bible into English, except with the approval of a bishop. Later in the year Arundel tried to enforce these measures, and Richard Courtenay, the chancellor of Oxford University, appealed to the Prince to defend its liberties. This may have been one of the factors leading to the breach between the Archbishop and the Prince. Certainly Lollardy was manifesting itself more as an anti-clerical than a doctrinal movement. The clergy were very unpopular, and Arundel's rigid interpretation of his duty to suppress heresy did not have the approval of the knightly class. Although a faithful son of the church, the Prince may well have shared some of the antagonism to the clergy, which was felt by many of the knights who had served under him in Wales, Sir John Oldcastle being the outstanding, but not altogether exceptional, example.

In the interval between the two convocations the Cardinal Archbishop of Bordeaux, who had taken his part in the defence of that city as a loyal subject of Henry, arrived in England as the spokesman of the cardinals assembled at Pisa. He was received by the King with all due ceremony, and preached before him, setting forth the cardinals' case for deposing the two rival Popes as a first step towards uniting the Church. In January Robert Hallum, Bishop of Salisbury, Henry Chichele, newly-appointed Bishop of St. David's, and Thomas Chillenden, the Prior of Canterbury, were chosen to lead the English delegation; and in the next month Nicholas Bubwith, the ex-treasurer, now in his third see of Bath and Wells, was given leave to attend, but there is no evidence that he ever did so. The council opened in Pisa on 25 March, but the main part of the English delegation only arrived a month later, and from that time Bishop Hallum acted as their leader. In June both rival Popes were deposed and a new one, Alexander V, elected, but he died within a year and was replaced by Baldassare Cossa as John XXIII.

In England the King's health was causing most anxiety. In 1408 David di Nigarellis of Lucca, a doctor of European renown, was called into his service and remained with him for some four years. If he did not cure Henry, at least he did not die, although the winter of 1408–9 seems to have produced the worst crisis before the fatal one of 1412–13. In December both the Prince and Thomas his brother were summoned to the court because fears were entertained for their father's life. After Christmas he was moved to Greenwich, in the hope that the fresher air by the river might be good for him. There on 21 January 1409 he made his will, which was witnessed by six members of the council, the chancellor, treasurer, chamberlain, keeper of the privy seal, Duke of York and Bishop of Durham, and amongst others, Sir Thomas Erpyngham, John Norbury and Robert Waterton.[1] The presence of the last three proves that Henry's old and faithful friends still followed his court, although now excluded from the council.

The will is short and written in English, doubtless the first royal will to be so. Henry confessed his sins and asked for forgiveness. He wished that he should be buried in Canterbury Cathedral, that his debts should be paid, and that the Queen's dower should for the future be charged against the revenues of the duchy of Lancaster. The Prince was to be executor, but could name such others to assist him as he wished. This will was eventually superseded, but the final one has not survived. Its hurried completion on this occasion proved to be unnecessary. Henry stayed at Greenwich for two months, slowly recovering. In mid-March he was able to return to Eltham, where there must have been more room for his court, to spend Easter as usual. On 10 March whilst at Greenwich Henry granted the castle and lordship of Queenborough in Sheppey to Archbishop Arundel for life. To save the chancellor from the embarrassment and difficulties which might arise from sealing his own grant the

[1] Nichols, *Wills*, p. 203; Weever, *Fun. Mon.*, p. 208

King sent for the great seal and had it applied to the letters patent
in his own presence and in that of Bishop Langley of Durham,
Sir Thomas Beaufort, the treasurer, steward of the household,
John Wakeryng, the keeper of the rolls of chancery, and others.
Seven days later, perhaps as a thank-offering for his recovery from
illness, Henry fulfilled a promise of some years' standing by
founding a chantry chapel with eight chaplains on the battlefield of Shrewsbury, to pray for the souls of those who had fallen
in the battle.[1] It was only a few weeks earlier that he had endowed
a similar chantry by the tombs of his parents in St. Paul's Cathedral
to pray for their souls.[2]

On Easter Saturday, 6 April, the Queen perhaps reminded him
of the difficulties which might arise if she were left a poor widow,
for a privy seal writ was sent to the chancellor about her dower,
and on it Henry wrote with his own hand:

> With al min trew hert, worchipfull and well beloved cosin, I grete
> yow ofte well and yow next God I thanke of the goode hele that
> I am inne, for so I may well without saying so. Reverend and well
> beloved cosin, I send yow a bylle for the Quene towchyng her dower,
> wych I pray yow micht be sped, and ye shall do us gret ese ther inne,
> wherfor we woll thank yow with al owre hert. Yowr trew sone
> Henrye.[3]

This letter was evidently successful, for on 1 July Queen Joan
received grants of lands and revenues to the value of 10,000
marks yearly, mainly from the possessions of alien priories,
which had with the sanction of Parliament been permanently
appropriated.[4]

Henry was now able to travel short distances, but he was to
make no more long journeys during the remainder of his life.
The furthest limits of his travel were to be Leicester and Kenilworth, but mostly he stayed within fifty miles or so of London.
At the beginning of May he went to Sutton by Chiswick on the
way to Birdsnest, his hunting lodge in Windsor Park, then to
Easthampstead, Swallowfield, Henley-on-the-Heath, Chertsey and
back to Windsor Castle by the end of the month, mostly journeys

[1] *Cal. Close* (1405–9), p. 498; *Cal. Pat.* (1408–13), p. 59
[2] *Cal. Pat.* (1408–13), p. 51
[3] P.R.O., C 81/1362/46
[4] *Cal. Pat.* (1408–13), pp. 85–7

of well under twenty miles. From Birdsnest on 9 May he answered a letter which Arundel had written to him with his own hand. He thanked Arundel for his letter, assured him that he was in good health and suggested candidates for appointment as a serjeant-at-law in place of Robert Tirwhyt, who had recently been made a judge of the King's bench. Once again Henry added a note in his own hand:

> My Dere Worshypfful and well beluved cousyn I thank you hertely of the grete besinesse that ye do for me and for my reaume and trust pleynly in yowre good conduit and hopynge to God to spek to you hastely and thank you with good herte
> Yowre true frend and chyld in God. H.R.[1]

These exchanges of letters written with their own hands suggest that at this time at least King and Archbishop were working together with a high degree of mutual trust.

June and July were spent by the court at the houses of the Archbishop of York and the Bishop of Ely in London, at St. John's House, Clerkenwell, or at the Queen's house of Havering-atte-Bower in Essex. At Clerkenwell the King, the Prince and the whole court sat for four days on a wooden scaffold to watch the parish clerks playing the story of the Bible; and for eight days at the end of July he watched a tournament at Smithfield between English knights and the followers of the young steward of Hainault, who was feasted at Windsor on 4 August.[2] Afterwards Henry went into Hampshire as far as Bagshot and Romsey, and in November he went by way of St. Albans, Stony Stratford and Northampton to Leicester, returning by the same road to spend Christmas for the seventh or eighth time at Eltham.

Most of the work of government was being done by Arundel and the council. They were treating with the Hanse, and with the Scots, and sending an embassy to France to arrange a further extension of the truce. With the recapture of Harlech and Aberystwyth Glendower had ceased to be a real danger to the King's authority. It was clearly only a question of time before the rebellion was finally put down, so that the Prince's presence was no longer needed in Wales. On 28 February 1409 he was appointed

---

[1] Rymer, *Foedera*, vol. viii, p. 584; R. *Letters, H. IV.*, vol. ii, pp. 275–7
[2] Wylie, *H. IV*, vol. iii, pp. 245–8

Constable of Dover and Warden of the Cinque Ports in place of Sir Thomas Erpyngham, and soon on the death of his uncle, the Earl of Somerset, he was to become Captain of Calais also. On 18 August he attended a meeting of the council at Westminster along with Arundel, the Duke of York, the Earl of Somerset, Sir Thomas Beaufort, the treasurer and the keeper of the privy seal. A meeting of the council without any bishops, apart from Arundel, was most unusual. Even Henry Beaufort of Winchester was absent, but in compensation both his brothers, John, Earl of Somerset and Sir Thomas attended. This was the first recorded attendance of Sir Thomas, and the last of Somerset, who died on 16 March following. Their presence was an indication of the increasing influence both of their own family and of the Prince.

This council discussed relations with Prussia and with Spain, the governance of Ireland and the expenses of Prince Thomas, the keeping of the Scottish march by Prince John, the truce with Scotland and the needs of Guyenne. The steward of Aquitaine, Gaillard de Durfort, and the mayor of Bordeaux, Sir Thomas Swynbourne, had come to London to confer with the council. After he had described the difficulties of the position in Bordeaux and the surrounding countryside, Swynbourne was sent back with a small force to restore the authority of the English King, and make the remains of the duchy as defensible as possible. After two and a half years there he returned to England in 1412 and died shortly afterwards. On 21 November the council arranged for certain sums from the wool subsidy and from tunnage and poundage to be allotted to the expenses of the royal household, amounting to about £6,500 up to the following Easter. But this council was breaking up. The treasurer resigned on 19 December and the chancellor two days later.

Chapter 16

Henry Prince of Wales, January 1410–October 1411

THE sudden resignation of the two principal officers of state, Arundel, the chancellor, and Tiptoft, the treasurer, just before Christmas 1409, shows that a crisis had arisen in the conduct of the government, but the nature of this crisis can only be surmised. The normal procedure was for the new officer to be appointed and take over on the day that his predecessor gave up office, but on this occasion a long interval elapsed, suggesting not only that the vacancies were unexpected, but also that there was no agreement on who should fill them. The King, who was as usual at Eltham for the holiday, kept the great seal with him for a month, causing writs and letters to be sealed with it from day to day until 19 January. On that day he gave it to John Wakeryng, keeper of the rolls of chancery, who applied it as necessary at the King's command until 31 January.[1] The office of treasurer was filled rather earlier, by the appointment on 6 January of Henry, Lord Scrope of Masham, nephew of the rebel Archbishop Scrope of York, and a newcomer to the royal council. It is clear that he now came in as a supporter of the Prince of Wales, for treason against whom as King he was to be beheaded in 1415; for there can be no doubt that the result, and perhaps also the cause, of the crisis was the accession to power of the Prince.

So long as he was fighting in Wales the Prince appears to have retained the full confidence of his father; but it is a tradition that all Princes of Wales, indeed all eldest sons, come into opposition to their fathers. This is a normal part of the jealousy felt by one generation for another, the desire of the younger to wrest authority from the elder, but in Prince Henry's case it was unfortunate that the two men who were most kind to him in his youth, and who became to some extent the heroes of his boyhood, Richard II and Hotspur, should have become his father's two principal enemies. It is significant that as soon as

[1] *Cal. Close* (1409–13), p. 115

226

he became king, Henry V caused the corpse of Richard to be carefully reburied, and although he remained loyal to his father at Shrewsbury – his future being tied to that of his father he had really no alternative – the sudden break with Hotspur must have been a great shock to him. A large number of Hotspur's servants and followers afterwards found places in the service of the Prince. Perhaps he sympathised with men who had devotedly served the Percies and lost their chief, and no doubt they tended to influence his mind in favour of Hotspur's memory. There was therefore constant tension and sometimes open opposition between father and son during the later years of the reign, and this was perhaps aggravated by the Prince's unruly behaviour. Between the ages of twelve and twenty-two he had been mainly occupied with the war in Wales, but from very early in the reign he had, in addition to the manors and castles of his duchy of Cornwall, his own house of Coldharbour in the City of London, and doubtless spent part of the year there. A number of chroniclers remarked on the reformation in his behaviour when he became king, implying that it had been notoriously bad before, and one said that he served Venus as eagerly as Mars,[1] but most of the stories of his riotous youth are based on legends which grew up long after his death, and some may well have originated in the deeds of other princes.

Most of the autumn of 1409 had been spent by the Prince at Berkhamstead, and there on 20 November he entertained his father, his brother Humphrey, the Duke of York, Lord Beaumont and other members of the court to dinner, on their way from St. Albans to Stony Stratford. After a short tour early in December which took him to Towcester and Daventry he returned to Berkhamstead and stayed there until the end of the year.[2] He was not therefore with the court when the chancellor and treasurer for whatever reason resigned.

As early as 26 October a Parliament had been summoned to meet at Bristol on 27 January 1410. On 2 December orders were issued for transporting rolls, records and other things required for the Parliament from Westminster to Bristol, and arrangements were made for the court to spend Christmas at Worcester, so as to be on the way to Bristol. Then on 18 December the place

---

[1] Elmham, *Vita*, p. 12
[2] Wylie, *H. IV*, vol. iii, p. 272; vol. iv, p. 247

of meeting was changed to Westminster. This was the moment that Arundel, who had no doubt hoped to dominate the Parliament at Bristol as he had done that at Gloucester, resigned, but whether there was any connexion between the change and his resignation there is no means of knowing. When Parliament did meet on 27 January the opening address, usually given by the chancellor, was delivered by Bishop Beaufort. As he had already held the office, was a bishop, and reputed supporter of the Prince of Wales, he was the obvious choice for the office; but it was in fact his brother, Sir Thomas Beaufort, who was appointed chancellor four days later. Possibly the Prince wanted someone less experienced, who would be more dependent on himself, or possibly it was thought better to appoint a layman, in view of the strongly anti-clerical feelings of the Parliament, which may already have become manifest. For whatever reason it was in the Parliament chamber of the Archbishop's own palace at Lambeth, where the King had taken up residence, that the great seal was given to Sir Thomas in the presence of both the Archbishop and the Prince.

The text chosen for Bishop Beaufort's opening address was '*Decet nos implere omnem justiciam*' or 'It becometh us to fulfil all righteousness.'[1] He made the usual declaration about the King's wish to preserve the liberties of the Church and of his subjects, and spoke of the need for good governance at home, of the truce with Scotland, and of the threat to Calais from the Duke of Burgundy who was now governing France. He then discussed two forms of government *de jure regiminis* and *de jure subjectionis*. Unfortunately we are not told what he said about them, and can therefore only conjecture that he was feeling the way towards a definition of constitutional monarchy, an anticipation of Fortescue's distinction between *jus regale* and *jus politicum et regale*, that is between absolute and limited monarchy. The only reported development of his theme was his telling how Aristotle is supposed to have said that the real defences of any state lie in the love of its people for their ruler. People, he said, should give honour and obedience, reverence and benevolence, and cordial assistance, to the King, who was asking for the advice and help of the estates.

The next morning at eight o'clock the Commons met at the

[1] Matthew, chap. 3, v. 15

abbey, and at nine they presented Thomas Chaucer, the Beauforts' cousin, as their Speaker once more. Almost the only business recorded for the first session of this Parliament was a request that a petition about the alteration of the statute against the Lollards should be returned to the Commons as nothing had come of it. The King agreed to this on condition that it was not taken as a precedent. The reform of the statute against Lollardy may have had very wide implications. Moreover it was not the only or even the main attack on the Church which this session produced. It is noteworthy that the Parliament Roll often records attacks on the King and his Government, but that those on the Church are almost always passed over in silence.

Since the meeting of the last Parliament there had been one important change amongst the Lords. Lord Cobham had died, and Sir John Oldcastle, having married his granddaughter and heiress, was summoned to Parliament in her right as Lord Cobham. Oldcastle, who had sat for Herefordshire in the first Parliament of 1404 and served under the Prince in Wales with some distinction, was well known for his Lollard opinions. His presence in the Lords would be at least an encouragement to those anti-clerical knights who wished to put forward their views in the Commons. As on several earlier occasions the confiscation of the wealth of the clergy was proposed, but this time some detailed figures were worked out or guessed at and a definite plan produced. The wealth of the bishops, abbots and priors would, it was believed, provide sufficient revenue to maintain 15 earls, 1,500 knights, and 6,200 squires, as well as £20,000 annually for the King as well. The larger religious houses were thought to be worth over £200,000 yearly, which would enable every township to maintain its own poor, and provide a hundred almshouses, whilst the revenue of the smaller houses would serve to maintain 15,000 parish priests.[1] But the time for such drastic measures was not yet. King and Prince must have been united by opposition to such proposals, and, as already said, they were not officially recorded at all by the clerk of the Parliament.

On Saturday, 15 March no progress having been made the Commons asked for an adjournment for Easter, promising to get down to business on their return, which was accordingly

[1] Wylie, *H. IV*, vol. iii, pp. 309–10; Galbraith, *St. Albans Chron.*, pp. 52–6

fixed for 7 April. The King was staying either at Westminster or at Lambeth with the Archbishop, who had nonetheless dropped out of the council for the first time since Henry landed at Ravenspur. The council had already been negotiating with the Regent Albany about the possibility of releasing his son, the Earl of Fife, but the first meeting of the year of which a record has survived, was held at the Prince's house, Coldharbour in the City, on 8 February. Only the Prince himself and the new chancellor and treasurer, Sir Thomas Beaufort and Lord Scrope, are known to have been present. The business of the meeting was to reach a settlement with the other Beaufort brother, the Earl of Somerset, on the financial implications of various grants which he had had from the King.

On 23 April, a fortnight after the reassembly of Parliament, the Commons presented eighteen articles. Almost all of them had been raised and agreed to earlier in the reign, and to most of them the King now assented without qualification. He was asked to appoint wise councillors, who would be sworn with the judges, and who would not accept presents or bribes. Statutes and common law should be enforced, and judges in special courts should not take common law cases. The marches towards Scotland should be properly guarded and the Welsh rebels subdued. If a grant were made it should be devoted to defence, and as war was likely with France, foreigners should either be kept out of the kingdom or supervised to prevent them from spying. To other articles Henry gave a qualified assent. As to purveyance for the household, he said that he wished to live of his own, and revenues which fell in to the Crown would be devoted to the expenses of his household. On the keeping of the seas and the truces, and on rumours and riots in the counties north of Trent, Shropshire and Devon, he would consult his council and then take such action as was thought necessary. The Commons claimed that as the revenue from the customs and subsidies had amounted to £160,000 in the fourteenth year of Richard II (1390–1) and was now very much less, the fault must lie with the collectors of customs, and alien merchants must be evading the cloth subsidy. In fact this figure was a gross exaggeration. The total revenue from customs and subsidies had rarely exceeded a quarter of this figure during Richard's reign, and almost certainly never a third. Henry expressed doubts. Some of his advisers may have been aware that there was a real falling-off in wool exports, and no more cheating of, or by, the collectors than in the past. He agreed that if a subsidy were granted three parts of it should be devoted to paying the garrison of Calais. Finally another pro-Lollard suggestion was rejected. This was the request that persons suspected of heresy and taken into custody at the instigation of the bishops and other religious dignitaries under the statute of 1401 should be arrested in the normal way with other accused persons, without suffering any injury or extortion whatsoever. Heretics could not expect to be treated merely as criminals.

On Friday, 2 May the Commons again asked to be told the names of the King's councillors. Henry said that certain lords that he had chosen and named for his council had asked to be excused for various reasonable causes, and he had accordingly excused them, possibly a reference to Arundel and Tiptoft. The remainder whom he had chosen as councillors were the Prince, Bishops Beaufort, Langley and Bubwith, of Winchester, Durham and Bath, the Earls of Arundel and Westmorland and Lord Burnell. In view of the exclusion of his uncle, the Earl of Arundel was perhaps a surprising newcomer. The Prince, echoing the words of the Archbishop on a similar occasion, said that the councillors would undertake their task only if a grant were made by the Commons. Then apart from the Prince himself, who was excused on account of his high rank, the members were sworn with the judges and others. Presumably the three officers, chancellor, treasurer, and keeper of the privy seal, were assumed to be members and included amongst the others. The swearing-in made the dropping of the Archbishop an officially accepted fact without, of course, ever mentioning his name. A week later, on 9 May, the last day of the Parliament, Henry Chichele, Bishop of St. David's, and the Earl of Warwick were added to the council because it was feared that the Bishop of Durham and the Earl of Westmorland might be needed on the Scottish march, and so be unable to attend.

The subsidies were then granted. The King, or his council, had asked for a regular grant of fifteenths and tenths for the rest of his life, thus freeing him, or them, from parliamentary control, but this was refused. Instead the grant was spread over three years, one and a half fifteenths and tenths, one half to be collected at Martinmas (11 November) in each of the three years, 1410, 1411 and 1412. The usual wool subsidy and tunnage and pound-age were also granted. Spreading the grant over three years meant that the King need not, indeed was not expected to, call another Parliament for three years, but as the grant was rather less than the minimum on which the government could reason-ably be conducted, the council was forced to spend most of its time contriving financial expedients, and in fact recalled Parlia-ment a little more than half way through the three years. The King was to have only £13,666 for his own expenditure, a lower figure by several thousands than the household actually received from the exchequer in any year of the reign, and probably less than two-thirds of what was really needed to cover all the King's expenses. The most important statute of this Parliament laid down penalties for sheriffs who did not hold elections in legal form, and enabled justices of assize to enquire into elections. Finally the Commons made their now customary suggestion that suitable advancement should be given to the King's sons. This time Henry thanked the Commons for their advice, and promised that he would advance his sons as soon as he could do so hand-somely. But it was not in fact until 9 July 1412 that Thomas, the second son, was created Duke of Clarence, and the other two had to wait for their dukedoms until their brother was king. Four days earlier Henry had made his only other addition to the upper ranks of the peerage when Sir Thomas Beaufort, then ex-chancellor, became Earl of Dorset.

Whilst the Parliament was engaged in debating anti-clerical measures, John Badby, a tailor, was burnt as a heretic at Smith-field. Arrested at the beginning of 1409 and examined before the Bishop of Worcester, Badby had been given a year in which to recant his heretical opinions, but having refused to do so, was now brought to trial before the convocation of Canterbury at Blackfriars. Besides Archbishop Arundel, eight bishops, the Duke of York, the chancellor, Sir Thomas Beaufort, Lord Roos and many other lords were present. In front of them all he stoutly maintained that the sacramental bread of the mass was merely bread and not the body of Christ. Brought before con-vocation again four days later, this time in St. Paul's, he refused to recant, was pronounced a heretic, and delivered to the sheriffs of London, who were ordered by a writ from the King in council to put him to death by burning. He was accordingly taken to Smithfield and burnt the same afternoon. The Prince himself was present, urged Badby to recant, and even had him dragged half dead from the flames, but the tailor withstood all entreaties and died for his own faith. Despite the current anti-clerical feeling his death was apparently accepted without demur. It was mainly the clergy who were unpopular rather than the faith.

The ending of the Parliament left the government for the first time entirely in the hands of the Prince and his council. Henry was probably too much handicapped by his health to assert himself with any regularity against his masterful son. The council met on 16 June at Blackfriars, on the 18th at Westminster and on the 19th at the Bishop of Hertford's house in the City, the Prince and the members sworn in Parliament including the three officers being present. On the first occasion it was agreed that three parts of the wool subsidy should be assigned for Calais, and detailed arrangements were made. The Prince had now succeeded his uncle, the late Earl of Somerset, as Captain of Calais, though he was not able to spend very much time there. Arrangements were also made for paying nearly £5,000, partly by assignments on the wool subsidy, partly in cash raised by loans, and partly in merchants' bonds, for the defence of Berwick Castle and the east march, which were in the charge of Prince John. Assignments were ordered for the royal household, and the raising of loans was organised. John Hende agreed to lend 1,000 marks and Italian merchants £500. As it was desired to give all lenders the best possible security these loans were given priority on the wool subsidy.

When the meeting was resumed on the 19th the council had a petition before them from Prince Thomas, who had claims amounting altogether to over £10,000. The council agreed that tallies which he had been unable to cash should be replaced, that if he produced the indentures for his service in Ireland they would endeavour to arrange for him to have what was due, and finally that his claims for pay as Captain of Guines in the march of Calais would be settled when the whole question of Calais came up for discussion. They also had to find £5,000 for Wales. It was probably in this year, 1410, that Glendower launched his last attack, which ended disastrously. In beating off the rebels the Constable of Welshpool Castle captured Rhys ap Griffith,

Philip Scudamore and Rhys ap Tudor, and in doing so brought the rebellion effectively to an end,[1] but there were still about a thousand men serving at the King's own expense, and the cost of keeping them in the field was nearly £1,000 per month. The Prince finally told the council that his father wished the chancellor to have a special reward above the normal salary of his office, but left the amount to their discretion. It was no doubt thought that not having the revenues of a bishopric to maintain his state Beaufort would need to be paid more than the chancellor usually received for his official duties. Almost daily until 30 July when they met in Robert Lovell's house in Old Fish Street the council went on discussing the defence of Calais and the raising of money, commissioners being appointed to raise loans in each county. The King had gone meanwhile to Woodstock and remained there for most of August. Limitations on the expenditure of the royal household and on royal grants had made the financial situation somewhat easier than in the early years of the reign, but it was still very difficult. It is evident that the council was now doing a great deal of planning of expenditure, with estimates of revenue and needful expenditure constantly placed before it. It was now reckoned that the half fifteenth and tenth voted by Parliament should bring in nearly £19,000, but the cost of Calais was £14,000, the two Scottish marches £9,000, Ireland £5,000, and the castle of Fronsac in Guyenne £1,600, making £29,600 for defence alone. Hence the need for loans and assignments on the wool subsidy.

After the death of John Beaufort, Earl of Somerset, in April 1410, Prince Thomas obtained a dispensation to marry his widow, Margaret Holland, daughter of the Earl of Kent, and this led to a quarrel with Henry Beaufort, who was his brother's executor. The Prince sided with Beaufort, and so caused a further rift in the royal family, Thomas tending henceforth to side with his father against the Prince.

From Woodstock Henry went to Leicester in September, spent October four miles away at Groby, and November and early December between the two. He went on to Coventry and Kenilworth in January and February 1411, and eventually to Windsor for April, and so back to the environs of London, Lambeth, Rotherhithe and Stratford for the summer from May

[1] Lloyd, *Glendower*, pp. 141-2

to September. For much of the time he was therefore as physically isolated from the government, as he was barred in theory by the powers entrusted by Parliament to the Prince and the council. By March 1411, however, the council were finding that the financial problem was too much for them, and recourse to Parliament not being possible, at least without a confession of complete failure, a great council was assembled instead. This met at Lambeth on the 19th, Henry himself presiding. Besides the Prince, both archbishops, ten bishops, two abbots, the Duke of York, four earls, ten barons, the chancellor, treasurer and keeper of the privy seal were present. Complicated financial statements, which now survive only in an obviously incomplete form, were put before them. It was shown that three-quarters of the wool subsidy being earmarked for Calais, only £7,500 was left, instead of the £20,000 that was needed towards the defence of the Scottish marches, Ireland and Guyenne, and the only solution suggested was to cut £3,000 off the amount to be spent on Guyenne, still leaving a deficit of £10,000. Other revenues which were listed, including a half tenth from the clergy, tunnage and poundage, the petty custom, the farms of alien priories and feudal incidents, were expected to produce £18,000, whilst the cost of the household and of the domestic administration of the realm would be at least £22,000, thus leaving a further deficit of £4,000, without providing anything for annuities payable at the exchequer, or for salaries for the councillors. There seems to be no mention of the half fifteenth and tenth from the laity due to be collected in November, and the evidence is insufficient to enable us to judge how critical the situation was, whilst the only remedy recorded as having been suggested by King or Lords was greater diligence by the tax collectors, which they hoped might help to bridge the gap.[1] Although a letter from a certain William Stokes at Middelburg in Holland to the council, dated 25 May, and supposedly in this year, listed a number of merchants who had evaded payment of customs and subsidies for wools which they had exported,[2] this could be no more than an extreme example of wishful thinking. No appreciable increase of revenue could be expected from this source. Some small addition to the revenues was however provided by

[1] Nicolas, *P.C.*, vol, ii, pp. 6–18
[2] R. *Letters, H. IV*, vol. ii, pp. 303–8

fines for failing to take up the order of knighthood, which all holders of £40 a year of land or rent had been ordered to do within three months in November 1410. Most of them apparently preferred to pay the fines which now on 20 May the exchequer was ordered to collect. But as these amounted to only about £1 or £2 each their contribution to the royal revenues was not great. As always there was no real solution except a large parliamentary grant, and failing that the exchequer had to carry on from day to day, anticipating the next year's revenues, and hoping that a sufficient number of loans could be raised to keep the machine working.

Arundel had continued meanwhile with his attempts to heal the schism in the Church, and at home to suppress the Lollards. In pursuance of the second objective he attempted a visitation of the University of Oxford, where heretical doctrines were supposed to originate. Courtenay, the chancellor of the university, forcibly prevented the Archbishop and his nephew, the Earl of Arundel, with other followers from entering St. Mary's Church, and deadlock was reached. After a good deal of argument it was arranged that the dispute should be referred to the King. Accordingly the chancellor and the proctors appeared with the Archbishop before the King at Lambeth on 9 September 1411. In spite of the Prince's and his own supposed friendliness towards the university, the King gave judgment for his Archbishop. The claim to visit and control the university was recognised, the chancellor was deposed, the proctors imprisoned, and university representatives had to apologise publicly in St. Mary's and seek the Archbishop's pardon.

In France the situation which was soon to enable the Prince, when he became king, to invade and conquer was already developing. In 1409 a formal reconciliation took place between the Duke of Burgundy and the sons of his murdered rival, Orleans, but this truce soon gave way to conditions of civil war. In July 1411, driven from Paris by the rival faction, Burgundy sought English aid against the young Duke of Orleans, and the King's uncle, the Duke of Berri. He offered to hand over certain Flemish towns, and to marry his daughter Anne to the Prince of Wales. Accordingly on 1 September Henry appointed envoys to treat with him. These were Henry Chichele, Bishop of St. David's, the Earl of Arundel, both members of the council,

Sir Francis Court, Hugh Mortimer and John Catryk, the last two being much experienced in such negotiations with the French. They were instructed to find out first of all what dowry the Duke was prepared to offer with his daughter, and what help he wanted against Orleans and Berri. Meanwhile despite all the financial difficulties preparations were going ahead for an expedition to France in defence of Calais, under the command of the King himself. This was one of several occasions when Henry proposed to take the field in person against the French, but as in earlier years nothing came of it. At the last moment he changed his mind, being probably too ill for such exertions. The English troops which did go across were put under the command of Arundel, who was playing the part of allied commander as well as ambassador at the Duke of Burgundy's court; and with their assistance the Duke, John the Fearless, was able to regain control of Paris and of the King at least momentarily. At the beginning of 1412, however, although negotiations for the marriage of the Prince to Anne of Burgundy were still going on, it was the turn of the Dukes of Berri and Orleans, Burgundy's bitter foes, to appeal to Henry for English help.

Chapter 17

The return of Arundel, the end, November 1411–March 1413

ON 21 September 1411 another Parliament, the ninth of the reign and the last of which any recorded proceedings survive, was summoned to Westminster for 9 November. For nearly two years the Prince and the councillors appointed with him had struggled to make the meagre grant of the last Parliament meet all the country's needs, and the calling of a new Parliament a year before the grants had expired suggests a confession of failure, which enabled the King and Archbishop Arundel to reassert themselves. However, when Lord Scrope, the treasurer of the Prince's party, gave up that office in December after spending only the very small amount of £7,000 since Michaelmas, there was over £8,000 in cash remaining at the exchequer.

Henry had been for some time at Windsor. Ill-health had prevented him from taking command of the expedition to France, and now in November being unable even to reach Westminster on the appointed day he empowered the chancellor, Sir Thomas Beaufort, to open Parliament in his name and to prorogue it. This was most probably the moment at which Bishop Beaufort suggested that the King should resign the crown, and the Prince have himself made king; Henry being unfit to rule, and Parliament being there to endorse the change. Because unsuccessful plots had no place in official records and chroniclers were naturally chary of saying too much about their details, nothing is really known about this Beaufort plot, if it may be so-called; but when accused ten years later Beaufort did not explicitly deny that he had suggested an abdication, and there is sufficient chronicle evidence to indicate that some such suggestion was made. Six knights, one of whom, Sir Roger Leche, was steward of the Prince's household, were arrested and sent to the Tower on 23 October, but they were very soon released, without, so far as is known, being charged with any offence. Plot or some other cause certainly roused the King to prompt action. After empowering the chancellor to open Parliament because he could not get there in time, Henry was in fact only one day late.

On Tuesday, 3 November when the members had been received by the steward of the royal household, as the custom was, the chancellor put off the opening until the next day; and then in the King's presence he made the usual speech, giving three reasons for the summoning of Parliament, the need for good governance, the due execution of the laws within the realm, and the defence of the lands outside the realm and of the seas. The first required loyal counsel, honour and obedience to the King, the second prompt remedy for infractions of the law, and the third exposition by the King of his needs, and speedy provision for them by Parliament. On Thursday the Commons presented Thomas Chaucer as their Speaker for the third time. As usual he asked to be excused, but Henry merely said that he accepted the choice of the Commons. Chaucer then asked to speak under protestation, to which Henry replied that he might speak under such protestation as his predecessors, but not otherwise. For, said the King, roused perhaps by the attack on his possession of the crown to take the initiative, and still resenting the restrictions imposed by the last Parliament on his freedom of action, he wanted no kind of novelty in this Parliament, but wished to preserve his liberty and prerogatives as fully as any of his predecessors. The Speaker then asked to have until the next day to put his protest into writing, but it was not in fact until Saturday that the King was able to receive it.

Archbishop Arundel and Richard, Lord Grey, the King's chamberlain, were appointed to arbitrate in a dispute between William, Lord Roos and Robert Tirwhyt, a justice of the King's bench about rights of common at Wrawby in Lincolnshire, in pursuit of which Tirwhyt had assembled armed men to lie in wait for Roos. As to the disputed rights the arbiters directed the parties to accept the judgment of William Gascoigne, the chief justice, but Tirwhyt was ordered to bring two tuns of Gascon wine, two fat oxen and twelve fat sheep to Melton Ross to provide a feast for all who had been present at the 'loveday' when he had staged his ambush. Before them all he was to apologise to Lord Roos, and to promise to pay him 500 marks. Roos, however, was to decline the payment and accept his apology. Despite this unlawful behaviour Tirwhyt was allowed to retain his place on the judicial bench for the rest of his life, nearly twenty years. That a judge might take part in such an affray is perhaps some indication of the lawless tendencies which at all times threatened the peace of the country. Another dispute that was formally settled in this Parliament was that between the Archbishop and the University of Oxford, the King's decision in favour of the Archbishop being enrolled. A number of private petitions were also answered, but of the King's own business there is very little record.

On 30 November the Speaker asked the King to thank the lords who had been appointed to his council in the last Parliament. Whereupon they all knelt before the King, and the Prince said that they had all done their duty as promised in that Parliament. The King thanked them, saying that he was satisfied with their good and loyal service, advice and duty whilst they were of the council. This presumably constituted their dismissal or at least discharge from office, though nothing was said according to the records of this Parliament about nominating a new council. If councillors were named the fact was not entered on the Parliament Roll; but probably the King, who was asserting himself more strongly than for many years, decided to keep their names to himself until after the Parliament had dispersed.

About taxation also there is no record apart from the terms of the grants which the Commons made. The subsidy on wools was granted at the usual rates for one year from Michaelmas 1412, three quarters being reserved for Calais, and the remaining quarter to be expended on the defence of the realm. Tunnage and poundage was also granted, but there was no mention of a fifteenth and tenth, presumably because there was still one half outstanding from the grant of the last Parliament to be collected in the following November, 1412. Instead a revised version of the taxation experiment of 1404 was imposed, in the form of a payment of 6s. 8d. on each £20 worth of land to be collected only from holders of at least that amount on 3 February 1412. Commissioners were however not appointed to assess it until 2 January with instructions to report before the end of February. Again the Commons asked that this grant should not be taken as a precedent, but in fact no Government was likely to wish so to take it, because the yield was so low. Some assessments, unlike those for 1404 have survived, and a comparison of eight counties with the corresponding estimates made by the council for the yield of a half fifteenth and tenth in 1410 suggests that this tax brought in a little over £2,000 compared with the £19,000 which they expected to get from the half fifteenth.[1]

The last day of the Parliament was Saturday, 19 December, on which it was said that the chancellor had been to show the Commons a certain article of the last Parliament, and the Commons were now asking through their Speaker what the King wanted done about it. To this Henry replied that he wished to keep his liberties and prerogative as fully as any of his predecessors. The Commons agreed, and the King thanked them, annulling the article and all its consequences. This mysterious article was evidently so derogatory of the King's standing and authority that even though it had been imposed by the last Parliament neither King nor council was willing to have its terms openly recorded.

The only other business of any importance was a slight devaluing of the gold nobles, because owing to their excessive value they were being melted down and taken abroad. Fifty instead of forty-eight were in future to be coined from a pound of gold. Their face value remained at 6s. 8d. each or three to the pound sterling. All this being accomplished the chancellor thanked the members in the King's name for their great labours, and the Parliament was dissolved.

The official account suggests a quiet session with the business peacefully done, but there can be little doubt that the official account was often written to conceal, as much as to explain what had really happened. Many bitter things must have been said, but somehow the King managed to re-establish his authority after the humiliations of recent Parliaments, the effects of his illness, and the usurpation of authority by his son and the council. Probably the Beauforts had gone too far, open contempt for the King, and support for the Prince produced a reaction. And there was always Archbishop Arundel. Henry IV had always been necessary to him, and now that he was on bad terms with the heir apparent, he must obviously be strongly for the King.

However it happened, the result is clear. Within two days of the ending of the session both the chancellor, Sir Thomas Beaufort, and the treasurer, Lord Scrope, gave up their offices. Sir

[1] *Feudal Aids*, vol. vi, pp. 391–551; Nicolas, *P.C.*, vol. i, pp. 344–5

John Pelham, who had served as one of the war treasurers in 1404, was immediately appointed treasurer. Keeping the chancellorship temporarily vacant once more, the King went off to Eltham to spend Christmas. Arundel had gone to Maidstone, but there was probably never any uncertainty about his appointment. On 5 January he came to the King to receive the great seal and become chancellor for the last time. He was to retain the office as long as the King lived. No new council had been named in Parliament, but in fact one was very soon constituted. In addition to Arundel as chancellor, John Pelham, the treasurer, and John Prophet, still keeper of the privy seal, it included Henry Bowet, Archbishop of York, Thomas Langley of Durham, Nicholas Bubwith of Bath and Wells, Richard Clifford of London, Ralph Neville, Earl of Westmorland, and William Lord Roos. The bishops were all officials with long service to the Crown behind them, and the two lords had served Henry from the beginning. But no attempt was made to bring back the knights and squires who had played a large part in the council before 1406. If Henry preferred them, the Commons had made it very clear that they did not, and perhaps in this respect Arundel agreed with the Commons, or thought it unwise to provoke them unnecessarily. From the last council not only the Prince, but also the two Beaufort brothers, Lord Burnell, Bishop Henry Chichele, and the Earls of Warwick and Arundel were all dropped. On 18 February the Prince was paid for his services as a councillor.

This was really the moment of Henry's triumph. Almost from the day of his accession he had been forced to contend both with a succession of armed rebellions, and with continuous opposition from his Parliaments, severely handicapped in both struggles by the lack of money, which only his Parliaments could make good. Each Parliament had attacked and limited his choice of councillors until in 1410 very little initiative was left to him, his son and his council being in control. Now only eighteen months later, after his last Parliament, not only were all the rebels defeated, but the King had also recovered his lost authority. Unhappily it was too late; he now faced his final struggle with his ill-health.

In the last fifteen months of his life the farthest that Henry travelled from London was to Canterbury and Windsor. In January 1412 he was at Eltham, and after a visit to Stratford-by-Bow returned there to receive the envoys of the Dukes of Orleans

and Berri, who were ready to offer him large territorial concessions, amounting to the entire duchy of Aquitaine, their sons,
daughters, nephews and nieces in matrimony, and their own
service in arms, in return for his help against Burgundy. Early
in February the Queen was with him at Greenwich, and after
a short visit to the Tower he went to Canterbury for March and
part of April, spending Easter there, no doubt as the guest of
the Archbishop and chancellor.

Returning to London, he went to Windsor for his last St.
George's Day, and then came back to Stratford, London and
Rotherhithe for the summer. Riverside places had the advantage
both of ease of access, a barge on the river being the most
comfortable form of transport for a sick man, and also of the
supposedly health-giving breezes. Moreover the summer jousts at
Smithfield had become a regular entertainment for the court.
This year Tanneguy du Chastel, who had been captured during a
Breton attack on the coast of Devon in 1404, was coming to
challenge Sir John Cornewaille, and John Kerneau to joust with
Sir Richard Arundel. But meanwhile more important matters
demanded Henry's attention. In London on 18 May agreement
was reached with the French envoys reversing the Prince's
policy of alliance with Burgundy. Henry promised to send a
thousand men-at-arms and three thousand archers to serve
against Burgundy, and in return was to receive large territorial
concessions in and around Guyenne. As a security various
towns in Poitou and Angoulême were to be handed over to his
forces almost immediately. Two days earlier he had written to
the burgomasters and echevins, or aldermen, of Ghent, Bruges
and Ypres, announcing his intention of making war in Guyenne
in his own person, and asking them not to assist Charles VI or
the Duke of Burgundy, but so far as Henry himself was concerned,
this was, like all his earlier proposed expeditions overseas, to
come to naught.

It was at Rotherhithe in July that Henry ordered the issue of
the charters creating his only two new peers, Prince Thomas
becoming Duke of Clarence, and Sir Thomas Beaufort, Earl of
Dorset; as the latter belonged to the Prince's party his promotion
balanced, perhaps, that of the Prince's brother and rival. The
witnesses were the same for both charters: the two Archbishops,
the Bishops of Durham and Bath and Wells, William, Lord Roos,

Henry, Lord Beaumont, John Pelham, the treasurer, Lord Grey of Codnor, the King's chamberlain, John Stanley, the steward of the household, and John Prophet, the keeper of the privy seal, that is members of the council and of the royal household. The Prince was again a very notable absentee, although he had witnessed a charter as recently as 1 June. On that day Henry also made some grants to his old friend, John Norbury. He had granted Cheshunt manor in Hertfordshire to the Earl of Westmorland for life, and Westmorland granted it to Norbury for the same period, with remainder to his wife, Elizabeth, his son Henry, the King's godson, and Henry's brother, John. At the same time Norbury was granted 'of the King's special grace and own motion, and not at his instance or supplication, and for a certain sum of money paid at the receipt of the King's chamber', for life with remainder to the same persons as the other grant, the alien priory of Greenwich and Lewisham with all its manors and appurtenances.[1]

Whilst Henry was at Rotherhithe his council was also meeting there on 8, 9 and 10 July. Henry having decided that he could not go to France, and the Prince being out of favour and perhaps opposed to the King's policy, the command of the expedition was to be given to Prince Thomas, the new Duke of Clarence. The council still struggling as usual to find enough money for the ordinary needs of government was thus confronted with the task of paying for a large expeditionary force as well. First Prince John was to have £1,000 for the keeping of the east march, and especially the repair of Berwick Castle, and Sir Thomas Swynbourne £2,300 for the castle of Fronsac. The cost of the expedition apart from the shipping would be about £200 per day, or £6,000 per month. The City of London had promised to lend 10,000 marks, the Archbishop £1,000, and certain other bishops, abbots, the staffs of the exchequer and chancery, and Italian merchants in London, £2,700 between them, making a total of £10,000; and letters were sent by the council to eight more bishops asking for a further £2,700. This would take care of the first two months, and this no doubt was as far as the council dared to look forward. Once the expedition was in France its members could live off the land and wait for their pay. Three knights, John Pelham, John Berkeley and John Popham, were

[1] *Cal. Pat.* (1408–13), pp. 404–5.

appointed by the council on 11 July to take the musters of Clarence's men at Southampton.

Clarence, who was now about twenty-four, had been lieutenant of Ireland for the whole of his father's reign, but had spent perhaps only a third of his time there, having also served in Wales and at Calais, where he was Captain of the outlying fortress of Guines. In 1410 and 1411 he and his brother, John, with their followers had been involved in riots in Eastcheap, which may have formed the basis of some of the stories of the Prince's riotous conduct, for it was easy enough to confuse the brothers, and blame one for another's misdeeds. Early in 1412 he was at Drogheda, but was evidently recalled to join the council, and eventually to take command of the expedition. His force landed in the Cotentin in August 1412, and after capturing certain towns joined Orleans at Bourges, but the changing policy of the French court led to an offer to buy him off, and in November he agreed to withdraw with his army to Guyenne. There in the following spring he learned of the death of his father, and that brought him hurrying home. The garrison of Calais taking advantage of the French dissensions had taken the offensive in his support, and by capturing Balinghem added one more to the ring of fortresses, on which the defence of the town depended.

The Prince of Wales, who had written a long letter from Coventry on 1 June explaining his position,[1] was accused of misappropriating the money assigned for Calais. He had, he said, gone to Coventry to discuss increasing his forces to enable him to serve in Aquitaine, and not in order to attack the King as had been suggested. He declared that he was loyal to the King and had no intention of attempting to seize the throne. The council having received two rolls of paper purporting to contain his accounts for Calais, declared that the charges of misusing the money were untrue. The Prince came before the King and asked for revenge on those who had slandered him, whereat the King promised that the matter would be referred to the next Parliament, the Parliament which owing to the King's illness was destined never to meet for business.

Henry's movements during the last months of his life are somewhat obscure. He was spending a good deal of time at one or other of the Archbishop's manors, either because he wished to

[1] Galbraith, *St. Albans Chron.*, pp. 65–7

be near his chancellor, or because his household cost less if he was enjoying at least the partial hospitality of the Archbishop. The difficulty is that very few letters have survived from this period, and when letters are dated from one of these places, it is not always clear whether this indicated the presence of the King, or merely that of the great seal and the chancellor. In August 1412 Henry was at Fulham and in London, but probably did not, as Wylie thought,[1] accompany the Archbishop to Canterbury in September. October he spent partly at Merton priory, and at the Archbishop's manor of Croydon.

On 21 October members of the council came to Merton to consult him on a number of matters. He confirmed that 100 marks should be spent on repairs to the walls of Berwick, and discussed the maladministration of Ireland, the payment of arrears due to the Prince's forces in Wales, and the offer of Sir Robert Umfraville to undertake the keeping of Roxburgh Castle; but the main topic was still the finances of Calais. Robert Thorley, the treasurer, and Richard Clitheroe, the victualler, had appeared before the council on the previous day, and then been told to come back in a fortnight's time with all their accounts and papers. Now Henry wanted Thorley to be suspended from his duties, money being received meanwhile by the treasurer of England, who was to pay the Prince as Captain of Calais, and also make available what was needed by the victualler. Thorley had already been committed to the Tower, but cannot have remained there very long, and does not in fact appear to have been suspended from his duties at all, because he went on receiving money from the exchequer until the end of the reign.

This last exchequer term of the reign, which ran from 3 October to 2 March, was a most remarkable one in that receipts (£44,000) exceeded issues (£39,000) by £5,000, the largest surplus so far as one can tell of the whole reign. Of the receipts £33,000 came from the wool subsidy and other customs duties, £6,000 from the lay and clerical subsidies, fifteenths and tenths, £3,000 from feudal and casual revenues, £1,000 from the subsidy of 6s. 8d. on each £20 of land granted in the last Parliament, and £1,000 from a loan from Richard Whittington. This last was to pay some of the Prince's arrears in Wales, which the King had discussed on 21 October. On the issue side the strict limitations which had

[1] Wylie, *H. IV.*, vol. iv, p. 100

been imposed on the expenditure of the household departments, and the limitation on the number of annuities granted by the King, were making the situation much easier. Nothing needed to be paid out for the expedition to France and the defence of Guyenne, since Clarence had been bought off; and less than £2,000 was spent on the Scottish marches and less than £100 on Ireland. No doubt aware that drastic changes might occur at any moment the treasurer and keeper of the privy seal took the precaution of getting their salaries paid up to 2 March on that day. Later, no doubt after the King's death, they drew what was owing for the remaining eighteen days.

On 19 November the council met in London to consider a petition from Robert Mascall, the Bishop of Hereford, and Henry was either present or not far away. His illness had now become acute – the skin disease on his face had made him personally repulsive – and it was realised that he would not live very long. Writs for a new Parliament were nonetheless issued on 1 December calling the members to Westminster on 3 February; and once again the King set off for Eltham, where a further bout of his illness seemed likely to end in his death, but he recovered for the moment, to celebrate Christmas as merrily as he could,[1] and to stay on until the end of January. Then he came to London, presumably for the Parliament, but because he was unfit this was never officially opened, and the members were left unable to claim their expenses, as was vainly pointed out in the first Parliament of Henry V.[2] On 3 February the two Archbishops, the Bishop of Durham, the Earl of Westmorland, the treasurer and keeper of the privy seal met in council. Pirates and privateers had been operating in the Channel for years, and all that the English Government could do was to issue licences to English merchants and seamen to take their share in the plunder. Now letters of marque were issued to William Walderne and other merchants of London, who claimed that they had been robbed of wool and other merchandise to the value of £24,000 by the Genoese, to enable them to recover its value. This decision of the council was noted as being made 'with the assent of the Prince of Wales.' Authority was clearly passing; the Prince was not a member of the council, but he was almost king. During

[1] Galbraith, *St. Albans Chron.*, p. 69
[2] *Rot. Parl.*, vol. iv, p. 9

the next month as Henry lay dying at Westminster, the business of the chancery gradually faded out. Grants, letters and executive orders dwindled, and by mid-March stopped altogether. Slowly the business of the kingdom came to a halt; officials of chancery and exchequer were quietly waiting for a new master.

The final scene of Henry's life has been many times portrayed, most vividly by Shakespeare. The King is said to have swooned whilst making an offering before the shrine of Edward the Confessor in Westminster Abbey, and to have been carried thence to the room known as the Jerusalem Chamber in the Abbot's lodging. As Henry Percy had died near the wrong Berwick, so must Henry of Lancaster die in the wrong Jerusalem. According to Monstrelet,[1] the crown was placed, as was the custom, on a pillow beside the King's head. Then the watchers by his bedside thinking that he had ceased to breathe covered his face, whereupon the Prince picked up the crown and took it away. But Henry awoke, opened his eyes for the last time, and asked for the crown. Being told that the Prince had taken it he called for both Prince and crown to be brought again to his bedside. Then he asked his son what right he could have to the crown, seeing that he himself had none, to which the young Henry replied, 'as you have kept it by the sword, so will I keep it whilst my life lasts.' John Capgrave relates that when John Tille, the King's confessor, proceeded to urge him to repent for his share in the death of Archbishop Scrope, and for his usurpation, Henry said that for the former he had already received absolution from the Pope, and as to the taking of the kingdom, his sons would never permit him to make that restitution.[2] The contemporary English chroniclers do not relate the Prince's taking of the crown, but concentrate on the King's supposed last speech of advice to his son. In this he is said to have contrasted his own youthful vigour with his present weakness, as an example or warning to the Prince. He then advised his son to be cautious in prosperity and patient in adversity, not to listen to evil counsellors, and to love his brothers. Finally he told him to love and fear God, and, after giving him his blessing, died.[3] The date was 20 March 1413.

[1] *Monstrelet*, vol. ii, p. 338
[2] *Memorials of Hen. V.* (Rolls ser.), vol. i, p. 307
[3] Kingsford, *First Eng. Life*, pp. xxvii–xxviii

The King's body was embalmed, and after lying in state at Westminster, taken down the river by barge to Gravesend, accompanied by his sons, Henry, now king, John and Humphrey, and all the leading magnates of the realm. From Gravesend the funeral procession continued its journey by road to Canterbury, where the King was buried in the cathedral in accordance with his own wish. The coffin was placed in Becket's chapel near the tomb of the Black Prince. His widow, Queen Joan, had an altar tomb built over the spot, with a full-length figure of the King in gilt and painted alabaster. Twenty-four years after his death her own coffin was placed beside it, and her effigy was eventually placed beside his. There they lay undisturbed for four hundred years until in 1832 the tomb was opened in the presence of the then Dean of Canterbury and others. Parts of the rough wooden coffin were cut away. Inside was a leaden coffin. A section of this was cut out, revealing wrappers, which being removed the lower part of the King's face was seen, with a red beard. On exposure to the air it immediately sank away. The coffin was resealed and put back in its place.[1] The tiny chantry chapel where two priests were to pray forever for his soul may still be seen close by the tomb.

---

[1] *Archaeologia Cantiana*, vol. viii (1872), pp. 294-9; *Archaeologia*, vol. xxvi (1836), pp. 441-5

Chapter 18

Character of the King

'CALM and fearless, he excelled as knight, earl and duke; a king distinguished alike for his bodily vigour, mind and stature . . .'[1] Apart from the suggestion of great strength and height conveyed by these words of Thomas Elmham, we know almost nothing of Henry's physical appearance. When his tomb was opened in 1832, the face, so far as it could be seen, was said to resemble the effigy on the outside, and this effigy, with its broad rather heavy face, forked beard and curling moustaches, is probably the nearest that we have to a likeness, for the age of portraiture was not yet come, and little faith can be placed in any other surviving representations. Carved in stone Henry appears on a corbel by a doorway in the south aisle of the choir of Southwell Minster, and above the window on the east side of Battlefield church, near Shrewsbury,[2] and there are a number of pictorial representations in manuscripts,[3] but these like the one on his great seal,[4] are little more than conventional representations of a king (or a duke) without any real claim to be considered as portraits. The picture which is exhibited at the National Portrait Gallery as that of Henry IV is one of a number of versions of a false portrait which was created at the end of the sixteenth century to fill a gap in the series of portraits of the Kings of England. This was done by adapting an existing foreign portrait, a wood engraving of his contemporary, Charles VI of France. A red rose was substituted for a falcon in his right hand, and a moustache and beard were added to his face. Otherwise the whole portrait, including a fleur-de-lys sceptre, was taken over.[5]

[1] *Pol. Poems*, vol. ii, p. 123
[2] Planché, *Costume*, vol. i, p. 127; W. G. D. Fletcher, *Battlefield Church* (Shrewsbury, 1889), p. 18
[3] B. M. Harley MSS. 1319, 4379, 4380
[4] N. F. Cantor, *The English . . . to 1760* (1968), plate x
[5] I owe this information to Mr J. F. Kerslake of the National Portrait Gallery

The only other known claimant to be a likeness of the King is in the decorated initial of a Cowcher Book of the duchy of Lancaster, now in the Public Record Office.[1] This was probably drawn by Richard Frampton, a contemporary artist, but gives little more than a general idea of a bearded face.

If then the detail of Henry's features continues to elude us, so very largely does the detail of his character. All that the French chronicler could find to say when Henry died was that he had been in his time 'vaillant chevalier, aigre et subtil contre ses ennemis', a valiant knight, sharp and cunning against his enemies.[2] The words 'in his time' emphasise the fact that in 1413 his time was long past, and however we look at Henry's reign there must be a sense of disappointment that the promise of success, even of greatness, inherent in the 'vaillant chevalier' was not fulfilled. Less than fourteen years separated the landing at Ravenspur from the burial at Canterbury, yet looking back on its sequence of events and the rapid ageing of the King, it seems a long reign. It is easy in looking for more spectacular successes to overlook the very real accomplishments, the establishment of a new dynasty, the suppression of rebellions, the removal of threats from abroad, and the gradual evolution of a working compromise with Parliament and council. Henry's real achievement lay in the fact that he died a king, and left his son a united realm to serve as a base for his great victories in France. The disappointment, to use no stronger word, nonetheless remains, partly because Henry always gave the appearance of being at the mercy of events rather than in control of them, and partly because disease had made him prematurely old just when his worst troubles seemed to be over. The appearance of helplessness may at times have been deliberate, an example of Henry's 'subtlety' or cunning, but his ageing was only too evident to all. In the fourteen years of his reign a vigorous man of thirty-two, whose father had lived to be fifty-nine, and his grandfather to sixty-five, had become an aged invalid at forty-six.

It is in this contrast between the able and successful man of thirty-two and the weary old man of forty-six that the whole problem, even tragedy, of Henry's personality is hidden; for there can be no doubt that in 1399 Henry was a man of great

[1] P.R.O., D.L 42/2
[2] *Monstrelet*, vol. ii, pp. 337–8

promise as well as of achievement. First of all he had proved himself a 'valiant knight', a young warrior outstanding in strength and skill, a champion both on the field of battle in Prussia, and in the lists in England and France, a leader of men, whose loyalty to his followers was as great as the loyalty he expected to receive from them. Secondly he had invaded England, raised an army, and won the whole kingdom without battle or bloodshed. Doubtless the opportunity was his. After his father's death everything seemed to happen right for him, but the ability to seize opportunities is the prerequisite of success; and if everyone welcomed him in England, this was in no small part due to the impression that his bearing and affability had created. Unlike, indeed in spite of, his father, Henry had won the hearts of the citizens of London by his charm and easy manners long before he went into exile, and their support was vital to him in the beginning of his reign.

Nor was it only the Londoners whose hearts Henry had won. During his journeys from Danzig to Venice and Venice to Calais, as well as during his exile in France, he had made a number of friends amongst the rulers and nobility of Europe. According to Froissart the French lords found him 'gracieux chevalier, doux, courtois et traitable.'[1] In Milan he had already won the friendship of the Duke and of the Archbishop, afterwards Pope Alexander V, and also the enduring devotion of the Duke's fifteen-year-old niece.[2] His biographer, John Capgrave, who although he perhaps saw Henry only once, when as a thirteen-year-old boy at Lynn in 1406 he witnessed the King's farewell to his daughter, Philippa, then setting out for Denmark, must have talked with many who knew the King, summed up this side of Henry's character with the word 'amicabilis' or friendly. But he was a great deal more than that. His strength, energy and courage were known to all. His first child was born when he was sixteen, and his wife died before he was thirty leaving him six small children. After that it may be supposed that a strong, handsome and charming man of the highest rank might have chosen as either mistress or wife from half the ladies of England, yet there was general praise for the remarkable chasteness of his life, so unlike that of his father, of most of his contemporaries,

[1] Bk. iv, chap. 68
[2] Wylie, *H. IV*, vol. iv, p. 128

and even of his sister, Elizabeth. He was nine years a widower before he was able to receive his second wife, Joan, in England; and then apparently rode with boyish eagerness to meet her, treated her with lavish generosity, and remained faithful to her for the rest of his life.

In religion Henry was conventional, pious and orthodox, scrupulous in his attendance at mass, a frequent pilgrim to the shrines of saints, the founder in 1409 of a chantry on the battlefield of Shrewsbury, to pray for the souls of those killed in the battle, and of another in St. Paul's Cathedral by the tombs of his parents, to pray for their souls. A regular supporter of the church with his offerings, he had the unquestioning faith of his age, so complete an acceptance of the church's teaching that any offence of his own, which political expediency might dictate, lay heavily on his conscience. Like almost all medieval kings he dreamed of uniting Christendom under his own command as a first step towards leading a vast army of Christian knights to recover the Holy Land, and unlike most of them he had actually been to Jerusalem. This preoccupation with the idea of a crusade was characteristic and medieval. Henry looked to the past rather than the future, always sought precedents in dealing with his Parliaments, and was jealous of the prerogatives of his predecessors, He had a lifelong series of learned confessors, one at least of whom was not afraid to write to him criticising his behaviour and policy, and remained on good terms with him after he had been promoted to be Bishop of Lincoln. Indeed Henry seems to have remained loyal to all his friends and followers throughout his reign.

Amongst these are generally numbered the three poets, Geoffrey Chaucer, John Gower and Thomas Hoccleve, yet here the importance of Henry's patronage may easily be exaggerated. Chaucer was a member of the family or household, being related by marriage to John of Gaunt, but he died a year after Henry's accession. Hoccleve's rewards from Henry were rather the pay of a civil servant – he was a clerk in the privy seal office – than the patronage of a poet; and Gower, although he claimed to be Henry's liege man, does not appear to have received any financial rewards. Henry is also said to have wished to persuade Christine de Pisan, the French poetess, whose son spent some time in England, to come to his court, but she preferred to remain in

France.[1] However that may be, Henry certainly believed in having his sons well educated, for Henry V, John and Humphrey were all ultimately to display their taste and learning. Moreover he was not uneducated himself. Letters quoted above show that he could quote Latin and write in both French and English, and for a layman his handwriting was clear and regular.[2] John Gower writing an address on his accession said:

> Thus tellen thei whiche olde bookes conne,
> Whereof, my lord, y wot wel thou art lerned.[3]

So at Bardney, his only visit to an abbey of which we have an eyewitness account, we are told that he examined the library and spent some time in reading. In exile in Paris he is supposed to have spent some time closely watching the teaching in the university there. But even so music was almost certainly a greater interest than literature or learning.

Musicians were certainly employed in Henry's household from his earliest youth. His minstrels accompanied him on his travels, and remained with his court when he became king. John Strecche, the canon of Kenilworth, who must often have met him when he stayed at the castle there, both before and after his accession, declared that Henry was himself a brilliant musician, and there is a suggestion that he played the flute or recorder, whilst his first wife, Mary Bohun, sang. Early in his reign the household chapel was reorganised with a large choir, and it has even been suggested that Henry himself was the 'Henry Roy' who composed a *Gloria in Excelsis* and other church music early in the fifteenth century.[4]

Such then was the man who became king in 1399, richly endowed with all the qualities which should have ensured success, a valiant soldier and leader, strong, handsome, religious and cultured. Why was the promise not more amply fulfilled? Was it simply illness that defeated him in the end, or did a gnawing conscience leave him without sufficient confidence in himself,

[1] Wylie, *H. IV.*, vol. iv, pp. 136–7
[2] Above, pp. 160–1, 223–4
[3] *Pol. Poems*, vol. ii, p. 5
[4] Harrison, *Music in Med. Britain*, pp. 22, 221, 230: Wylie, *H. IV.*, vol. ii, p. 487; vol. iii, p. 325; vol. iv, p. 158

questioning the rightness of his own actions, and losing all firmness of purpose?

As Earl of Derby Henry was far from sympathetic towards his cousin, King Richard, but even so he probably regretted his own entanglement with the appellants, and might well have remained staunchly loyal to the King, as his nature surely dictated, but for Richard's unpardonable actions. The sentence of exile pronounced at Coventry, and the seizure of the Lancaster estates after the death of John of Gaunt could be justified on no grounds, even in the long run on those of political expediency. A mild contempt for his cousin was converted by these actions into hatred. Suddenly deprived of his own loyalties, to his father and to his king, Henry could henceforth look to no one but himself. Soon after the landing at Ravenspur he must have realised the loneliness of his own position. No one stood between him and his God, for even Archbishop Arundel had become a dependant. Nothing had prepared him for this position, and hence he made serious mistakes. The oath at Doncaster, perhaps extorted from him by the Percies, was the first of these.

Having sworn that he would not seize the throne he soon came to realise that seizing the throne was the only practicable way out of the situation which his own and Richard's actions had created. He then discovered that by making rebellion successful he had made it respectable, and for most of his reign he had to contend with the rebellion of others. Where swift action was needed he showed that he was second to none; rebellions in 1400, 1403 and 1405 were speedily suppressed. But although successful in rapid movements Henry did not have the patience to deal with guerilla tactics or siege warfare, and it was left to his son, generally reputed to have been head-strong and violent, to subdue Wales slowly and firmly. At first Henry showed himself lenient towards enemies and rebels. The revolution of 1399 was almost bloodless, demotion in the peerage, or deprivation of a see, being the roughest measures employed against the supporters of the fallen King. In 1400 and 1403 only the rebel leaders were executed, the rest quickly forgiven. But with Archbishop Scrope in 1405 it was different. Henry was perhaps beginning to think that there would be no end of rebellion, and that he must make an example, even amongst the highest and most sacred of his subjects. The Archbishop had been captured by a ruse, and the King's conscience cannot have been clear. When Arundel came to plead for his brother archbishop, Henry was in no mood to listen to reason. As he ordered the execution he was doubtless obstinately aware of his sin. Already he had doubts about his usurpation, and now Scrope began to haunt him. When shortly afterwards he was taken ill, he probably agreed in the secrecy of his own heart with those who said that this was God's punishment. The execution was his biggest mistake, not only because of the odium which he incurred, but because of his knowledge that he had succumbed for once to his own hot temper.

In Parliament and council Henry faced another kind of opposition. His instinct led him to rely on his own loyal followers, but a kingdom was not a duchy, or even an army; the magnates had a claim to be heard in the council before the King's friends, and in enforcing it they were supported by the Commons in Parliament. Opposition to a self-made king seemed more acceptable than opposition to one of undoubted right. Henry had wished to claim his throne by hereditary right, but his followers would not allow him to adopt a far-fetched theory, or even to claim by conquest, lest this upset their own territorial rights. So Henry was driven back on a parliamentary title, somewhat disguised and mixed up with his other claims though it was; and the members of his Parliaments probably thought that what they had given they could take away, or at least regulate and limit. That was where the financial situation had its part to play. Henry for his part was perhaps too conscious of the limitations of his position, but quite unaware at first of the financial problem.

Up to 1399 Henry had been a wealthy man, probably with his father the richest in England. Money had never been a problem. All that he could need the Lancaster estates had been amply able to supply. On becoming king he promised with all the rashness of an opposition leader not to ask for grants of subsidies, and so suggest a contrast with his extravagant cousin. Then he proceeded to spend lavishly on his household, and to reward large numbers of his friends, as well as many whom he hoped might become his friends, with annuities. He was very soon faced with, and no doubt surprised by, a financial crisis, which endured throughout the reign, a crisis which placed him very much at the mercy of the knights of the shire in Parliament, men whose ideal king would give them good governance, law and order at home, and an aggressive policy abroad, all preferably without levying any taxation to pay for it.

Thrust unprepared, as he was, into kingship, Henry found it easier to deal with rebellion than with the constitutional opposition of those knights and magnates in Parliament and council. His personal authority was never sufficient to outweigh the weakness of his title, and instead of dominating his Parliament as a king, he came to them as a petitioner, almost begging for money to pay for his household and his Government, thus unwittingly providing precedents for the development of the constitution. By 1406 the most dangerous rebels were defeated, and his year-long struggle with Parliament, apparently a defeat, really prepared the way for his victory because he had made no irrevocable concessions and perhaps exhausted the Commons. But from that time, although he was always hoping to lead an army to France or even to the Holy Land, Henry was subject to recurring bouts of illness. He seemed to have lost faith in himself, and to be content to leave the government very largely in the hands of Archbishop Arundel or the Prince of Wales, asserting only occasionally his own authority.

List of officers

1 Chancellors

5 Sept 1399 John Scarle

9 March 1401 Edmund Stafford, Bishop of Exeter

28 Feb 1403 Henry Beaufort, Bishop of Lincoln to Nov 1404, thereafter of Winchester

2 March 1405 Thomas Langley, dean of York, Bishop of Durham from 8 Aug 1406

30 Jan 1407 Thomas Arundel, Archbishop of Canterbury, dismissed 21 Dec 1409

31 Jan 1410 Thomas Beaufort, knight, dismissed 20–21 Dec. 1411

5 Jan 1412 Thomas Arundel, Archbishop of Canterbury

2 Treasurers

3 Sept 1399 John Norbury, esquire

31 May 1401 Lawrence Allerthorpe, baron of the exchequer 1375–1401

27 Feb 1402 Henry Bowet, Bishop of Bath and Wells

25 Oct 1402 Guy Mone, Bishop of St. David's

9 Sept 1403 William Roos, Lord Roos of Hamelak

5/9 Dec 1404 Thomas Neville, Lord Furnival, died 14 March 1407

15 April 1407 Nicholas Bubwith, Bishop of London

14 July 1408 John Tiptoft, knight

6 Jan 1410 Henry Scrope, Lord Scrope of Masham, dismissed 20 Dec 1411

23 Dec 1411 John Pelham, knight

3 Keepers of the privy seal

14 Nov 1397 Richard Clifford

1401 Thomas Langley, Dean of York

2 March 1405 Nicholas Bubwith, keeper of the rolls 1402–5, Archdeacon of Dorset

4 Oct 1406 John Prophet, Dean of York

4 King's secretaries

1401/2 Nicholas Bubwith, to 24 Sept 1402

1402 John Prophet, until 4 Oct 1406

  1406 William Pilton, receiver of the chamber and keeper of the King's jewels in 1405

  1412 Richard Holme

5 *Chamberlain of England*

7 Nov 1399 John Beaufort, Earl of Somerset, died 16 March 1410

6 *The King's chamberlains*

  1399 Thomas Erpyngham, knight

9 March 1401 Thomas Brounflete, knight

  1404 Richard, Lord Grey of Codnor

7 *Stewards of the household*

10 Oct 1399 Thomas Rempston, knight

1 March 1401 Thomas Percy, Earl of Worcester, dismissed 12 Feb 1402

3 June 1402 William Heron, Lord Say

21 Feb 1404 Thomas Erpyngham, knight

29 Jan 1405 John Stanley, knight

8 *Treasurers of the household (keepers of the wardrobe)*

1 Oct 1399 Thomas Tutbury, treasurer of household of John of Gaunt, 1389–90

9 March 1401 Thomas More, cofferer of the household of Richard II, 1395–8

7 Jan 1405 Richard Kingston, Dean of the chapel in the household, 1400–2

8 Dec 1406 John Tiptoft, knight

18 July 1408 Thomas Brounflete, knight, formerly controller and King's chamberlain

9 *Controllers of the household*

  1399 Robert Litton, esquire

  1401 Thomas Brounflete, knight

  1404 Roger Leche

  1408 John Lestrange, knight

10 *Admirals of England*

15 Nov 1399 Thomas Percy, Earl of Worcester

20 April 1401 Richard, Lord Grey of Codnor (north and east)

20 April 1401 Thomas Rempston, knight (south and west)

5 Nov 1403 Thomas, Lord Berkeley (south and west)

28 Nov 1403 Thomas Beaufort, knight (north and east)

20 Feb 1405   Thomas of Lancaster, the King's son
28 April 1406   Nicholas Blackburn (north)
28 April 1406   Richard Clitheroe (south)
23 Dec 1406   John Beaufort, Earl of Somerset
8 May 1407   Edmund Holland, Earl of Kent, died 15 Sept. 1408
21 Sept 1408   Thomas Beaufort, knight, Earl of Dorset from 1412

11 Constables

30 Sept 1399   Henry Percy, Earl of Northumberland, to July 1403
10 Sept 1403   John of Lancaster, the King's son

12 Marshal

30 Sept 1399   Ralph Neville, Earl of Westmorland, for the whole reign

13 Captains of Calais

1399   Peter Courtenay, knight
April 1401   John Beaufort, Earl of Somerset
1410   Henry, Prince of Wales

14 Treasurers of Calais

1399   Nicholas Usk, died 2 Feb 1403
5 March 1403   Robert Thorley, dismissed 5 April 1405
9 May 1405   Thomas Neville, Lord Furnival, treasurer of England, Richard Clitheroe, deputy
March 1406   Robert Thorley
7 July 1407   Richard Merlawe
28 Dec 1409   Robert Thorley

Bibliography and list of abbreviations

Add. Chart.   Additional Charters

Anglo-Norman Letters   *Anglo-Norman Letters and Petitions,* ed. M. D. Legge (Anglo-Norman Text Soc.). Oxford, Blackwell 1941

Annales R. II et H. IV   *Annales Ricardi II et Henrici IV* in *Chronica Monasterii S. Albani,* ed. H. T. Riley, vol. iii *Johannis de Trokelowe etc.* (Rolls Ser.). 1865

Anonimalle Chron.   *The Anonimalle Chronicle, 1333 to 1381,* ed. V. H. Galbraith Manchester U. P. 1927

Armitage-Smith, *Gaunt*   S. Armitage-Smith, *John of Gaunt,* Constable 1904, reprinted 1964

Aston, *Arundel*   M. E. Aston, *Thomas Arundel,* O.U.P. 1967.

B.M.   British Museum

Bean, 'H. IV and the Percies'   J. M. W. Bean, 'Henry IV and the Percies', *History,* vol. 44, 1959, pp. 212–27

Bekynton Corres.   *Correspondence of Thomas Bekynton,* ed. G. Williams, 2 vols. (Rolls Ser.). 1872

Beltz, *Garter*   G. F. Beltz, *Memorials of the most noble order of the Garter.* 1841

Boucicaut   *Livre des faits du bon messire Jean le Maigre, dit Boucicaut,* ed. J. A. C. Buchon. Paris 1835

Bourgeois de Paris   *Journal d'un Bourgeois de Paris, 1405–1449,* ed. A. Tuetey (Société de l'histoire de Paris). Paris 1881

Brut   *The Brut, or the Chronicle of England,* ed. F. W. D. Brie (Early English Text Society, orig. ser. vols. 131, 136). 1906–8

Buchon, *Collection*   J. A. C. Buchon, *Collection des Chroniques françaises,* 47 vols. Paris 1824–9

Bull. I.H.R.   *Bulletin of the Institute of Historical Research*

Bull. J.R.L.   *Bulletin of the John Rylands Library,* Manchester

C 57   P.R.O. Chancery, Coronation Roll

C 76   P.R.O. Chancery, Treaty Rolls

C 81   P.R.O. Chancery, warrants for the great seal

C. Med. Hist.   *The Cambridge Medieval History.* 8 vols. C.U.P. 1911–36

Cal. Close   *Calendar of Close Rolls in the P.R.O.* H.M.S.O. 1900–

Cal. Docs. Scot.   *Calendar of Documents relating to Scotland in the P.R.O.,* ed. J. Bain. 4 vols. 1881–8

Cal. I.P.M. *Calendar of inquisitions post mortem in the* P.R.O. H.M.S.O. 1904–

Cal. Pat. *Calendar of Patent Rolls in the* P.R.O. H.M.S.O. 1901–

Cal. S.P. Venice *Calendar of State Papers ... relating to English Affairs ... in ... Venice.* H.M.S.O. 1864–

Capgrave, *Chron.* John Capgrave, *The Chronicle of England,* ed. F. C. Hingeston (Rolls ser.). 1858

Carus-Wilson and Coleman E. M. Carus-Wilson and O. Coleman, *England's Export Trade 1275–1547,* O.U.P. 1963

Chaucer G. Chaucer, *Complete Works,* ed. Skeat. 1894

Chaucer Life-Records *Chaucer Life-Records,* ed. Martin M. Crow and Clair C. Olson. O.U.P. 1966

Chrimes, *Admin. Hist.* S. B. Chrimes, *An introduction to the administrative history of medieval England,* 2nd edn. Oxford, Blackwell 1959

Chrimes and Brown S. B. Chrimes and A. L. Brown, *Select documents of English constitutional history, 1307–1485.* Black 1961

Chron. J. de Reading *Chronicon Johannis de Reading et anonymi Cantuariensis 1346–67,* ed. James Tait. Manchester U.P. 1914

Chronographie Regum Francorum *Chronographie Regum Francorum,* ed. H. Moranville (Société de l'histoire de France). 1893

Clarke, *Fourteenth Cent. Studies* M. V. Clarke, *Fourteenth century Studies,* ed. L. S. Sutherland and M. McKisack. O.U.P. 1937

D.K.R. *Annual Reports of the Deputy Keeper of the Public Records,* H.M.S.O.

D.L. 28 P.R.O. Duchy of Lancaster, Receivers' Accounts

D.L. 29 P.R.O. Duchy of Lancaster, Accounts

Davis, *H. IV* J. D. Griffith Davis, *King Henry IV.* Barker 1935

Davis's Chron. *An English chronicle of the reigns of Richard II, Henry IV, Henry V and Henry VI,* ed. J. S. Davis (Camden Soc. orig. ser. no. 64). 1856

Devon, *Issues* *Issues of the Exchequer from King Henry III to King Henry VI* ed. Frederick Devon. Murray 1837

Dict. Biog. Franc. *Dictionnaire de Biographie française,* ed. J. Balteau and others. Paris, Letouzey 1933–

Douët d'Arcq, *Pièces inédites* L. Douët d'Arcq, *Choix de pièces inédites relatives au règne de Charles VI* (Soc. de l'hist. de France). 1863–4

Dugdale, *Mon. Ang.* William Dugdale, *Monasticon Anglicanum,* ed. Caley, Ellis and Bandinel. 6 vols. in 8. 1817–30

E 28 P.R.O. Exchequer, council and privy seal files

E 101 P.R.O. Exchequer, King's remembrancer, accounts various

E. 135 P.R.O. Exchequer, King's remembrancer, ecclesiastical documents

E 327 P.R.O. Exchequer, Augmentations Office, Deeds series BX

E 364   P.R.O. Exchequer, lord treasurer's remembrancer, foreign accounts enrolled

E 401   P.R.O. Exchequer of receipt, receipt rolls

E 403   P.R.O. Exchequer of receipt, issue rolls

E 404   P.R.O. Exchequer of receipt, warrants for issues

E.H.R.   *English Historical Review*

Ellis, *Orig. Letters*   *Original letters illustrative of English History*, ed. Henry Ellis, 2nd ser. 4 vols. 1827. Reprinted, Dawson 1969

Elmham, *Vita*   T. Elmham, *Vita et Gesta Henrici V*, ed. T. Hearne. 1727

Eulogium   *Eulogium Historiarum sive Temporis Chronicon* . . . ed. F. S. Haydon, vol. iii (Rolls ser.). 1863

Feudal Aids   Inquisitions and assessments relating to Feudal Aids preserved *in the Public Record Office, 1284–1431*. 6 vols. H.M.S.O. 1899–1920

Fortescue, *Governance*   Sir John Fortescue. *The Governance of England*, ed. Charles Plummer. O.U.P. 1885

Froissart   Jean Froissart, *Chroniques*, various edns and translations

G.E.C.   G. E. C[ockayne], *The Complete Peerage*, new edn. by Vicary Gibbs and others. 13 vols. in 14. 1910–59

Galbraith, *St. Albans Chron.*   *The St. Albans Chronicle 1406–1420*, ed. V. H. Galbraith. O.U.P. 1937

Gaunt's reg. 1372–6, 1379–83   *John of Gaunt's register, 1372–76*, ed. S. Armitage-Smith (Camden 3rd ser. nos. 20, 21), 2 Vols. 1911; *1379–83*, ed. E. C. Lodge and R. Somerville (Camden 3rd ser. nos. 56, 57). 2 Vols. 1937

Giles's Chron.   *Incerti Scriptoris Chronicion de regnis . . . Henrici IV . . .* ed. J. A. Giles. 1848

Hakluyt, *English Voyages*   Richard Hakluyt, *Collection of the early voyages, travels and discoveries of the English nation*. Various edns

Hanserecesse   *Hanserecesse. Die Recesse und andere Akten der Hansetage von 1356–1430*, ed. Karl Koppmann. Leipzig 1880

Hardyng, *Chron.*   John Hardyng, *Chronicle; with the continuation by Grafton to 34 Henry VIII*, ed. H. Ellis. 1812

Harrison, *Music in Med. Brit.*   F. L. Harrison, *Music in Medieval Britain*. Routledge 1958

Hist. du roy Richard   *Histoire du roy d'Angleterre Richard . . .* [attributed to Jean Creton], ed. John Webb, in *Archaeologia*, vol. xx, pp. 1–423, 1824; another edn in J. A. C. Buchon, *Collection des Chroniques françaises*, vol. xxiv, pp. 321–466. Paris 1826. 'Poëme sur la déposition de Richard II'.

Hist. MSS. Comm.   Historical Manuscripts Commission

Historians of York   *Historians of the Church of York*, ed. J. Raine. 3 vols. (Rolls ser.). 1879–84

Jacob, *Fifteenth Cent.*   E. F. Jacob, *The Fifteenth Century, 1399–1485* (Oxford History of England vol. vi). O.U.P. 1961

Kingsford, *Eng. Hist. Lit.*   C. L. Kingsford, *English Historical Literature in the Fifteenth Century.* O.U.P. 1913. Reprinted New York, Burt Franklin

Kingsford, *First Eng. Life*   C. L. Kingsford, *The First English Life of Henry the Fifth, written in 1513.* O.U.P. 1911

Kingsford, *London Chrons.*   C. L. Kingsford, *Chronicles of London.* O.U.P. 1905

Kunze, *Hanseakten*   K. Kunze, *Hanseakten aus England, 1275 bis 1412.* Halle 1891

Lapsley, *Crown, Community & Parlt.*   G. T. Lapsley, *Crown, Community and Parliament in the later Middle Ages*, ed. H. M. Cam amd G. Barraclough. Oxford, Blackwell 1951

Leland, *Collectanea*   John Leland, *De rebus Britannicis Collectanea.* 6 vols. 1774

Leland, *Itinerary*   *The Itinerary of John Leland in or about the years 1535–43*, ed. Lucy Toulmin Smith. 6 vols. Bell 1907–10

Lit. Cant.   *Literae Cantuarienses, the Letter Books of the monastery of Christ Church, Canterbury*, ed. J. B. Sheppard. 3 vols. (Rolls ser.) 1887–9

Lloyd, *Glendower*   Sir J. E. Lloyd, *Owen Glendower.* O.U.P. 1931

Lobineau, *Hist. de Bretagne*   C. A. Lobineau, *Histoire de Bretagne.* 2 vols. Paris 1707

McFarlane, *Wycliffe*   K. B. McFarlane, *John Wycliffe and the beginnings of English Nonconformity.* English Universities Press 1952

Madox, *Formulare*   T. Madox, *Formulare Anglicanum.* London 1702

Memorials of H. V   *Memorials of Henry the Fifth*, ed. C. A. Cole. (Rolls ser.). 1858

Michaud et Poujoulat *Mémoires*   *Nouvelle Collection des Mémoires pour servir a l'histoire de France*, ed. J. F. Michaud et J. J. F. Poujoulat. 12 vols. Paris 1850

Monk of Evesham   *Historia vitae et regni Ricardi II angliae regis a monacho quodam de Evesham consignata*, ed. T. Hearne. Oxford 1729

Monstrelet   *La Chronique d'Enguerrand de Monstrelet . . . 1400–1440*, ed L. Douët d'Arcq (Société de l'histoire de France). 1857–62

Nicolas, *P.C.*   *Proceedings and ordinances of the Privy Council* [1386–1542], ed. Sir N. H. Nicolas (Record Commission). 7 vols. 1834–7

Nicolas, *Scrope and Grosvenor*   Sir N. H. Nicolas, *The Scrope and Grosvenor Controversy.* 2 vols. 1832

Nichols, *Wills*   J. Nichols, *Collection of the wills of the kings and queens of England.* 1780

Otterbourne, *Chron.*   *Chronicle of Thomas Otterbourne,* ed. T. Hearne, *Duo Rerum Anglicarum Scriptores.* 1732

P.R.O.   Public Record Office

Planché, *Costume*   J. R. Planché, *A Cyclopaedia of Costume.* 2 vols. 1876–9

Pol. Poems   Political Poems and Songs . . . Edward III to Henry VIII, ed. T. Wright. (Rolls ser.) 2 vols. 1859–61

R. *Letters, H. IV   Royal Letters, Henry IV,* ed. F. C. Hingeston. (Rolls ser.) vol. 1 (1399–1404), 1860; vol. 2 (1405–13), printed with corrections 1965

Religieux de Saint-Denys   Chronique du religieux de Saint-Denys contenant le régne de Charles VI de 1380 à 1422, ed. M. L. Bellaguet (Collection de Documents Inédits), 6 vols. Paris 1839–52

Report on Foedera   Report on Rymer's Foedera, appendices A–E (Record Commission), ed. C. P. Cooper. 3 vols. *c.* 1836

Roskell, *Speakers*   J. S. Roskell, *The Commons and their Speakers in English parliaments, 1376–1523.* Manchester 1965

Rot. Parl.   Rotuli Parliamentorum. The Rolls of Parliament. 6 vols. and index. 1783–1832

Rot. Scot.   Rotuli Scotiae in Turri Londinensi . . . asservati. 2 vols. (Record Commission) 1814–19

Russell, *Eng. Intervention*   P. E. L. R. Russell, *The English Intervention in Spain and Portugal in the time of Edward III and Richard II.* O.U.P. 1955

Rymer, *Foedera   Foedera, conventiones, litterae etc.,* ed. Thomas Rymer. 20 vols. 1704–35

S.C.1   P.R.O. Ancient Correspondence

Smith, *Expeditions   Expeditions to Prussia and the Holy Land made by Henry, Earl of Derby (afterwards Henry IV): accounts kept by his treasurer during the years 1390–91 and 1392–93* (Camden Soc. new ser. no. 52), ed. Lucy Toulmin Smith. 1894

Somerville, *Dy of Lancaster*   R. Somerville, *History of the Duchy of Lancaster,* vol. 1 (1265–1603). Duchy of Lancaster 1953

Steel, *R. II*   A. B. Steel, *Richard II.* C.U.P. 1962

Stubbs, *Constit. Hist.*   W. Stubbs, *The Constitutional History of England.* 3 vols. O.U.P. 1873, and later edns

Traïson et Mort   Chronicque de la traïson et mort de Richart Deux Roy Dengleterre ed. Benjamin Williams (English Historical Society). 1846

Trans. Devon Assoc.   Transactions of the Devonshire Association

Trans. R.H.S.   Transactions of the Royal Historical Society

Usk   Chronicon Adae de Usk, A.D. 1377–1421, ed. Sir E. M. Thompson. 2nd edn. O.U.P. 1904

Walsingham, *Hist. Angl.   Chronica Monasterii S. Albani*, ed. H. T. Riley, vol. 1: *Thomas Walsingham Historia Anglicana*. 2 vols. (Rolls ser.). 1863–4

Weever, *Fun. Mon.*   J. Weever, *Ancient Funeral Monuments*. 1631

Wilkinson, *Constit. Hist.*   B. Wilkinson, *Constitutional history of medieval England 1216–1399*. 3 vols. Longmans 1948–58

Wylie, *H. IV*   James Hamilton Wylie, *History of England under Henry the Fourth*. 4 vols. Longmans 1884–98

Ypodigma Neustriae   Chronica Monasterii S. Albani, ed. H. T. Riley, vol. vii, Ypodigma Neustriae (Rolls ser.) 1876

NOTE: References to manuscripts in the British Museum and the Public Record Office are prefixed by the letters B.M. and P.R.O. respectively. All other references are to printed books or articles in periodicals.

Index

Index

Westmorland, Earl of, *see* Neville, Ralph
Whittington, Richard, 84, 95, 108, 116, 212, 246
Wight, Isle of, 124, 161, 163, 171
Wilbram, 37
Williams, Benjamin, 7
Willoughby, William, Lord Willoughby (1396–1409), 30, 35, 38, 55, 68, 72–3, 79–80, 82, 147, 167, 169, 172, 197, 203
Wiltshire, Earl of, *see* Scrope, William
Wilycotes, John, 205
Winchcombe, Tideman of, Bishop of Worcester (1395–1401), 92, 126, 139
Winchester, 126, 135, 150; Bishops of, *see* Wykeham, William of (1367–1404), Beaufort, Henry (1404–47); Cathedral, 151; College, 82; Prior of, 151
Windsor, Berks., 25, 47–8, 78, 85, 87, 89, 108, 119, 129, 140, 149–50, 154, 162, 165, 170, 182, 184, 195–6, 210, 220, 223–4, 234, 238, 242–3; Dean of, *see* Kingston, Richard
Woburn, Beds., 170; Abbot of, 190
Wodecock, John, 139
Wodehouse, John, 155
Woodstock, Oxon., 159, 184, 234
Worcester, 119, 129–30, 158–60, 171–2, 184–5, 188–9, 199, 227; Bishops of,

see Winchcombe, Tideman of (1395–1401), Clifford, Richard (1401–7); Earl of, *see* Percy, Thomas
Wotton, Nicholas, 205
Woxbrigg, John, Abbot of Bardney, 203
Wycliff, John, 19, 214
Wydcombe, William, 216
Wygomor, Richard, 153
Wykeham, William of, Bishop of Winchester (1367–1404), 19, 27, 82, 84, 95–6, 144, 181
Wylie, James Hamilton, 2, 246

York, 57, 98, 102, 116, 158, 165, 185–9, 195, 213, 218; Archbishops of, *see* Scrope, Richard (1398–1405), Bowet, Henry (1407–23); convocation of, 201; Dukes of, *see* Edmund (1385–1402), Edward (1402–15)
Young, Richard, Bishop of Bangor (1400–4), 84, 116, 128, 139–40, 169, 183; Bishop of Rochester (1404–18), 175
Ypodigma Neustriae, 4

Zölner von Rotenstein, Konrad, Grand Master of the Teutonic Knights, 31–2